Mark Stanley

THE SACRED SPRING OF THE BLOOD ROYAL

Available on Amazon in Paperback and Kindle

During World War II, an American paratrooper on a covert mission drops into eastern France to find mystery, romance, murder, espionage and becomes involved with the Prieuré de Sion, an ancient secret order that has been quietly influencing western society for centuries.

And that is only the beginning.

For over a thousand years, members of the Prieuré de Sion have been the targets of assassinations. Why? The tale weaves a thread that begins in the alpine meadows of the Jura mountains, and moves into mystical journeys of self-realization in the labyrinth and secret underground temple complex near Rennes le Chateau in southwestern France.

Mystical, Magical, Esoteric Entertainment--Edward J. Barton-VineVoice

This was one of those books I couldn't put down. It seemed to have a little bit of everything. A thriller, a love story, a spiritual quest, a fantasy, a history primer, and a travelog all rolled up into one grand adventure. Charles

Well Done--Riveting--Inspector 12

Stanley has woven a mystic tale with a historic background and mysterious throughout. This is a story of love and intrigue but it seems with a underlying content of the spiritual development of the soul. Roger

All elements were there for an entertaining and enjoyable book. I found it a plus that the writing style took me into the environment in a refreshing way. I would enjoy further efforts by this author VanDeMark

Creating World Class Red Wine

Creating World Class Red Wine
Copyright © 2014
Mark Stanley
Ascension Press

ISBN 9781500825416

Graphics by Chris Miller

Cover design and images by Mark Stanley

Creating World Class
Red Wine

Mark Stanley

Ascension Press

CONTENTS

Author's Note

This book is written for the casual reader to enjoy, but also contains what I deemed the most important technical information for professionals. Wine lovers and beginning winemakers will notice special text boxes throughout the book with Tech Talk headers containing more technical info. This layout allows casual readers to avoid the more technical information if they choose.

Some sentences may seem isolated—in their own paragraph; a statement that does not necessarily flow well with the body of the text. I chose to leave them in. These are valuable little statements that represent notes I saved from opinions made about or by world-class winemakers, or ideas I felt were poignant.

The winemaking chapter begins with "Red Winemaking Simplified", an outline presented in a linear time line. Each step refers to a page containing in-depth discussions on that particular step or topic. The Red Winemaking Simplified section can therefore be used as an overview of the process, by beginning winemakers as it is, and also as a table of contents for further discussions in the vinification chapter.

This layout is intended to simplify what can be a rather daunting process for those not familiar with it—a process even further complicated due to my habit of presenting different options for the winemaker to choose from.

There are times when I will make a simple command statement, like: "Never allow aluminum to contact wine". There are technical reasons behind those statements that I chose not to bore the reader with. I prefer to say "no" to tedium.

Temperatures are important in winemaking. For the international audience, most temperatures are expressed in both Fahrenheit and Celsius scales. To simplify throughout the text, I have chosen to abbreviate---69 degrees Fahrenheit/20 degrees Celsius is abbreviated to: 69F/20C

At some point the reader may notice that some of the most mundane aspects of grape growing and winemaking are absent from the text: How deep is the planting hole? How does one build a sturdy trellis? How to use a siphon hose? These are topics very well covered by other authors and easily found with a search engine. What is less covered by other authors is how the best grapes are grown and how the finest wines are made. That is the center of the focus here, the hub the mandala wheel rotates on—and like a sacred spring, I keep gravitating back to the watering hole.

INTRODUCTION

If life smiles at you
Enjoy it completely
Never let the golden cup
Wait in the moonlight

Li Bai 701-762 A.D.

How rare those pivotal experiences which shape our lives, appearing out of the mist like the muses of the ancient world--unexpected, perhaps unwelcome to most but the courageous or very foolish few.

Inspiration, insight, passion? No—there is no word to describe it. And yet, I have learned to recognize that elvan craft, bedecked with flowers, as an invitation, and impulsively embark; choosing not to step once again onto the shore until my spirit has been satiated.

Allowing our passions is to honor life itself, as during those times we really know we are living. Whatever the manifestation, whether it be a piece of music, a new design, or even a well-crafted meal; it is the creation process itself that is the fuel of the artist.

One could say the journey began in 1971. I had a friend who later, when it came time to function as an adult, somehow couldn't handle it well. But at sixteen years of age he was as great a friend a teenager could hope for.

The setting was a sleepy Seattle suburb near the Puget Sound. We were perched on the railing of a grey weathered back deck at his parent's house.

It was one of those bright early summer days, with just a hint of coolness blowing in from the north across the water, bringing with it a salty, nose-twitching clam and octopus fragrance. Sweet and sour—that gentle heat and almost goose bump breeze.

His father (who was not at home) had a wine rack in the dining room. On that particular day, since we had nothing else to do, my buddy said, "Let's drink a bottle of my dad's $20-a-bottle French wine!" I was game.

Oh, those days of youth—that fleeting moment in time when one is blessed with the luxury of zero responsibilities. The most important thing I did not do was to roll out the prayer rug every sunset and thank whomever for yet another day of freedom.

I remember him struggling with the cork and handing me a glass. Those were two "firsts" for me: wine with a cork and drinking it from a wine glass. Prior to that time, except for unmentionable screw-top encounters, the only beverage I had partaken in that resembled genuine wine had been filched from the gallon O'Cribari rouge that my mother kept in our refrigerator.

Cold Cribari. I do honor my mother for being a red wine drinker. She was half French.

What Geoff produced was a genuine bottle of French wine. I confirmed that because I had studied three years of the language, but that didn't help me understand but very little of the exaggerated script on the label—like: "Appellation Musigny Contrôlée." That sounds nasty.

Or: "Mis en bouteille au domaine." What? *Lions* have domains. There was obviously plenty of bragging going on in the French language all over the label. However, I did note the shape of the bottle. That was the clue. Twenty-seven years later Sherlock and I put the pieces together and we discerned that it had to have been a Bourgogne (Burgundy), crafted from the Pinot Noir grape.

One can only speculate, because the spent bottle probably got unceremoniously tossed into the laurel bushes, but a similar bottle of wine today would most likely cost well over $300.

My friend disappeared somewhere. The wine was not deeply colored—red, not purple. It tasted kind of earthy, gritty, floral, delicate and powerful all at the same time.

I must have drank a couple of glasses because my veil came down. Little beads of sweat were forming on my forehead from the sun beating on it, and I found myself staring at the glass. Thoughts began to flow in unhindered: "Wow, we're like Europeans", "This is wine", "This is good!", "*This is what I remember*". Wait a minute. Remember from when? Remember from whence? I let that one roll over me as I chewed on it for a few moments.

At this point the reader may choose to close this book with a snap, reach for a bookshelf and insert it between two new age dust collectors. I will not discourage the reader from doing so, but I must say that upon reaching fifty years of age I made a vow to speak my truth no matter what others thought, and let the chips fall as they may.

Whether it was a soul memory or some kind of genetic memory I do not know, but one thing is unwaveringly clear; I remembered that taste. The experience was very powerful for me, because I knew I'd momentarily stepped out of the box of ordinary reality, goaded on by that wonderful wine.

We finished that bottle, and Geoff said, "Let's drink another!" I recall nothing whatsoever about the second bottle except heading for the beach afterwards, staggering down to the Old Indian Trail that went around Three Tree Point. From that experience I learned two valuable life lessons:

1. Out there somewhere is red wine that is extremely good.
2. Quality wine may help give us a quality experience.

Why quality wines harbors those potentials remains unclear, as little empirical data exists to support the notion. However, remarkable stories related by those fortunate enough to sample well-aged famous wines are numerous. I shall digress, and relate one from memory from some old wine lovers book.

A vertical tasting was scheduled years ago at one of the five Bordeaux first growths. I can't remember which one, but it doesn't really matter. They all historically produce world class wines. The tasters were a small handful of important folks fortunate enough to receive an invitation. As with all vertical tastings, the oldest wine was tasted first, and others from the same producer followed along a linear time line. They tried five or six wines, all pulled from the cellar where they were made—as pristine as they could be.

The first bottle was from the Chateau's 1899 vintage. It was still quite good, but showed some oxidation. It was on it's way out.

The second bottle was from 1921. When the wine was poured and they began to sample it the room became silent. You could hear a pin drop. The tasters were still, as if frozen in time.

Now these were people who could probably easily determine the difference in taste between Chateau Mouton and nearby Chateau Lafite. They were those who can vociferously come up with a seemingly unlimited vocabulary of adjectives to describe a wine. And yet they had nothing to say. They were dumbstruck. The wine was so good it simply did not compute. There were no neurons in the brain that could make the connection. Afterwards, one of them said something like, "It felt as if the wine was cool liquid fire that melted—flowing down the throat, continuing throughout the body until I felt warm from the tips of my toes to the top of my head."

Remarkable wine--Health food.

A friend and colleague (and not a Merlot fan), had a chance to taste a Chateau Petrus (*the* Merlot) at a tasting. When I asked him what it was like, he thought for a moment and said, "It was an experience." That pretty much sums it up in a nutshell.

Many years passed, during which time I always enjoyed wine but knew very little about it. Then, out of the blue, I had a remarkably similar experience to the "encounter with the Burgundy kind" 27 years prior. This time the call was much more insistent, heralded by trumpets instead of violins.

In 1998 I was enjoying a bottle of Syrah with my sister Terri, who is shall we say, a singularly unique person--an eastern European gypsy woman somehow born into an American family.

We were relaxing on her 1905 Bainbridge Island veranda surrounded by foliage and flowers.

I was holding the bottle which felt somehow compelling. "What is Syrah?"

"It's a grape", said the garden designer before wandering off.

Once again, much like 27 years before, I found myself alone with the bottle; staring at it… Syrah… What is it about Syrah?

Time stopped. I entered a kind of singularity—a black hole. A tsunami, quietly rolling through the ocean, unnoticed in the hour before dawn swept me up. It was irresistible, pulling me.

Too overwhelmed to struggle—I swam. *Syrah*. I sensed it was a key to a mystery. Out of nowhere, with a bedrock kind of determination like from an old movie intro in huge block letters up in the sky I thought, "I'M GOING TO FIND OUT ABOUT THIS!"

That time I leaped onto the elvan craft.

My sister was unaware of the metamorphosis that had occurred on her back porch until I informed her years later. To this day I still do not understand why, but I launched myself into a massive ten hour per day, seven days a week, in depth study of Syrah, wine in general, vinification, and finally viticulture. It was all I wanted to do. I consumed it, or was consumed by it.

After a while I began to realize that I'd become almost completely Syrahphilatcd, and after six months of it, honestly, at a low point considered just checking in to the hospital with the full intention of receiving a Syrahtomy. Why not download the information directly into my brain, or if it was deemed that too many brain cells were missing, implant a chip in there somewhere. Alas, the coward that I am, that did not occur. So I continued with the full immersion campaign, and finally upon surfacing, found that I had become a very knowledgeable self-taught enologist.

I had read everything I could get my hands on in the English language, and continued to max out the inter-library loans from three different library systems.

I have at times pondered about that bottle of vin de pays Syrah from the Languedoc my sister produced that turnpike day. Perhaps it was actually the brew of some southern French sorceress, cleverly concocted, intending to induce prolonged madness. But I was a happy lunatic, immersed in my fuzzy scholarly pursuit. Now, I must admit to remain unsatiated, as to this day the malady still persists. If I someday encounter the sorceress it is unclear whether I will strangle or kiss her.

As a small part of the study I took notes when an opinion concerning techniques was offered by one of the great winemakers of the world. If a newer, recent vintage bottle of wine retails for $8000, I think it behooves us to pay attention when that winemaker speaks. Even though there are almost as many opinions about how wine should be made as there are winemakers, slowly I realized that there are common threads. Eventually I learned how the best, most expensive wines in the world are made. Thus the seeds for this work were first sown.

The first factoid that struck me hard was concerning the predominant use of indigenous yeasts in world class wines. That unleashed a back-study, and I found that at that time (2000 A.D.) virtually all of the best wines in the world were made on their own yeast. Wow. That tidbit of information was what actually birthed the idea for *Creating World Class Red Wine*.

We shall discuss yeasts later, but I must mention now that I am not a purist, and love to work with different commercial yeast strains, as well as allowing the natural yeasts to do their thing.

Working in wineries, I was surprised to find that the information available to home winemakers was limited, inaccurate, and often in juxtaposition to methods used by professionals. The home wine making world and the professional wineries seem to have evolved along independent lines, but from similar origins.

American wineries emerged predominantly from the post-Prohibition industrial sector, eventually incorporating a few older European methods, and developing new ones. But there was no single, simple, modern comprehensive text. Professional vinification and viticultural information is a huge body comprised of studies and university textbooks—leaning heavily towards the technical side. Some of the wine chemistry is so intense that it is only palatable by other wine chemists. There is more focus on ideas than techniques--and as you can imagine, the professors do not necessarily agree on many issues--but we should consider that a healthy dynamic. One way or another, the professional scholarly wine world is difficult for the lay person to assemble and digest.

The home winemaking world appears to have been born from the Prohibition bathtub gin era, gleaning from a distance some, but not all of the professional winemaker's techniques, and oftentimes generating it's own mediocre ones. It is hard to believe how poor some of the information is. If one performs a search for winemaking techniques, what appears are predominantly home-grown ideas. The sad part is, they-all keep passing the same ideas around until they become regarded as truth. It reminds me of something William Shakespeare wrote:

The wine cup is a little silver well
Where truth —*If truth there be*
Doth dwell

I therefore felt compelled to create a manual and treatise, based on the techniques used by some of the best professional winemakers and viticulturists— focusing solely on red wines.

I love white wines, but they represent a distinct body of winemaking disciplines. Also, I have observed how some texts can be confusing because it is difficult at times to tell whether the author is referring to reds, whites, or kit wines made from concentrates.

On that note, I will not pull any punches concerning kit wines. Please do not be swayed by the magazine advertisements depicting handsome male and beautiful female models enjoying a wine made from concentrate by candlelight. Beauty does not necessarily equate to good taste. Wines made from concentrates are jug wines.

When I mention $1000 bottles of wine to my consumer-level wine drinking friends, it can illicit an furious knee-jerk reaction: "That's not worth it!"

Who has ever claimed that the luxury goods market has anything to do with sane valuation? A $100 wine is not going to be 10 times better than a $10 bottle. It's not a linear-based valuation.

Let's say a hard working couple brings home $300 clear per day after taxes between the two of them. Their budget is tight, but they like wine and spring for a $10 bottle to share most evenings.

The consumer-level market is huge. Big wineries fiercely compete in that $9-$13 range, and the consumer generally gets what they pay for--a decent drinkable table wine.

Another couple is more abundant, and brings in $1000 per day. Unless they are particularly poor money managers, they should have some surplus cash to spend. They love wine, and it is not unusual for them to split a $100 bottle with dinner. They can afford a bit of luxury. $100 wines express much more variability in perceived (subjective) quality than consumer-level wines.

Another couple brings in more than $50,000 per day. No, you say? Next time you are waiting in the doctors office peruse through Forbes magazine and consider reassessing your attitude. Check out the ads—private jets, yachts etc. There are plenty of couples in that income bracket. No envy—stop that—it's bad for your health. The high roller couple either literally does not care what the wine costs, or it is important that it is pricey—for psychological reasons we dare not venture into. That couple is not merely engaging in the luxury market—they are driving it, and they are competitive. Wine buyers are hired.

The price of wines sold at international fine wine auctions represent what the market will bear. Let's face it—there will always be a market for the best of the best, and the prices will be astronomical.

The high roller couple that tastes well actually helps urge the producers of $200+ wines to be both on their toes and honest. If they are going to pay that much for a wine it better be good! So although world-class wines will certainly be variable in perceived quality; if they are aged and cellared well, and from a good vintage, they should express some remarkable characteristics.

The rest of us look for a good value in a bottle of wine. As we are all aware, price can only be used as a general guideline as to the quality of any given bottle. Many wines costing far less than $100 express some of the finer wine qualities we seek, while others costing far more may not—at least to our taste—today. The following year that same wine may offer more expression. Once again, the whole discipline is far from linear. When friends are raving about a wine they tried that is both good and very reasonably priced, my response is always the same: Buy now—and lots of it. Invest in cases and store it in a cool place.

I make fine wine. I do not make world class wine. I simply don't have access to world class grapes. Very few winemakers do—and the two go hand in hand. That should not stop us from making the best wines we can. Here we will examine the various ways that the finest wines are made on planet Earth, and incorporate some of those techniques for ourselves. I am offering the winemaker and winegrower options, through knowledge and techniques. This treatise is not a simple recipe for making a great wine. As far as I know, there is no recipe, no arcane alchemical formula, and no closely-guarded technological secrets.

So what is world class wine? What are the typicities that historically great wines share?

The data is data, irregardless of what you or I or anyone else believes.

In brief:

The grapes are grown in vineyards with high mineral content—commonly limestone, schist, slate, or granite etc., with a soil pH above 6.90.

Vineyards of low fertility, but deep, rocky soils.

Healthy soils with high beneficial microbial content.

Soil types that augment the particular grape variety.

Predominantly dry-farmed vineyards.

Grapes from old vines (over 20 years) with naturally low yields.

Vineyards where the grapes barely ripen fully towards the end of their normal season.

The vineyard is possibly situated on a power spot—on a ley-line or an intersection (speculative)

Well ripened, but not over-ripened fruit with phenols still in a monomeric state.

Grapes with high, but well-balanced phenolic content.

Spontaneous fermentations

Malolactic fermentations

Wines well aged in wooden barrels, whether neutral or new, large or small.

Wines built to age, that improve dramatically with time.

Powerful aroma profiles.

Multi-dimensional flavor characteristics.

Phenomenal health benefits and effects on the body.

It is the taste of wine that captures most of our attention. The better the wine, the more distinct flavors and aromas it can express.

A good single dimensional wine may smell predominantly of oak, with a pleasant, rich taste--one taste.

Add a dimension—the bouquet, which originates from the grapes, not the oak. Too much oak aroma can compete with the bouquet, and should not be considered a replacement for it. We taste mostly with the nose, and one can wallow in the complexity of a fine powerful bouquet.

Add another dimension—fruit, in its many forms, which may take a moment to begin to blossom in the mouth.

Following the fruit, more subtle, mature flavors begin to open up, capped by smooth tannins clinging to the tongue. Finally, when you think it's over, you realize there is yet another dimension, hovering in the background. The finish of a fine wine can morph into an aroma that lingers in a cloud around the body for hours, like a perfume.

My definition of a fine wine is one that expresses more than one dimension, while a world class wine can express many.

In The *Romance of Wine* published in 1932, H. Warner Allen offered his personal belief that pre-Phylloxera wines were superior to 20th century examples, due to the new vines not growing on their natural roots. Allen had tasted plenty of wine from the 19th century, including Tokay Essence from the famous vintage of 1811, "Year of the Comet". In his floral style, he relates some tasting notes in the midst of an evening devoted to Bordeaux's:

"The tapestry like purples of the Latour 1869 contained that sheen of molten gold which only comes after many years of secret ripening in the still darkness of the cellar…Beautiful to the eye, this great wine breathed forth a perfume worthy of the gods. It was compounded of a multitude of subtle fragrances, the freshness of the sun ripened grape, etherealised by the patient work of Nature into a quintessence of harmonious scents. The palate recognised a heroic wine, such a drink as might refresh the warring archangels, and the perfection of its beauty called up the noble phrase 'terrible as an army with banners.' The full organ swell of a triumphal march might express its appeal in terms of music."

"The Margaux 1871 that followed is a wine apart. After the thunderous heroism of the epic Latour, it comes with the dainty sweetness of lyric poetry. Its magic bouquet envelopes the senses in a cloud of airy fragrance, raspberry-scented like the breezes from the Islands of the Blest, a dream of grace and delicacy, the twinkling feet of dancing nymphs, suddenly set free in our tedious world."

Most of us mortals can only hope that once, perhaps twice, in our lifetimes we could drink a wine that made us dream of, "the twinkling feet of dancing nymphs".

Philosophy

Great winemakers intuitively know that their wine is a living, evolving entity– literally, not philosophically.

In Quantum Physics, the experiment conducted in the early 1950's which led to the controversial observer effect theory may in fact effect every aspect of our lives. If it is true that the electron spin around the nucleus of an atom is altered merely by our observation of it, then the ramifications of this effect are enormous.

What the observer effect theory suggests is that we are not merely animals reacting to our environment as in Newtonian physics theory, but rather commanders and commanderesses of the very fabric of our world.

I are promoting both a Newtonian materialistic approach coupled with a Quantum Physics determination. Great vintners carefully craft their wine using impeccable physical techniques, like a Japanese tea ceremony, while at the same time loving and nurturing their wine as if it were a child.

In the vineyard the vigneron expresses both the same attention to detail but also allows the vines to flourish as individual entities. Great wines are forged with a seamless amalgamation of art and science.

Philosophies differ.

Some of the best wines in the world are made using what has been termed Burgundian style. In essence it's a traditional style, beautiful in it's simplicity, mirroring the techniques used to create some of the great wines of Burgundy in France.

The style is essentially based on the idea that excessive manipulation tends to generisize the wine, removing subtleties and complexities we associate with fine wines. Burgundian techniques work very well for coaxing a great wine out of the singular, enigmatic Pinot Noir grape.

More tannic, thick skinned grape varieties, like Cabernet Sauvignon may require a different approach, with attention focusing on choreographing the complex dance of phenolic tannins— encouraging them to eventually evolve into floral aromas and luscious flavors.

It has been said that there are as many techniques as there are winemakers.

Yes--here we bow to winemaking as an art. There is no secret—no single formula that will automatically produce a great wine. Flexibility therefore is an asset of the winemaker who, at times must be almost chameleon-like in nature.

We must honor the tenacity of one who adheres to an ideal, but not to such an extreme that it becomes ones own demise.

In a old wine travel book, the author described a small winery in southern France where the owner needed more cellar space, so decided to have his existing cellar dug out further. In doing so, they uncovered an archaeological treasure: a series of ancient vats with connecting spillways—all chiseled out of the solid bedrock, and designed to make wine utilizing the simple gravity feed principle. How old the vats were was not determined. They could have been carved out by a Merovingian, Sicambrian Frank, or even a Roman or Greek era winemaker. One way or another, every season the current owner now makes his best vin de garde wine in them.

We shall begin with a few snippets of history—vignettes really. I have kept it simple: The interesting, the poetic, the poignant, the anecdotal. Getting a grasp on the history of wine is paramount in the making of great wines. It helps tie the pieces together.

For the vineyard owner, understanding the history of Phyloxera is very important; the American aphid that destroyed all of the vines in Europe in the late 19th century, and still afflicts our vines today.

For the American winemaker, Prohibition is still very much with us, manifesting not only in puritanically restrictive federal laws, ridiculous absurd state and county codes, but also how we choose to make wine.

Call it sophistry if you will, but I believe that the winemaker who can step back and put time into perspective makes a more interesting wine—with more spice and character, more depth and nuance. A wine to contemplate.

HISTORY

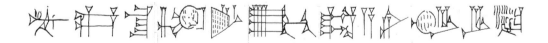

Whomever Has Walked With Truth Generates Life

Sumerian Proverb

In the ancient Sumerian language *tin* meant both "life" and "wine"-----and as a verb "to cure", "to be healthy", and "to live".

Sumeria is touted as the oldest civilization by conventional archaeologists, pre-dating the Egyptian culture by about 800 years. Only a fraction of the hundreds of thousands of clay writing tablets recovered from Mesopotamian archaeological sites have been translated, but the ones that have provide us with a wealth of information about these amazing people.

The Sumerian gods drank wine, and taught humans to make beer from barley. Fermented barley was a nutritious and easily digestible food. Practical and alcoholic, it helped keep the populace healthy and happy. A daily ration 5000 years ago amounted to about 1 liter of low-alcoholic beer.

The Sumerians made claims that are difficult for contemporary archaeologists, and ordinary people to accept as nothing more than mythology. They insisted that their overlord "gods," the Nephilim, or Anunnaki, lived amongst them, but were humanoid beings who came to Earth hundreds of thousands of years prior from another planet to colonize and mine for gold.

The Sumerians also related that the Anunnaki had been making wine since time immemorial, and it was they who brought grapes as well as other foods to Earth. Because of uncomfortable claims such as these, Sumerology is oftentimes ignored or glossed over in favor of the more monumentally impressive ancient Egyptian civilization.

However, the oldest of heroic tales cuts through time to somehow touch us, causing us to wonder, and ponder about the nature of life itself.

In the Epic of Gilgamesh, the hero challenges some of the core issues we have as humankind. Gilgamesh was the young king of Uruk, a city state near the Persian gulf. His mother Ninsun, was an Anunnaki, and lived in the palace attended by ladies in waiting. By human standards, the lifespan of an Anunnaki was extremely long, perhaps thousands of years, but Gilgamesh's father Banda, was half human, so he was uncertain what the length of his lifespan would be. It seems that the Epic of Gilgamesh is really about the hero's quest for his own immortality.

In the fourth part of the tale, he embarks on a great journey to meet Ziusudra (Noah), whom it was said had survived the Deluge millennia before.

Passing through the vast garden of the gods, Gilgamesh encounters Siduri, the Anunnaki lady winemaker, who sits by the sea with her golden bowl and golden vats. Rough, unkempt, and arrogant he tries to push his way through her vineyard gate. The elegant, enigmatic Siduri speaks very directly to him, "Why is despair in your heart and your face like the face of one who has made a long journey? Yes, why is your face burned from the heat and cold, and why do come here wandering over the pastures in search of the wind?"

After he tells her of his quest, she offers him some practical advice, "As for you, Gilgamesh, fill your belly with good things— day and night, night and day, dance and be merry, feast and rejoice. Let your cloths be fresh, bathe yourself in water, cherish the little child that holds your hand, and make your wife happy in your embrace; for this too is the lot of man."

Eventually, after crossing the sea, Gilgamesh finally meets Ziusudra, who reveals to him a mystery--a secret of the gods. The Semitic tale of the Deluge and the survival of Noah is familiar to us, but the much older Sumerian/Akkadian/Assyrian/Babylonian versions are far more complete and detailed. Ziusudra hired workers to help him build the arc, "I gave the shipwrights wine to drink as though it were river water, raw wine and red wine and oil and white wine."

If there are seeds of truth within the mythological framework of the Gilgamesh epic, then one could say that Ziusudra's tale of the building of the arc and giving his workers wine to drink is arguably the oldest literary reference to wine. It also suggests a relatively sophisticated Antediluvian wine culture.

In the Sumerian king lists, Gilgamesh reigned as ruler of Uruk (Erech) for 126 years circa 2700 B.C. He was the last king to rule for longer than a normal human lifespan.

Like the Sumerians, the ancient Egyptian royalty and upper classes favored wine, while the common people tended to drink more beer. Red wine symbolized the rebirth of the dead, and was closely associated with Osiris, who was called "The lord of wine through the inundation."

Lady Rennutet, a cobra goddess was the patroness of winemaking.

Wine in ancient Egypt was predominantly red, but a 2006 Spanish study showed that 6 of the 26 jars found in the 1330 B.C. tomb of Tutankhaton contained white wine, with the type of wine, place of origin, and winemakers names clearly identified on the outside of the jars. The jars are of different types, and 15 vintners are represented on the labels: seven from Syria, and two with Semitic names. This pre-dates the French AOC appellation labeling system by over 3200 years.

Along with some of the earliest written records in Egypt, 700 seven liter imported wine jars were found in the tomb of Scorpion I, from dynasty 0—circa 3150 B.C.. The dig was under the direction of German archaeologist Gunter Dreyer. Archaeologist Patrick McGovern and his team from the University of Pennsylvania determined that the jars were from the Levant, a more likely source for good wine than Egypt, where the climate is generally too hot. In fact, a vignette from the tomb of Thutmosis III depicts slaves picking grapes from overhead trellises, a typical trellising system used in hot climates.

The mapping of the human genome has its roots in wine yeasts. Bob Mortimer, professor emeritus of genetics and development at the University of California at Berkeley was instrumental in the 1950's study that eventually led to the genome mapping of the wine yeast *Saccharomyces cerevisiae* by more than 100 laboratories around the world in 1996. The study paved the way for the mapping of the human genome. Bob Mortimer, in association with Patrick McGovern recently found that yeast samples taken from the Scorpion I jars suggested that they may have been a precursor of *Saccharomyces cerevisiae*. A team in Florence, including molecular biologist Duccio Cavalieri isolated intact strands of the ancient yeasts DNA.

In his book *Ancient Wine; The Search for the Origins of Viticulture,* Patrick McGovern states, "The 840 base-pair fragments of ribosomal yeast DNA that were isolated were some of the largest fragments of ancient DNA ever recovered." And, "*Saccharomyces cerevisiae* was the first eukarote to have its genome sequenced. The genome is composed of about 13 million bp and contains 6,275 genes. It is estimated that the yeast shares 23% of its genomes with humans."

Calligraphy   Lu You (1125-1210 A.D.)
All my money has gone on three thousand gallons of wine,
Yet they cannot overcome my infinite sadness,
As I drink today my eyes flash fire,
I seize my brush and look round, the whole world shrinks,
And in a flash, unwitting, I start to write.
A storm rages in my breast, heaven lends me strength,
As when dragons war in the waste, murky, reeking of blood,
Or demons topple down crags and the moon turns dark.
In this moment all sadness is driven from my heart,
I pound the couch with a cry and my cap falls off
The fine paper of Suzhou and Chengdu will not serve,
Instead I write on the thirty foot wall of my room

Classical artistic renderings of the eight Taoist immortals always depict Li Tie Guai carrying a gourd of wine.

As the story goes, Li Tie Guai liked to go out-of-body for long periods of time.

Once, his body was immobile for an unusually long time. His family thought he was dead and burnt his body as was customary. Upon returning he found he had no body, so took the body of a cripple who was dying. Therefore he is always shown with a crutch as well as the gourd.

In Mandarin, grape wine is "putao jiu". Wine from *Vitis vinifera* grapes was being made at least as early as 126 B.C. in China, when General Chang Ch'ien brought wine grapes from Bactria. Prior to that time, wine was made from Chinese native species *Vitis thunbergi* and *Vitis filifolia* as mentioned in the 5000 year old book titled, *Classical Pharmacopeia of the Heavenly Husbandman.* However, traditionally wine, or "jiu", as a regular part of Chinese culture is actually any fermented beverage other than beer.

To date, the Chinese people have acquired quite a taste for western style grape wines, and tracts of land are devoted to the planting of popular international cultivars inspired in part by studies done at Wuxi University of Light Industry in Jiangshu province.

Along with their gorgeous architecture and art, the Minoan civilization on Crete may be one of the earliest Greek wine cultures. Dating from the later Cretan period, a fairly sophisticated, partially gravity-fed winery including earthenware stomping vats and fermenters was found at a site near Vathypetro, in the Archanes hill country.

Naturally, Homer had much to say about wine, as it was so much a part of Greek culture. Laertes, the father of Odysseys, boasted that he had fifty rows, each of a different variety; arranged so that his grapes ripened in succession. This suggests a relatively sophisticated viticultural prowess.

During the siege of Troy, Nestor's mistress Hecamede gave his wounded friend *Kykeon*—a combination of nebulous herbs, possibly barley, honey, and the most famous of ancient Greek wines—*Pramnian* . The mixture was purported to have amazing curative powers, much like the more modern, but legendary Hungarian *Essentia*.

In the Odyssey--it was in fact her own special mixture of *Kykeon* that the enchantress Circe enticed Odysseys's men with, so she could transmute them into swine and claim him for her lover (I hate it when that happens). But our hero was clever, tricking her and negotiating his own terms to be her lover.

That leads us to an often unrecognized fact that many, or most ancient wines actually contained additives such as: resin, barley, pepper, wormwood, capers, saffron, opium, honey, and many other herbs and spices. By far the most common was tree resin, which acted as a preservative by impeding the reproduction of acetic acid/vinegar producing bacteria. Wine was also the most common ingredient in ancient medicines, as many of the additives' compounds would be passively extracted by the alcohol or the water in the wine, and lightly preserved.

Oenotria, the Greeks called it. "The land of wine".

Italy is one of the largest producers of wine in the world today, and boasts so many cultivars, microclimates, and wines that it could be a lifelong study to fully master it--if that's possible.

Some claim that the Greeks originally introduced grapes to Italy. The Greeks were aggressive seagoing traders, planting vineyards wherever they colonized. However, the origins of the early Italian Etruscan culture remains unclear. We do know that they were already making wine when the Lydians and Phoenicians arrived on their shores. One way or another, by the time the sun set on the Greek era of dominance, the western Mediterranean had established thriving wine cultures, which the Romans expanded and capitalized on.

The wealth of Pompeii was firmly rooted in wine production and trade, providing Rome with much of its wine prior to the eruption of Mt. Vesuvius in A.D. 79. 2000 Years ago Pompeii was the Bordeaux of southern Italy, with vines planted on the slopes of Mt. Vesuvius and a superb harbor nearby. Twenty-nine out of the thirty-one villas surrounding Pompeii were devoted to wine; the "chateau" of their era. Within the town are the remains of wineries, with earthenware *Dolia*—fermenters an arms length deep and wide sunken neatly into the ground. The ground temperature would serve to modulate the fermentations, slowing down excessive vigor by reducing the naturally occurring heat. The destruction of Pompeii partially altered the nature of wine the Romans drank, favoring more red wines from newer vineyards planted near Rome.

Much later, the grape growing and wine making techniques used by the Italians in the 19th century differed very little from the basic process used by their ancestors millennia before.

It wasn't really until Angelo Gaja in Piedmonte and producers in Tuscany crusaded for modern-ization in the 1970's that Italian wines began to flower into the incredible examples we have today.

The heartland of a grape variety usually produces what many consider to be its best wine.

Italian wines made from two of Italy's flagship grapes, Sangiovese (Chianti, Brunello di Montalcino), and Nebbiolo (Barolo and Barbaresco) still somehow have finer dimensions in flavor compared to new world examples made from the same cultivars.

Spain has a very old history of producing both olives and wine.

In the 8th century B.C. Phoenicians, under the threat of Assyrian conquest fled from present-day Lebanon into the Mediterranean. Some established colonies in Carthage (Tunisia), planting vineyards and reestablishing their traditional wine trade. Carthage eventually developed some of the most sophisticated viticulture the world had known. That skill, dovetailed with their considerable seafaring and mercantile prowess allowed to them to grow quite wealthy. Carthaginian traders took grapevines and technology at least as far north as the Iberian peninsula. 700 years later the Roman agronomist Lucius Columella deemed Carthaginian viticulture the basis for wine growing in the Mediterranean.

Contrary to orthodox history, the Moors, during their almost 700 year control of Iberia did not curtail the indigenous wine culture to a great degree. In fact, Christians and Jews lived in relative peace under Moorish rule. Islamic culture, along with the Cathars on the other (French) side of the Pyrenees were the most sophisticated and wealthiest in Europe during the "Dark Ages" and early medieval periods. The open-minded Cathar society in the south of France made wine and traded freely with the Moors and the rest of the Mediterranean cultures.

Later the Cathar culture was destroyed and conveniently written out of history because of their unorthodox, non-centralized religious beliefs. It was from the Cathar troubadours the we heard the earliest versions of the Grail legends, forming the roots of our modern popular music. From the Cathar monastic music we get some of the earliest forms of musical notation. They were the hub of culture in Europe in their day.

During that period two important Iberian grape varieties came into southern France: Garnacha (Grenache), and Monastrell/Mataro (Mourvedre). Over a millennia later, the Rioja region received a technological boost. In the late 19th century Bordeaux vintners, endeavoring to escape the Phyloxera scourge temporarily moved to Rioja to make wine for a few years until the aphids finally reached northern Spain. The winemaking techniques of the Bordelaise and Rioja producers do therefore share some similarities. Today, the aristocratic Spanish grape known as Tempranillo produces the finest wines of Spain in Rioja, but never made its way into France. The variety does travel well, as excellent wines are being made from it in both California and Washington State.

As of this writing, Spain has become the largest producer of wine worldwide, edging out Italy and France.

In the Early 1700's in Portugal, the Marques de Pombal, Jose de Carvhallo e Mello became aware of a wine fortification technique used at a monastery in the mountains of the Douro. The monks had been adding brandy to partially fermented musts which arrested the fermentation, resulting in thick, sweet, highly alcoholic wines. The Marques, having formerly served as ambassador to London, and well acquainted with British tastes, saw this as a marketing opportunity. He eventually established his own company, shipping the wine out of Oporto, then the largest city in Portugal. The Marque de Pombal, Jose de Carvhallo e Mello then proceeded to set up the first government controlled regional demarcation for wine production in Portugal, focusing on improving quality at the vineyard level. The Portuguese model served to become one of the major inspirations contributing to the creation of the important French AOC system two centuries later.

Eleanor of Aquitane was one of the most historically enigmatic individuals from the middle ages. The feisty, beautiful, politically savvy young woman inherited the Duchy of Aquitaine when her father, the duke, died on a pilgrimage into the Pyrenees Mountains. She married the northern French prince who, in 1137 became King Louis VII. After accompanying him on the second crusade, she returned to give him two daughters, but to his great disappointment, no sons. In an age of unenlightenment, when women were treated like cattle, Eleanor managed to divorce Louis, and several months later marry Henri Plantagenet who became Henry II, King of England.

So in her lifetime, Eleanor was both Queen of France, and Queen of England, as well as Duchess of Aquitaine. She bore Henry sons, including the infamous John, Geoffrey, and the celebrated Richard Coeur de Lion. When Henri Plantagenet was crowned king, Eleanor's duchy of Aquitaine fell under the control of the British crown, and their heirs. Aquitaine was a vast, wealthy region in southwest France which boasted many wine growing areas, the most renowned at the time in Cahors, producing deeply colored wines from the old Malbec and Tannat grapes.

The British hired Dutch engineers to drain the swamps in the Medoc near present day Bordeaux. There they planted vast vineyards and created an easy drinking wine for export to England. The Brits called the lightly pigmented wine "Claret"; and they still use that term today when referring to a wine from the Bordeaux region.

Bordeaux was under English control for 277 years until finally acquiescing to the French (who were aided by Joan d'Arc) in 1431 following the Hundred Years War. By that time, the Brits had developed quite a taste for wine, the supply of which was abruptly cut off (rough times for the British). In response to the demand, merchants began importing wine from Spain and Portugal, and were instrumental in developing Port as a commodity.

Port was made by encouraging a quick, high temperature fermentation for three days with continuous maceration by foot. Then, early enough in the fermentation to leave some residual sugars, it was then fortified with strong Brandy, which effectively terminated the ferment.

This yielded a powerful wine resistant to spoilage, which was a persistent problem in that era. A common wine from the renaissance may have harbored so much vinegar and other spoilage organisms that a modern consumer would consider it undrinkable.

Wine was shipped in the summer months, and entire ship-loads would sometimes spoil before delivery could be completed. Whether they gleaned the information from the ancients remains unclear, but by the 1600's, Dutch traders were burning sulfur wicks in barrels to reduce spoilage.

Wine was shipped in three barrel sizes: the 60 gallon *barrique*, the 120 gallon *pipe*, and the 240 gallon *tonneau*, as well as the 80 gallon *hogshead*. Traditionally, the capacity of a sailing ship was defined by how many barrels of wine it could carry. "She's a 200 tonner", meant that the vessel could fit 200 tonneau of wine in her hold, using it as ballast.

In days of yore, wine was typically poured directly out of an amphora or barrel for drinking.

As the level in the barrel decreased, the oxidation of the wine increased, encouraging spoilage. Thus we have the old term, "bottom of the barrel."

The development of high quality bottles and corks is a relatively recent luxury.

As beautiful as some ancient glassware was, it tended to be brittle. In the 1630's techniques to produce harder glass bottles were developed in England by the alchemist, author, and sometimes pirate Sir Kenelm Digby. Digby figured out how to use a wind tunnel attached to a coal-fired glass kiln to raise the temperature. This allowed the increase of the ratio of sand to potash and lime, which rendered the bottles more durable. Still, it wasn't until 1700 that the French adopted the "English method" of making glass, and not until about 1800 that wine began to be systematically put into bottles for storage.

This development dramatically altered the nature of wines because they could then be created to lay down and store for longer periods, much like the Romans and Greeks had done millennia before in earthenware amphorae. The shape of bottles from the 1600 era was very short and squat. They were almost as wide as they were tall, and designed to sit on a table without tipping over. The next 200 years saw the shape gradually becoming taller and narrower, as it became more common to lay the bottled wine on its side for storage, thus keeping the corks wet.

Today we see many variations of two basic bottle shapes used for red wines. We have the Bordeaux bottle, used in western France for Cabernet Sauvignon, Merlot, Cabernet Franc, Malbec, and Negrette. The other major bottle shape is the Burgundy bottle, from eastern France. Burgundy bottles are used for Pinot Noir, Gamay, Syrah, Cabernet Franc from the Loire valley, and all of the Grenache dominated blends from the southern Rhone valley. Most wineries worldwide tend to loosely follow the traditions—particularly concerning Cabernet Sauvignon, which always comes in a Bordeaux bottle, and Pinot Noir in Burgundy bottles.

The priest Dom Perignon is generally attributed to be the first to use corks in Champagne bottles, which essentially allowed for the development of sparkling wines. The Romans were however, using cork to seal their six gallon amphorae in the latter part of the Roman Empire. Today there are not enough cork trees in Portugal and Spain to meet the demand, which cause the price we pay for high quality corks to be high.

In the middle ages European monks were considered by many to be nothing more than slovenly drunkards, blatantly living off the goodwill of others.

Martin Luther summed it up, "Monks are the fleas on the beard of God Almighty".

We do owe monastic orders our thanks however, for contributing to the systematic development of viticulture, horticulture, and to a lesser degree, vinification. The Benedictine order owned vast vineyards in Champagne, Burgundy, Bordeaux in France, and in the Reingau in Germany.

The Cistercian order was created in 1098, at the inception of the first crusade. There were four levels of rank in the order, the highest level made up of noblemen, who were closely aligned with the Knights of the Temple of Solomon, both purportedly involved in high finance.

Both the Cistercians and the Templars became extremely wealthy, and are the obvious candidates responsible for the technology and financing necessary to build the great cathedrals of Europe. However, to the outside world, what appeared to be the singular occupation of the Cistercian order was viticulture and vinification . They grew grapes and made wine.

The lowest rank of monks in the Cistercian order wore brown robes and performed the bulk of the manual labor. For over 600 years they planted, grafted, pruned, experimented with cultivars, selections, took careful notes, and passed the data down to further generations.

The Cistercian and Benedictine chapters in France were disrupted during the French revolution, but their legacy lives on. The French are arguably still the fussiest viticulturests anywhere.

Today, French wineries whose name begins with "Clos de", were probably once monastic holdings. "Clos" is the root for "enclosure", which suggests the vineyard was once surrounded by a wall, typical of an old monastic vineyard.

Today, monks of the Cistercian order produce the famous Trappist beers in Belgium, Austria, Holland, and now in Massachusetts at St. Joseph's Abbey.

One could say that the French revolution was a harbinger of changes to come in the Oenological sphere. In a mere 100 years, a handful of developments followed; the use of glass bottles and corks, the industrial revolution, Phylloxera and mildew attacks, and the birth of modern chemistry.

Ideally, grapes are crushed immediately after harvesting, as subtleties in the fruit degrade as rapidly as mold and bacteria grow. Healthy, dry grapes will however hold up fairly well for several days depending on their temperature and acidity.

With the industrial revolution came the advent of the railroads, enabling grapes to be transported long distances. This particular technological advancement helped increase the production, but was eventually detrimental to the quality of French wine.

A new type of merchant emerged, called a negociant, who today are merchants dealing in wine, perhaps purchasing wine in barrels, cellaring, bottling, and marketing it. But in the 19th century "negociant" was somewhat of a dirty word. Negociants were notorious for manipulating markets, and remarkably creative in their sordid, underhanded business deals. The ability to transport grapes to auction houses by rail gave negociants the power to pit one grower against another, mercilessly bidding the prices down.

Typical grape growers in Europe were barefoot peasants--subsistence farmers just barely putting food on their tables. For them, surviving lower prices meant overcropping--allowing the vines to bear higher yields; which in turn encouraged the planting of higher yielding varieties like Carignan, the Spanish and French jug wine grape.

By the 1920's the situation was abysmal. The south of France was described as a "vast lake of cheap wine".

In 1928 Chateauneuf du Pape, the most famous wine growing area in southern France, endeavored to correct these issues by defining their borders, and created rules to be followed focusing on quality and accountability. In 1936, the French government, following Chateauneuf du Papes lead, created the AOC regulatory system which, though bureaucratic, helped improve the quality of French wine in general.

The French AOC system divided the country into legally defined viticultural areas. Germany, Italy, Austria, and Spain soon followed with their own regulatory systems, using the French AOC as a model.

Chateauneuf du Pape has always distinguished itself as a trend setter in French regulation concepts.

Following a spate of alleged flying saucer sightings in France in 1954, the mayor of Chateauneuf du Pape issued the following decrees, which are still enforceable today:

Article 1. The overflight, the landing and the takeoff of aircraft known as "flying saucers" or "flying cigars", whatever their nationality is, are strictly prohibited on the territory of the community.

Article 2. Any aircraft, known as a "flying saucer" or "flying cigar", which should land on the territory of the community will be immediately impounded.

One can only imagine how tourists from outer space would react to having to stand in line waiting to pay their fee in a greasy little French towing company office. Welcome to planet Earth!

Microbes were first observed by Anton van Leeuwenhoek, a Dutch trader and talented lens grinder. With his unique hand held microscope, he was first able to observe cells in 1673, and finally bacteria in 1677. In a scraping of plaque from his own teeth, he observed, "Many little living animalcules, very prettily a moving."

Almost two hundred years later, in 1861, 39 year old Louis Pasteur won a prize offered by the Paris Academy of Science concerning the persistent idea that germs grew by "spontaneous generation". The theory was discreetly linked to the then predominant belief in Creationism, and held to the idea that microbes simply popped in out of thin air. Pasteur proved the idea incorrect, illustrating that microbes do have reproductive capabilities, and can be introduced into a culture medium from the air as well.

Louis Pasteur could be called the first Zymologist, when in 1857 he connected yeast to fermentation. Leeuwenhoek may have been the first to observe yeasts under a microscope, but Pasteur was the first to get a good grasp of the life cycles of microbes.

In 1863, Napoleon III hired Pasteur to investigate why 25% of all French wine went bad before reaching the consumer. At the time France produced much more wine than they do today. 25% of the total production equated to millions of bottles of spoiled wine annually, resulting in a national travesty that hampered the French economy.

Pasteur then produced his famous treatise *Études sur le Vin*, which became a cornerstone of modern microbiology. He discovered the role that oxygen plays in wine, which set the stage for understanding the differences between aerobic and anaerobic microbes.

A small gradual influx of oxygen contributes to the maturation process in wine, but too much at the wrong times encourage the growth of vinegar producing bacteria and other undesirable microbes. Pasteur suggested heating the finished wine to 140° F. to subdue the microbes. Unfortunately, that would not only ruin the flavor, but would also volatilize off some of the alcohols which helped protect the wine in the first place. However, the technique did work well with milk, helping to give it a longer shelf life in an era prior to refrigeration. Thus we have the simple process which still bears his name.

French vignerons, curious about the sturdy native American grape species, began obtaining imported vines from American nurseries in the 1840's. It was, in a sense, a harmless hobby, expressing that uniquely human urge to tinker and experiment.

Unheralded came the disastrous events that followed. The imported American vines were accompanied by downy mildew, powdery mildew, and by far the most infamous stow-away, the *Phylloxera vastatrix* aphid. The Eurasian *Vitis vinifera* grape species, the vines of which then almost literally covered Italy and France, had little or no resistance to these new afflictions.

Chemistry was a rapidly emerging science, so fortunately, by 1885 the mildews were partially kept under control with the use of sulphur and copper products, but no genuine cure existed or exists today for the Phylloxera root louse.

The aphid was single-handedly responsible for killing almost all grapevines planted on their own roots in Europe between 1850 and 1905. Who knows how many obscure grape cultivars were lost in the melee? The statistics are staggering. In 1868 the enologist Dr. Jules Guyot wrote, "The vineyard occupies in France 2,500,000 hectares, almost half of the worlds total, representing the sixteenth part of our cultivated soil. The culture of the vine maintains six million farmers, and about a further two million suppliers, manufacturers, carriers, and storekeepers."

The spread of Phylloxera throughout Europe, and how it was dealt with is, in itself a pragmatic study of human nature. Beginning in 1862, for over 10 years the brick & mortar scientists in Paris denied first the existence of the aphid, and then insisted that it would never be a problem.

Meanwhile letters poured in from desperate vignerons whose vineyards were dying by the hundreds of thousands of hectares.

The most ardent crusader battling the spread of the Phylloxera aphid in France was the botanist Jules Emile Planchon. He recognized the seriousness of the problem immediately, but unfortunately his relentless work was hindered by the "experts" in Paris who were clearly in denial, choosing to bury their heads in the sand.

No one knew how the aphid moved from vineyard to vineyard. In the summer of 1868 at the Mas Fabre vineyard owned by viticulteur Louis Faucon the vines began to sicken. He posted his two young nephews to watch over the vineyard. The sharp-eyed boys observed microscopic yellow specks moving across the surface of the sun-baked soil. Planchon reported the boy's observation, "These spirited youngsters told their uncle they had seen the insects, 'strolling along like good bourgeois going into a restaurant with walking sticks in their hands'".

The discovery was discounted. How could children know anything compared to the ordained, educated, bearded experts in Paris? (beards were in fashion) Actually, the boys were correct; one of whom, upon maturing into an adult became involved in Phylloxera research.

French nurserymen were more practical, as they perceived early on that vinifera vines could be grafted onto American rootstock which was inherently Phylloxera resistant.

The drama continued. Enter the purists: "How could we even consider grafting our noble Pinot Noir onto vulgar American rootstock?"

Resistance was futile, and in the end that is exactly what happened, and is the current situation. Today almost all vines in Europe are planted on grafted rootstock resistant to the Phylloxera vastatrix aphid. The modern entomological term for the aphid is *Dactylasphaera vitifoliae*, but the wine world still refers to it using the older common term: Phylloxera.

At the present time, Phylloxera has managed to circumnavigate the globe. In California and Oregon it is considered impolite to walk into a vineyard without permission because ones shoes and clothing can serve as temporary hosts for the nymphs and eggs. Some believe that pre-Phylloxera wines were superior to 20th century examples, due to the "new" vines not growing on their natural roots. The subjective nature of wine tasting renders the question difficult to answer, and complicated by many factors, including the superb string of Bordeaux vintages from 1864-1878, the loss of all of the old vines, and the poor viticultural practices of the early 20th century.

The Antedeluvians were all very sober
For they had no wine, and they brew'd no October;
All wicked, bad livers, on mischief still thinking,
For there can't be good living where there is not good drinking.
Derry down
Twas honest old Noah first planted the vine,
And mended his morals by drinking it's wine;
He justly the drinking of water decry'd;
For he knew that all mankind, by drinking it, dy'd.
Derry down
From this piece of history plainly we find
That water's good neither for body or mind;
That virtue and safety in wine-bibbing's found
While all that drink water deserve to be drown'd
Derry down
So for safety and honesty put the glass round.

A drinking song by Benjamin Franklin—circa 1745

Why should it be a revelation to us that the American founding fathers drank wine and had a good time doing it? The majority of those gentlemen shared a love for French wine, and collaborated in not only the acquisition of it, but the planting of experimental vineyards in Virginia.

Thomas Jefferson, a lover of Bordeaux wines, tried seven times to plant *Vitis vinifera* vines on his estate—unsuccessfully. Those early would be, well meaning vineyard owners were unfortunately ignorant to what we know today about the susceptibility of Eurasian vines to Phylloxera, mildews, black rot, and Pierces disease.

Jefferson has been hailed as the first American wine connoisseur, having traveled throughout France, Germany and Italy with the specific intent to seek out quality wines with which to stock his 600 bottle per year cellar. Upon arriving in Paris in 1784, he dined with Benjamin Franklin and tasted a selection from Franklins' 1100 bottle cellar in Passy prior to serving as America's first minister to France between 1776-1785.

The early English and French settlers did try to grow imported wine grapes in the northeastern seaboard, but to no avail. The native American grape species they encountered were tough, hardy, beautiful vines, but unfortunately did not produce good wine.

The saga of the American colonial's quest to grow European wine grapes on the eastern seaboard is a testament to the sheer tenacity, strength, and determination of early Americans.

Thomas Jefferson is perhaps the best known would be vigneron, but his efforts were not the first, nor the last to fail. Shortly after Jefferson's final attempt, Nicolas Longworth imported 5000 plants from Madeira and 10,000 from France and Germany, planting them in carefully prepared beds in Ohio. Longworth writes in 1846, "All failed; and not a single plant is left in my vineyards. I would advise the cultivation of native grapes alone, and the raising of new varieties from their seed."

Even today, with our knowledge of the Phylloxera aphid, downy and powdery mildews, and cold winter tolerance issues, vineyard acreage east of the Mississippi river is still dominated by hybrids and native varieties.

The California wine renaissance had already begun when Longworth wrote those bitter words in 1846. California, for a time at least, was free of the Phylloxera scourge, and being dryer, the vines did not suffer as much from mildews and diseases.

Vines of the Mission variety had been growing at the San Diego Mission since the Franciscan Junipero Serra planted them in 1769, which was simply a northern expansion of a two hundred year old tradition in the Mexican Baja. Therefore, the history of California wine actually goes back almost 400 years.

Agoston Haraszthy bought the Sonoma Buena Vista Ranch in 1856 creating the now famous wine estate. Even in that era neighboring Napa valley was recognized as having promising potentials as well.

San Francisco became a hub of the new wine culture, which buoyed with it the excitement of the west—a truly brave new world. Much of the Californian wine from the late 19th century may have been of decent quality, so much so that very little of it left the state. It was consumed so quickly and locally by thirsty Californians that the nature of most of it has been lost to history. Since California was a frontier, with few laws regulating production in rural areas, some wine growers and producers from that time are also forgotten.

In Washington State French trappers were growing a few grapevines east of the Cascade mountain range in the early 1800's. An artist's drawing of Fort Vancouver at the mouth of the Columbia river depicts grapevines growing on orderly trellises. By 1905 good wine was being made in Washington State, mostly by immigrants who brought traditional skills with them.

But a few years later, the wine would turn sour with the unsavory events that were soon to follow. One might hope that we could use our history as a measure of our wisdom so as to avoid repeating mistakes of the past, such as the scourge of religious intolerance that inspired the American prohibition movement.

An environment devoid of alcoholic beverages —"Irish Hell".

American school children are routinely spoon-fed some of the most ridiculous historical nonsense. Columbus discovered America? Hogwash. Plenty of Europeans had already visited the shores of North America.

With scissors, colored paper and glue, children snip out and paste together charming renditions of tiny ships bearing black-clad Puritans with funny hats. "Those poor sweet Puritans trying to find a better life away from that nasty old England".

That is the furthest thing from the truth.

English history can be particularly boring, but some of it is important for North Americans, and the development of wine culture on the North American continent.

When Queen Elizabeth jettisoned the Roman Catholic Church and formed the Church of England it was both a shrewd political move as well as a social move on the chessboard.

Yes, there was the obvious political antipathy towards Spain and France, but there also ran deeper underlying currents. It was also a move away from religious extremism which, for the most part was supported by the English populace.

There are however, always those that are uncomfortable with freedoms.

The Spanish Inquisition had always been a hard pill for the Brits to swallow. In fact, they never really did, even at the height of the pressure from Rome and the Dominican order. Finally, they spit it out and let it sink to the bottom of the English channel along with the Spanish fleet.

But once again the creature reared its ugly head, this time in a Protestant format—Thou shalt not do almost everything. The Purist movement embraced some of the ugliest aspects of Christianity. They were a dour lot. Women, the human body, dancing, drinking, laughing, and having any kind of fun was considered the work of the devil.

Oliver Cromwell's army of Puritan Roundhead's campaign in Ireland was particularly brutal, massacring civilians and cutting out the tongues of women. Why? "Women tongues wag".

Yes, in the middle ages armies routinely behaved with that level of barbarity or worse, but not in the 17th century. European consciousness was evolving.

Prior to 1641, over 20,000 Puritans had already emigrated across the Atlantic. Finally, following Cromwells death in 1658, the English people grew completely intolerant of the Puritans and forced them out of the country. Essentially, Britannia pooped out the Puritans and the turd landed in North America.

Unfortunately, the hard-line religious extremism seeped into American culture like a virus. The long-term affects run deep, and are with us still today, but Americans cannot generally see it, since we grew up inside of the permeation.

Any ideology cooked up by an insecure A-type male fanatic inevitably leads to the same outcome. Somehow there is always the suppression of women, and an unhealthy attitude towards sexuality. The sexual repression creates an explosive—an incendiary expressed outwards by the young men—violence. We are observing that same tenant today in international struggles.

How about teaching our children a more accurate version of history: The Puritans were religious extremists with a pronounced violent streak.

Consider American television programming. Nudity is unacceptable, while violence is commonplace. In fact, violence is the order de jour—it is served with almost every meal.

Statistics illustrate how northern latitude grain producing countries citizens engage in more binge drinking than those in grape growing wine regions. In wine drinking cultures there is more of a tendency for alcoholic beverages to be consumed regularly, but not to excess.

19th century America had little imbedded wine drinking culture. For those that did imbibe, it was predominantly a country of hard liquor drinkers. The Anti-Saloon League was formed to address a genuine problem. The saloon habit had become obnoxious—rough men drinking, smoking, gambling, fighting, whoring, and swearing loudly all night—every night.

It was all upsetting for those living nearby in otherwise peaceful towns. Something had to change, but like Oliver Cromwell's deplorable actions, the fix was too extreme.

Prohibition only lasted from 1919 to 1933, but the effects of it were devastating to the fledgling American quality wine industry.

Life and wine for the likeness of nature are most agreeable. And this is the cause
I think why men by nature so greedily covet wine; except some odd Abstemius, one
amongst a thousand perchance, degenerate and is of a doggish nature; for dogges of
nature do abhor wine.

Thomas Cogan—physician—(1545?--1607)

The language of the Eighteenth Amendment was clear and severe:

> The manufacture, sale, or transportation of intoxicating liquors within, the importation thereof
> into, or the exportation thereof from the United States and all territory subject to the jurisdiction
> thereof for beverage purposes is hereby prohibited.

The National Prohibition Act passed by Congress on 28 October 1919 became known as the
Volstead Act. Both the amendment and the act were directed at the producers and "traffickers" of
"intoxicating liquors". The purchase, possession, and consumption of alcoholic beverages had no
penalty attached to them. The heads of families were allowed to make up to 200 gallons annually
of "fruit juices" exclusively for drinking at home. This facet of the act is still with us today, and
as we shall see so is much of Prohibition. Americans still live under the pall of a post prohibitive
environment, and the history of wine in America is bound up with the drama of those times.

The Volstead Act was a triumph for teetotalers and the religious right who, spearheaded by the
Anti-Saloon League admonished the wickedness of the "Demon Rum".

"Long live Prohibition!"

Evangelist Billy Sunday proclaimed that you could no more repeal the amendment, "Than you
could dam Niagara Falls with toothpicks". Not to be outdone, Texas senator Morris Sheppard
declared that, "There is as much chance of repealing the 18th Amendment as there is for a
hummingbird to fly to the planet Mars with the Washington Monument tied to its' tail."

They had their day in the sun, but while they were blustering, the ship was steadily sinking, and
the tepid water had already covered their patent leather shoes.

Meanwhile, most wineries simply went out of business, except for the rare and lucky ones able to
jump through the legal loopholes associated with becoming producers of sacramental or medicinal
wines. Vineyard acres however, actually increased during the fourteen years of prohibition; but
new vineyards were inevitably planted with table and raisin grapes which tolerated the rigors of
shipping better than the more delicate wine grapes.

Thus, the seeds were sown for the growth of both the infamous American jug wine industry
as well as home winemakers. To say that home winemakers flourished in the 1920's would be an
understatement. In 1927 alone, 72,000 rail cars filled with grapes rolled out of California destined
for distribution in cities such as Chicago, Boston, and Newark.

No one will ever know how much wine was actually produced, but members of the Wickersham
Commission made a conservative estimate that an average 111 million gallons of wine was made
each year from 1922 to 1929 in American homes.

In California, Fruit Industries, a company created in 1929 began making grape concentrates in response to the annual surplus of California grapes. The product, called *Vine-Glo* was marketed aggressively, selling over a million gallons the first year. Probably a clever promotional stunt; when Vine-Glo entered the Chicago market in 1930, the media reported that gangster Al Capone was preparing to treat it with a strong-arm.

After prohibition was repealed, new wineries appeared, and in a fervor began making wines predominantly of questionable quality. California produced over ten times as much wine as the rest of the country combined, most of which was sold in 8000 gallon rail tank cars and shipped anonymously to other states where it was bottled and marketed under a plethora of local names. European place names were shamelessly purloined, such as: "Haut Sauterne", "St. Julien", "Margaux", "Chateau Yquem", "Moselle", and of course the infamous "Burgundy".

One can only wonder what the Europeans thought of this level of ignorance and audacity. It cannot have improved America's reputation as a country populated by annoyingly resourceful cowherds.

When Dr. Maynard Amerine and his associates from the University of California at Davis analyzed the wines submitted to the California Fairs and the Golden Gate Exposition of 1939 they found that none of the wine type names really meant anything at all. As Dr. Amerine observed, "The consumer has no way of knowing… what kind of wine he is getting except that it is red!"

Quality wineries were few, and most of those quickly went out of business. The marketing problem was a two-edged sword. After prohibition, an entire generation had never even tasted decent wine. Any quality wine culture America had developed before 1920 was either greatly diminished or entirely lost. It was during the Depression. Consumers wanted something cheap, sweet and alcoholic. Fortified wines made from cheap table grapes dominated the market until 1967, when dry wine sales finally eclipsed the sale of fortified wines in the U.S.

Another factor contributing to declining quality concerned the relationship between vineyards and wineries. At harvest time, there was usually a surplus of raisin grapes that became part of the blend, distilled into brandy or industrial alcohol during WWII. Wineries became a dumping ground for unsound fruit. Believe it or not, they saved the best for raisins and table grapes, and left the worst for wine. Table grapes dominated in California, and the Concord variety in the rest of the country, neither of which make quality wine.

Beginning in the 1930's, winemaking was performed on an industrial scale in mechanized wineries built to the new model: concrete floors, concrete fermentation tanks, and automatic cooling systems. They were the largest wineries on the planet, some with over 10 million gallon capacities and more.

Then, as volcanoes spewed forth magma in the distance, the corporate buyout era began. In typical Godzilla-like fashion, they swallowed each other up until, by the late 1950's only a few of the most dominant carnivores remained. What caused the climactic change that ended the age of the dinosaurs is up for speculation, but we do know one thing; after drinking jug wine for forty years Americans wanted something better.

The number of smaller wineries had been in a sharp decline in the 1950's and early 1960's, but by 1970 small wineries began to appear rapidly, endeavoring to produce quality wines. New vineyards were planted, and old ones planted or grafted over to vinifera grape varieties like Riesling,

Chardonnay, Cabernet Sauvignon, Merlot, and Zinfandel. The University of California at Davis was vindicated, as they had been promoting the planting of quality varieties for over 30 years.

Up until that era, wine was made in an industrial format, with technical support provided by UC Davis, which has historically been funded by the jug wine industry.

Somehow American mainstream consciousness had gravitated towards embracing the most mundane aspects of classical physics. Scientific fact had become the holy grail, even though in reality the "facts" that were in vogue tended to be what physicists had been working on 200 years prior.

An attitude usually accompanying materialism is the belief that we understand almost all there is to know about our world and that science has proved it. One could consider that this rather inflexible attitude is actually fostered by the fear of change, the unknown, and ultimately the fear of death itself. I am not attacking science, rather putting into perspective the attitudes which keep scientific development from naturally moving forward. This was of course the distasteful flavor of sterile materialism that baby boomers finally rebelled against.

In that intellectual climate, most large American wineries that were built after WWII definitely followed a technological approach to winemaking, using industrial standards as a model. Many traditional methods were simply thrown out. New world winemakers somehow thought they could make better wine than the Europeans did with whatever grapes were provided based solely on superior American technological prowess and the scientific method.

It was an ignorant and arrogant attitude.

Since the 1960's, American wineries have been gradually gravitating back towards more traditional viticultural and vinification techniques. By trial and error, they have experienced the validity of some of the practical wisdom accumulated over centuries of winemaking. Coupled with improved technology and greater understanding of wine chemistry, we are making some of the best wines ever. In the new millennium, winemaking technology is international, and tradition and technology are manifested as a unified whole.

So what does the famous British queen of the renaissance Elizabeth I have to do with modern American wine? The long term ramifications of religious extremism on American society.

Try applying for a county use permit to build a winery. Fill out the perpetual reams of federal paperwork for the ATF required for a winery (that's alcohol, tobacco, and firearms—the unholy triad). Dealing with bureaucracy is becoming increasingly more difficult. The more of them there are, the more they-all get paid, and the more annoying they become. Over-pensioned pests. They have descended on Napa valley like a cloud of locusts.

Recently, as reported by *winebusiness.com,* an inspector from the FDA showed up during crush season at a California winery with rubber gloves and a hair net on (but no hard hat, orange vest, dust mask or goggles). She looked around, and told them that they had to be wearing the gloves, the hair net, and that they could not process the fruit outside. What? What planet are bureaucrats from? She then admitted that it was in fact the first winery she'd been sent out to inspect. Who sent her? *You're Terminated!* Where is the governator when we so desperately need him?

As a private individual, try shipping wine via USPS or UPS. Nope. Shipping has become even more restrictive in the last decade.

Try opening up a wine tasting room across from a church. Good luck. But that same church could theoretically be built across the street from an existing tasting room, and eventually muscle the tasting room out of business. How does that work?

But it's more than just a separation of church and state dysfunctionality. Prohibition bit a fourteen year chunk in time out of America, which stunned and altered the fledgling wine culture. How we make wine today is still being affected by that.

Considering the thousands of profitable wineries operating in America, and more vineyard acreage being planted, one could say that we now have a thriving wine culture. I agree, but from a historical perspective it is still in a young adolescent stage. If we observe the movement as we would from 200 years in the future, we may note how quickly changes occurred during the closing chapters of the 20th century, and the beginning of the 21st.

It is very exciting. The young adolescent is charged up and ready to tackle life, but he is not quite sure as to how to go about doing so. The body matures rapidly, then wisdom is accumulated gradually.

Both America and Australia have in the past had a near-sighted techno-winemaking bent. But now it seems the adolescent is rebelling--usher in the ideology of the natural winemaking movement. Following standard procedural protocol for rebellion, the teenager is threatening to ignorantly throw all of that hard-earned technical knowledge out of the window. Hopefully the delicate lab equipment will not all be broken. When the teenager matures a bit, he may go outside and gather it up, realizing that it is in fact valuable.

But the young adult never quite forgets that vision, the idea they imaged when their mind was active and unencumbered by weighty accumulated baggage.

I honor our teenagers. Those fresh ideas drive society forwards. I believe that it is the vision of young adolescents that is responsible for the forward progression of the evolution of mankind. That belief is supported by the latest discoveries in the neurology of the human brain, and the ever-evolving science of Quantum Physics.

Thus we have the marriage of art and science. The couple may quarrel at times, but when they get together to make wine, their focus becomes unified through the excitement of creation, like a finely laminated steel—or a well made wine.

Grape Taxonomy

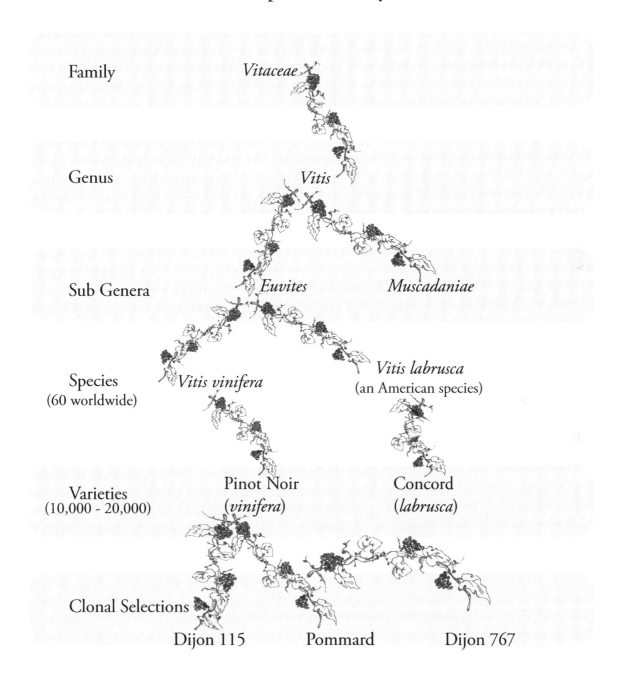

Family   *Vitaceae*

Genus   *Vitis*

Sub Genera   *Euvites*   *Muscadaniae*

Species
(60 worldwide)   *Vitis vinifera*   *Vitis labrusca*
(an American species)

Varieties
(10,000 - 20,000)   Pinot Noir   Concord
(*vinifera*)   (*labrusca*)

Clonal Selections

Dijon 115   Pommard   Dijon 767

THE ART OF VITICULTURE

The wine-grower, if his wine is of good report, loves his vines with a personal affection the deeper for all the pains they give him, as a mother will make a delicate and naughty child her favorite.　　　H. Warner Allen - 1932

Taxonomy

Depending on which ampelographer or University is used as a reference (these numbers vary), there are ~60 known species of grapes worldwide, ~20 of which are native to the American continents. What is a grapes species? The grape taxonomy chart on page 27 illustrates clearly how all grape species are in the family of *Ampelodaceae,* and in the *Vitis* genus.

American grape species such as *Vitis labrusca*, and *Vitis riparia* may be beautiful, hardy, and disease resistant, but unfortunately do not make quality wines. One can see from the chart how the Concord variety is thought to be predominantly from the American *Vitis labrusca* species.

The queen of fine wine is undeniably the Eurasian species *Vitis vinifera*, varieties of which make up over 97% of all vineyards on our planet. It has been estimated that almost 20 million acres (over 8 million hectares) are planted in grape vines, the vast majority of which are devoted to wine, resulting in an annual worldwide production totaling over 7 billion gallons (265 million hectoliters). Spain boasts the most vineyard space in hectares, while Italy and France are usually neck to neck in yearly production, with Spain recently reigning victorious, receiving the annual honor of being the world's largest producer of wine.

The species *Vitis vinifera*, roughly translated as "the wine grape", has between 10,000-18,000 *varieties* (also termed *cultivars*), depending on how we define them. Some of the best varieties are common, and recognizable to us because American wine is typically marketed using the varietal name boldly stated on the front of the bottle. Pinot Noir, Cabernet Sauvignon, Merlot, Zinfandel, Chardonnay, Cabernet Franc, Syrah, Grenache, Tempranillo, and Sangiovese are just a few of the better varieties of *Vitis vinifera.*

A grape variety can even be further divided into *selections*, which is a group of plants that share a common origin. Usually they originate from a single vineyard block that was selected for some desirable characteristics, and are often named from the source vineyard.

Clones are also plants that share a common origin, but in this case the origin is from a single plant. I used Pinot Noir as an example on the taxonomy chart, where one can observe that the clones Dijon 115, Dijon 767, and Pommard are simply different kinds of Pinot Noir.

In fact, there are over 40 different legally recognized clonal selections of Pinot Noir in Burgundy, France, and many more elsewhere. Each clone has its own unique character, both in growth habit and flavor. The Oregonians honor Pommard as one of their most commonly planted Pinot Noir selections. But Pommard is actually a village, surrounded by an appellation (wine growing area) by the same name in the Burgundy region of France—famous for its delicate, aromatic wines where the original cuttings were taken from—hence the name. Depending on growing conditions, Pommard selections of Pinot Noir tend to make wines mirroring those characteristics whether they are growing in New Zealand, New York State, South Africa, Oregon, or Sonoma County.

Many Pinot Noir producers like to have different clones in their vineyard that can be blended, resulting in wines with more complex flavors. That same theme is reiterated by wineries in all regions, where oftentimes more interesting wines are created by the blending of clones, grapes from various parts of the vineyard, different varieties; and as we shall discuss in the vinification chapter—the use of different yeast strains.

Since we are discussing the nature of grapes which eventually are transformed into great wine, let's dig one level deeper in our quest for quality.

It has been said that a grape variety is really just a group of vines that are genetically similar enough to be called by a single name. In reality, each vine is an individual, and old vignerons claim they know every one in their vineyard personally.

As practical as the discipline of taxonomy is, it seems to be spurned on by western science's necessary, but slightly neurotic need to classify.

In Bordeaux, there are old vines that are difficult for the experts to discern whether they are Cabernet Sauvignon or one of its genetic parents—Cabernet Franc. The ampelographer, also bearing the need to classify may do just that, or deem the vine to be so far to the extreme right or left as to be considered a genetic anomaly. Another vine in the same vineyard may bear red grapes, but look suspiciously like Sauvignon Blanc, the other parent of Cabernet Sauvignon.

Some clonal selections are the result of spontaneous bud mutations. In simpler terms, some vines will mutate right on the spot, possibly reacting to environmental stress. Pinot Noir in particular is one of the most readily mutable varieties. They say that a Pinot vine can mutate just by someone looking at it! At some time in the past Pinot Noir vines mutated into Pinot Blanc, Pinot Gris, and Pinot Meunier. It is well known that genetically older varieties mutate readily. Syrah is a good example, being one of the genetically oldest red varieties known to man.

Flowers on cultivated varieties of *Vitis vinifera* are hermaphroditic, expressing both male and female reproductive parts, which renders them self-pollinating. They will cross-pollinate, but grape plants are always propagated through cuttings, except for breeding purposes.

It should be mentioned that most cultivated *Vitis vinifera* plants are grown on special rootstocks they were originally grafted onto in the nursery. The rootstocks were specially bred to resist the Phyloxera aphid, reduce vigor, and accommodate different soil types.

However, in Phyloxera-free Washington state most vines are still grown on their own natural roots.

Viticulture

There is no doubt that the quality of the grapes is paramount in achieving great wine. The nature of the grapes is first and foremost that which defines the essence of a wine. One simply cannot make premium wines out of ordinary grapes.

Every grape variety has a heartland, a place where the vines thrive and offer the finest example of wines from that particular type of grape. The origins of grape varieties is lost in the fabric of time, but somehow each variety has found a place where it has evolved and mutated into; a place it claims as it's own. The concept of terroir is well known to wine lovers, as wine expresses the nature and particular character of the physical environment where the grapes are grown.

Some grape varieties—like Cabernet Sauvignon—travel well, and produce good wines in many viticultural regions worldwide. Others are poor world travelers, and stubbornly refuse to do well outside of their heartlands.

How does one grow great grapes? Legions of researchers from wine universities have devoted entire careers endeavoring to answer that simple question. The extensive continuing analysis of terroir and soil types of vineyards worldwide and how it relates to the quality of wine is in part inconclusive, as much debate ferments between researchers, whose quest is to unravel the mysteries of terroir.

Driven by the excitement of the hunt as well as the search for El Dorado, enologists careen into the vineyards, measuring, testing and theorizing. It is both challenging and exciting. If one could re-create the soil type of a famous vineyard in a carefully chosen area, could the wine be as tasty as the wine from the model vineyard?

I am dubious, but let's do some math and use Chateau Petrus in Pomerol, France as an example. Chateau Petrus is the heartland of the Merlot grape, producing arguably the best Merlot anywhere, and certainly the most expensive. The retail price for one bottle of recent vintage Petrus in 2014 is about $4000. The old rule of thumb in Bordeaux is: one vine (one plant) produces enough juice to make one bottle of wine. At Chateau Petrus they typically thin to only eight clusters per vine. Even figuring at ten clusters; if there are about forty grapes per cluster that would equate to each grape having a potential market value of $10.00 Wow!

How about the most expensive wine in the world: ~$12,000 bottle of Romaneé-Conti from Domaine de la Romaneé in Bourgogne (Burgundy), France. Each small Pinot Noir grape would have a potential market value of $30.00--worth their weight in gold! El Dorado indeed.

In Napa valley wineries are paying premium prices—some from $6000—$15,000 per ton. Apparently there is a Napa vineyard getting $20,000 per ton—$10 per pound.

The studies of famous vineyards worldwide has helped improve the quality and health of existing vineyards and aided in the determination of potential vineyard sites. When assessing the potential for a new vineyard, the professionals have a detailed soil analysis performed by an enologist who specializes in that field.

Soil Quality

Prior to planting grape vines the wine grower should, at the very least determine the pH of the soil. Ideally, *Vitis vinifera* vines will produce the best wines when the soil pH is at 7.0, while American species do well at 6.5 pH. Generous calcium uptake from the roots into the grapes is a very important factor for quality wines. Lime may be added to existing vineyards between rows and plants slowly year after year so as not to shock the vines, or as liquid calcium in drip irrigation. One of our goals is to create wines with good, higher natural acidity.

It is interesting that the acidity of the soil actually has an inverse affect on the acidity of the wine. Acidic soils yield low acid wines, while more alkaline soils produce higher acid wines.

Ideally, vines should be planted in dry, rocky soil of low fertility but with high mineral content. Wine grapes are traditionally grown on the gravelly hillsides of river valleys, leaving the rich alluvial valley soils for fruit and vegetable production. The poor soil causes the vines to be stressed into producing small quantities of highly concentrated fruit, and forces the roots to penetrate as much as 60 feet into the ground in search of moisture and nutrients. The massive root systems allow the plants to be drought tolerant, and function as potential energy reserves.

The soil, because of it's power of retention, can store up water. The best vineyards are those where the soil can provide water to the vine during it's growth period, but is fairly dry at the time of ripening. Limestone is particularly good at retaining a moisture reserve without being soggy. Vines growing in wet soils will be excessively vigorous and suffer. The underground water level governs the depth of the soil the roots will use, and also influences the cluster's susceptibility to rot.

There exists a relationship between the presence of water in the subsoil and acidity in the grapes. In soil that retains too much humidity, ripening is delayed, resulting in higher levels of malic and tartaric acids. Conversely, in permeable soils which are deep, the grapes ripen more quickly with lower acids.

Classic European vineyard soils are usually built on limestone, schist, slate, or decomposed granite. This leads us to the dodgy subject of minerality.

The Phenomenon of Minerality

There has been a lot of press time devoted to the perceived taste of minerals in wines, with plenty of disagreement concerning the mechanism of how these tastes get into the wine, and if it is even minerals we are tasting or merely our perception of them. There are a few things most enologists agree on:

Soil matters. Wines from the better European soils lend themselves to pronounced minerality. Wines with good minerality come from vines grown in healthy, living soils with high populations of mycorrhizal fungi. The fungi facilitate trace mineral uptake by expanding grape rootlet surface, ushering in a symbiotic exchange of minerals for sugars.

Minerals oppose oxidation in a finished wine. Wines with great longevity possess pronounced minerality, which decreases with time in the bottle.

High pH grapes subjected to excessive hang time exhibit lower levels of minerality.

Some of the current research suggests that minerality can be related to mineral discharge. We may in fact actually be tasting the minerals. What we are sensing on the palate may very well be the flow of electrons released from metallic elements of the periodic table as they move to higher valences. Many elements have an oxidized state as well as a reduced state, and can move from one to the other by giving up an electron. The cascade of that flow could be what we are tasting.

At the onset of veraison, when the berries begin to turn color, a dramatic shift occurs in the metabolism of the plant. For a brief but important time, the roots and trunk, like a mother nursing her young, gives everything it has to the ripening fruit.

Sucrose moves up from the roots into the trunk, converting into fructose and glucose before arriving at each cluster. Along with the sugars, the roots provide the grapes with minerals they have metabolized from the soil. Then, after the initial surge of energy from the roots, the leaves of the vine complete the ripening process by providing the clusters with even more sugars for another month or so—the magic of photosynthesis.

Therefore, we should not be surprised why old vines, having larger root systems and trunks, tend to make more complex, tannic, longer lasting wines. Wines from young vines may be adolescent, fruity and spirited, but will not store as long in the cellar. They do not possess the complex compliment of minerals and phenols such as wines made from older vines.

It's also understandable why great wines are always made from low yielding vines. One plant has a limited amount of energy to give to its grapes.

Secondary clusters that formed later than the primary clusters are culled, and dropped to the ground along with clusters that are ripening slower, or are in less-than-optimum positions on the vines. What remains are a few (typically 10-20) well-positioned clusters that are honored to be the beneficiaries of all the sugars and minerals the plant provides.

It is not always that elementary though—some tempering may be needed. Too rigorous a cluster thinning regimen can result in excessive canopy vigor, with little improvement in grape maturity or complexity. In Napa valley, many vines are actually over-thinned in a fanatical competition to produce the best wines. It is based on a single-minded idea: The lower the yield the better the wine. In reality the physiology of grape vines is far more complicated than that. As in much of nature—the vines need to remain in balance. Perhaps we should adhere instead to a different single-minded idea: Healthy vines produce fine wines.

Most rows are planted away from frost pockets, with good air drainage, and in a north/south orientation. Therefore, the morning sun shines on the east side of the row, while the west side benefits from the warmer afternoon sun.

The hillsides or slopes (côtes or côteaux in French) are ideally south or southeast facing to trap the most heat, with the steepest vineyards being the hottest. However, in Burgundy some of the best sites are slightly east facing. The east-facing theory is that the ripening grapes will receive direct sunlight in the morning when they are naturally cool, warming them better. In the warm evening when the sun descends into the west, the grapes will cool down gently. The gradual warming and cooling give the grapes finer tannins, compared to grapes ripening under rapid temperature changes, which—endeavoring to protect themselves will produce harsher tannins.

Vineyard Floor Management

There are two distinct camps concerning how to manage the vegetative growth on the floor of the vineyard between the rows. The predominant technique used in commercial vineyards is maintaining bare soil. A compact, moist, bare soil surface absorbs more heat by day and radiates more heat at night than vineyards with a vegetative floor. The difference in temperature can be as much as 3F/2C greater. In the event of a frost, cold air drains easily out of the vineyard, moving low along the ground. Weed killers are often used to maintain bare soils.

Those that adhere to the idea of a vegetative vineyard floor maintain that the grape vines are healthier due to the high population of beneficial soil microbes encouraged by the presence of diverse plants and their root systems.

Microbes are the alchemists that break down organic matter into smaller building blocks.

In a natural environment, soils tend to host an extremely wide range of bacteria, fungi, protozoa, and nematodes. Their populations are actually so diverse that we do not even have species names for most of them. We have learned enough however, concerning the life cycles of various microbes and fungi to begin to grasp the importance of these sometimes symbiotic, and sometimes competitive organisms.

In many ways plants are not so different from humans. When we perspire, the sticky compounds on our skin are actually considered good eating by various microbes. Likewise, plants use some of the energy from photosynthesis to "perspire" in both the root zone, or *rhizosphere*, and in the leaf zone, or *phyllosphere*. The perspiration, or secretion is known as plant *exudates.*

The nutrients, carbohydrates, and proteins in root exudates are a basic microbial food source, fostering a veritable feeding frenzy amongst bacteria, fungi, protozoa, nematodes, arthropods, and ultimately birds, reptiles and mammals. Some of the microbes feed on the plants exudates, some on exudates given off by each other, while many feed *on* each other.

The majority of this microbial feast occurs within the rhizosphere, an area extending out only about 2 mm from the roots. The plant benefits from all of the activity around it's roots by taking in nutrients produced by the exudates and decomposition of the participants at this microbial dinner party. In fact, what is truly remarkable is how the plant actually controls the guest list, as to whom is invited and when they shall come to the table—all based on the needs of the plant. The plant regulates who attends by altering the enzymic nature of its exudates secretions, kind of like playing different music to attract the appropriate guests.

Microbes are regular food for insects. Therefore, a vegetative vineyard floor is also an entomologists field day, as the ground cover supports more beneficial insect species.

Oftentimes vineyard groundcovers are planted, and tilled under much like vegetable farmers will do. The premier artifice for plowing a vineyard between the rows is a horse. The beasts are smarter than a tractor, causing less damage to the vines and far less compaction to the soil. A skilled plowman can trim the top feeder roots, forcing the plant to strike deep with its main roots.

Other viticulturists prefer planting grass between the rows. Some use rye grass, but wild grass species native to the environment may be the best to plant, due to their typically low nutrient needs, toughness, and minimal invasive characteristics. An online search will yield companies that specialize in wild grasses, particularly in the US grasslands, but there are some who have seed from species native to the Pacific west coast and others with seed from the northeast.

The use of grass is typical where erosion is a problem due to steep sites, and in vineyards with too much moisture in the soil. The grass evaporates moisture skywards, removing excess humidity, so reducing the incidence of rot. Grass covering also stifles undesirable weeds, eliminating the need for herbicides and reducing hand weeding. Grass also helps controls vine vigor, especially young vines, by competing with their prolific lateral surface roots for soil nutrients, forcing the important tap roots to strike deeper for nourishment.

There are some that contend that grassing encourages darker and more concentrated wines, but with less finesse.

Tech Talk

Propagation

Vitis vinifera varieties have been cultivated for millennia, so long in fact that the vines are now all hermaphroditic, and thus self pollinating, as the tiny flowers contain both male and female parts. Typically grape vines have been propagated by cuttings instead of by seed. Over the ages vines have been rogued by what is called *massal* selection, which is simply choosing to propagate new plants with cuttings from vines that exhibit particularly desirable characteristics.

In modern times the process is repeated in a more sophisticated way, termed *clonal* selection, which is performed in the laboratory. Cuttings are grown at high temperatures (100F/38C), quickly producing a growing tip which is then cut off and rooted as a green cutting. The advantage of this technique is that the grape diseases inherent in the cutting do not quite have time to infect the growing tip before it is removed, rendering the young plant theoretically virus-free.

Trellising

There are a myriad of trellising systems used for wine grapes, some tailored for the variety, and some that work well in a specific area or soil type.

Even though it is interesting to study old-world traditional systems like Gobelet, Taille Guyot, or the rarely used academic labor-intensive divided canopy systems like Scott Henry and Smart Dyson; we will focus on systems common and effective in the new world. What growers in Australia, South Africa, South and North America have actually done is to modify European systems like Double Guyot and Cordon de Royat to suit their own particular environments. Therefore, to avoid confusion, here we will dispense with local and regional trellising names.

Common trellising systems can be divided into two forms: single cordon or double cordon; and two pruning types: spur pruned or cane pruned systems. (see pages 36-38)

Single systems are well suited for lower vigor areas. Single cordon systems are known to produce high quality grapes, and are more productive per acre. However, because the vines are planted closer together, one runs the risk of overcrowded canopies when planting in an untested site with potentially too much vigor.

Because of the higher fertility levels of the soils in most American vineyards, we see far more double cordon trained vines than single systems. The vines are spaced further apart.

Spur Pruning

Spur pruning is favored in warmer climates, where spring frosts are not a regular threat to the delicate young shoots. The horizontal arms that are tied to the bottom wire are permanent, eventually growing quite large in diameter. Dormant pruning involves the removal of all of the vertical canes from the previous growing season, leaving buds every few inches for the potential new growth. In spring the shoots arise from those renewable spurs. (see illustration, pg. 36, 38)

Spur pruned vines are less vigorous than cane pruned vines. In Burgundy vigorous young vines are typically spur pruned for the first 20 years, then are switched over to a cane pruned system when the plant ages and begins to loose vigor. Spur pruning encourages more consistent sugar levels in all of the bunches, and yields tend to be reduced.

Cane Pruning

Cane pruning is used in cooler climates such as Oregon. When a double cane pruned vine is dormant pruned in early spring all but two canes from the previous years growth are removed. The two renewal canes near the center trunk are bent down and tied to the bottom wire, and become the current years' fruiting canes. From every node on the fruiting cane a shoot will grow.

Ideally, the renewal canes were earmarked for that purpose the previous year. They were chosen for their position near the center, upward growing orientation, and medium vigor. Grape clusters are ideally not allowed to grow on them. It is important that enough sunlight gets to them so they can get to 77F/25C during the growing season. Why? That is the temperature required for the *primordial clusters* to form inside of each node. The primordial clusters are the beginnings of what will be flowers and hopefully grapes the following year. Under a microscope they look like tiny clusters.

The advantage that cane pruned systems have in cool climates is based on the fact that the young shoots arise not all at once, but in succession, so a freak hard frost may damage some, but not all of the young green growth. (see illustrations on pages 37, 38)

One of the most common problems in North American vineyards is the increased vine vigor associated with higher fertility soils. Therefore, in new world vineyards, the plants are usually further apart, and trellising systems tend to be taller than their European counterparts, allowing for more vegetative growth.

In Italy and France, vigor is often so low that the rows are only one meter apart, and the vines are planted on a one meter spacing. Industry terms that a 1 X 1 meter spacing. The bottom wire on the trellis is low, where the grapes can get more heat. The top wire is often only one meter from the ground.

The idea is that if plants are close-spaced it will de-vigor the vines due to the root systems having to compete for moisture and nutrients. This is unquestionably true—to a point, with higher fertility soils tipping the scales. Some new world vineyards endeavoring to emulate Europe by planting on a 1 X 1 meter spacing have learned some hard, expensive lessons in ideology versus practicality when the vineyard ends up as a mess of tangled unmanageable vines.

 In contrast, the older un-irrigated vineyards in Spain were planted with wide row spacing and very wide plant spacing. The dry-farmed vines had to compete for moisture. That is why Spain has traditionally boasted having the most vineyard space of any country, but has fallen short in production. With new irrigation systems in Spain the country is eclipsing Italy and France in total wine production.

New world trellising systems are more like those used for years in Germany, with higher bottom wires, much higher top wires, and larger plant and row spacing.

Spur Pruned Grapevine

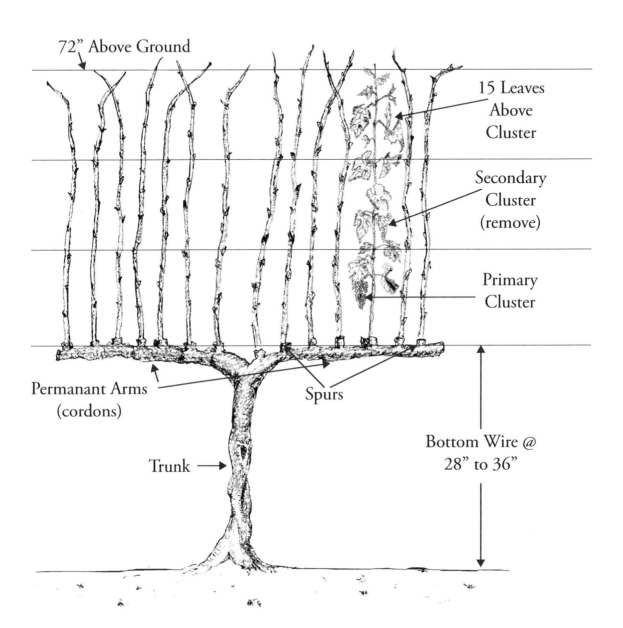

72" Above Ground

15 Leaves Above Cluster

Secondary Cluster (remove)

Primary Cluster

Permanant Arms (cordons)

Spurs

Trunk

Bottom Wire @ 28" to 36"

Cane Pruned Grapevine

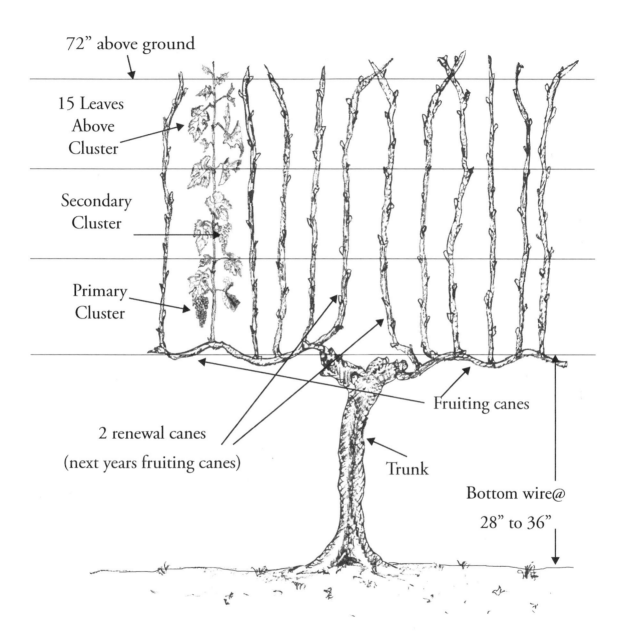

72" above ground

15 Leaves Above Cluster

Secondary Cluster

Primary Cluster

2 renewal canes
(next years fruiting canes)

Fruiting canes

Trunk

Bottom wire@
28" to 36"

Dormant Cane Pruning

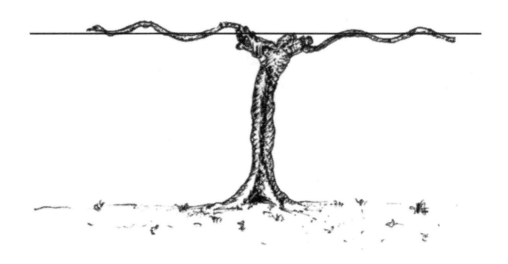

Dormant Spur Pruning

Shoot Morphology

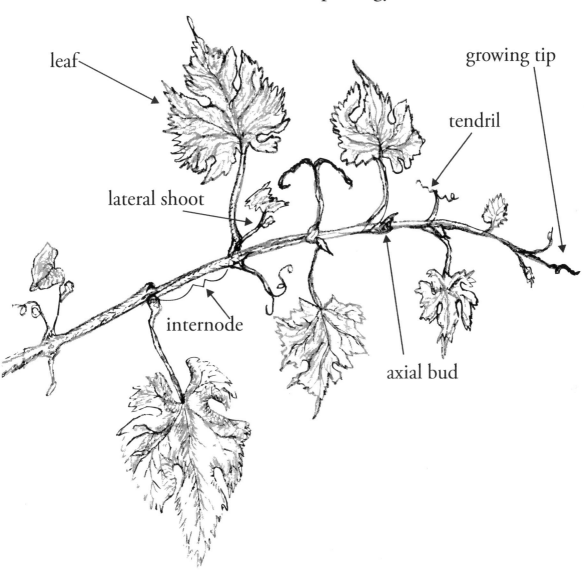

leaf

growing tip

tendril

lateral shoot

internode

axial bud

Sunlight

How much sunlight do grape clusters need? Different varieties have their varied needs, but in general, grapes grown in hot climates require more leaf shading than ones in cooler areas. Vignerons want the fruit to ripen fully but gradually, endeavoring to avoid sun-burning the clusters.

However, excessive shading contributes to lower levels of sugars, anthocyanins, other phenols, tartaric acid, and decreased varietal or fruit characters. Shade may also cause higher pH, potassium, malic acid levels, herbaceous flavors, and increased incidence of fungal problems.

Both heat and light are also important for the following years crop. With cane-pruned systems, two shoots nearest the trunk in the center of the trellis are allowed to grow, but the young clusters may be removed from them. These are termed *renewal shoots*. It is important for the renewal shoots to receive enough heat and sunlight because they will become the following year's fruiting canes.

Tucked inside each node along the shoot is the *cluster primordia*, the tiny beginnings of what will become grapes the following year. The primordial clusters are photo-reactive; they must receive ample sunlight and get to 77 degrees F. or they will not develop into grapes 12 months later.

Row Spacing

Technically, the spacing between rows should be at least as great as the height of the top wire on the trellis—rows need to be at least 6 feet apart for a 6 foot tall trellis. The further apart the rows, the more sunlight will reach the vines. In practice the row spacing is more often dictated by the tractor width, and often ends up at 9 feet or more. Ordinary tractors are certainly not that wide, but 9 feet accommodates vegetative growth that billows outwards from the trellis towards the end of the growing season. Smaller American tractors can barely work inside of 8 foot rows, depending on how vigorous the growth in the canopy gets.

I am recommending as a general guideline for new world vineyards: 6 foot tall trellises with 4 wire locations, and the rows spaced at 9 feet apart . Home vineyards that will not be worked with a tractor can place the rows as close as 6 feet apart.

Plant spacing

Plant spacing decisions are influenced by several factors: soil fertility, grape variety, and rootstock selection. From 5-7 feet is a good range to plant in, with 6 feet being very common, and 8 feet on vigorous or dry sites.

So lets say your vineyard is laid out in a 9 X 6 arrangement, the trellises are 6 foot tall with four wires. The bottom wire is 32" from the ground, with successive wires at 45", 58", and 72".

You have decided to start out using a spur pruned system until you can assess how much vigor is inherent on your site. In the winter of the second or third year you will choose two shoots that will become permanent arms which come out of the small trunk at 28", or at least 4 inches below the bottom 32" wire. You want the arms-to-be to smoothly bend up and grow along the bottom wire. If the bend is above the wire, causing you to pull the arms down to the wire, too much vigorous growth will persistently sprout from that area. You will cut the end of each new arm so that it almost touches the arm on the adjacent plant.

Canopy management

In the spring buds will appear and begin to grow. As they do throughout the growing season you will be guiding them straight up and tying them to the wires above in as orderly a fashion as you can.

The beauty of a tall trellising system is the generous amount of sunlight that is available to the leaves on each shoot, which typically are lined up vertically, eventually spilling over the top wire. Studies have shown that it takes at least 11 leaves beyond the cluster to bring one cluster to full morphological maturity. Vignerons prefer to see 13, or even 15 leaves above the cluster, particularly if they are allowing secondary clusters to ripen. Secondary clusters are those that emerge from a node further along the shoot than the primary cluster. In the highest quality low-yielding vineyards, secondary clusters are removed to enable the primary clusters to receive all of the energy from the plant. This is however, not a definite rule. Some varieties, like Cabernet Franc will ripen secondary clusters almost as well as the primaries. There are also times when the crop load is light, allowing the plant to have the energy to ripen two scant, loose clusters per shoot.

But in normal situations, one cluster per shoot will make the best wine.

How the green summer growth on the trellis is dealt with is termed *canopy management*, and is one of the art forms of the vigneron. As the green shoots arise from the cordon or fruiting cane some are selected to be allowed to grow and others are snapped off before they reach the second wire. This is termed *de-budding*. Well positioned medium-vigor shoots are selected in favor of weak or overly vigorous shoots. The goal is to end up with a shoot arising about every 4 inches from the arm or fruiting cane with a grape cluster on each one. This task should be performed judiciously, because once the tendrils form and begin to latch onto everything they can—the job becomes far less pleasant.

By the time you tie or tuck the shoot into to the second wire(s) you should see the flowers forming, which look like tiny grapes. The shoots are very delicate at this stage so must be handled carefully.

In many vineyards, the second wire is actually two wires side by side, about an inch apart and termed *catch wires*. Sometimes they are also adjustable vertically and are called *moveable catch wires*. Whether they are moveable or not, the shoots are guided between the catch wires, eliminating the need to tie the delicate shoots yet. It makes the whole job easier.

Eventually the shoots will grow up and over the top wire and may have to be hedged if they are spilling into the row and shading the vines too much.

A big part of the discipline of canopy management is the removal of unwanted growth from the vine in the form of suckers arising from the ground, water sprouts coming out of the trunk, and laterals continually trying to grow from the leaf nodes above the clusters. Even though much of this excessive vegetative growth contributes to the expansion of the root system, little of it helps the grapes to ripen. The tricky part is to try to find the balance for a vine; and yes, that means each individual vine, as they all express vigor uniquely.

In late summer—early September in the northern hemisphere, the berries begin to turn color. The English speaking world has adopted the French term *veraison* to describe the transformation, since we have no such term of our own. When veraison begins to occur, vigorous green growth slows to a stop, while the plant directs energy towards the grape clusters.

Irrigation

In old-world wine grape growing areas, irrigation is rarely needed, except perhaps to help young baby vines get off to a start. However, veraison is one time the vines might need irrigating for a very short period. Viticulturists determine if and how much water the vines need based on observed stress of the plant, through visual assessments of shoot density and shoot length, and often in conjunction with the data from below ground moisture sensors.

In many new world wine grape growing regions irrigation is necessary. Viticulturists working with WSU, UC Davis, and University of Adelaide have refined the technique termed *regulated deficit irrigation*. The goal is to irrigate a grapevine so the crop size and vegetative growth are balanced. Drip systems are used to give the vine barely enough water to control growth and berry size, saving critical water supplies. The final results are lower yields, and wines with more concentration.

However, the roots of vines that have always received irrigation congregate near the surface, rather than striking deep into the soil, increasing their dependence on water supplies, as well as their sensitivity to water stress. One must wonder how much water would need to be withheld to force the tap roots deep enough to render the vines less dependent on irrigation.

On that note, dry farming, as it is termed is becoming a movement in some of the finer appellations in California, where the availability of water has become scarcer. The focus of course, is on lower yields and higher quality, with the added benefits of not having to pay for water and fuss with irrigation systems. The movement has that distinctive flavor the Californians have gained notoriety for—a ready willingness to break with tradition, but doing so carefully with smart scientific backing.

Ripening

Prior to veraison, the clusters will not sun-burn, but once the berries color they can. Decisions are made as to how much exposure to the sun the clusters will receive. In hot climates, or in a year when the fruit might ripen easily, the vigneron may decide to leave the clusters partially shaded, so as to extend the hang time. Wine complexity is favored when the fruit takes longer to ripen, but not overripen. We shall discuss the perils of overripening later. Conversely, fruit that ripens unnaturally early tends to result in jammy, single dimensional wines. Once again, balance and harmony is our holy grail.

Most of the best wine-growing areas are located towards the extremes of ripening zones in relation to the varieties grown. Too much leaf shading may not only delay ripening, but can result in elevated malic acid levels in the ripe grapes. In many years, a few lower leaves in the fruit zone around the clusters are pulled to allow more sunlight to directly strike the grapes. Typically, the clusters are given more exposure to the morning sun, since temperatures in the afternoon can spike and burn the grapes on the outside of the clusters. More leaves are thus pulled off the east side of the vines than the west.

Traditionally, grapes are ideally picked in the morning so are cool when ready to be crushed. Chateau Petrus however, prefers to pick in the afternoon, both for concentration and to ensure there is no dew on the grapes.

Picking

In the olden days, vignerons would begin picking the grapes when they tasted ripe, and used dead reckoning to try to predict the weather. The old skills are still important, but today we are graced with weather satellites, refractometers, pH meters, and acidity tests to help us make the critical decision as to when to remove the grapes from the vines and bring them into the winery.

In practice, most vineyard blocks are picked when the grapes are as ripe as they can be; but the question arises: What really is the definition of ripe? Some vineyards have the luxury to be able to allow the grapes ripen to very high sugar levels, but is this automatically conducive to making the best of wines?

Generally, the answer to the question is no, but is complicated by both stylistic choices and varietal differences. Stylistically, many consumers prefer soft, low acid wines, but our focus favors world-class wines over consumer level wines. World-class wines are typified by possessing more tannic structure, minerality, balanced acids, and the ability to age gracefully.

There are as many varietal peculiarities as there are varieties. Understanding a variety well is a key to refined winemaking. Grenache is an example of a cultivar that benefits by being well ripened, becoming silkier and earthier as it softens up into the 24-25 Brix range. Cabernet Franc on the other hand, tends to turn flat and uninteresting if ripened above about 24 Brix.

Biodynamic Viticulture

Since we are discussing how the finest wines in the world are made, biodynamism stares us in the face, and cannot be ignored. In fact, the winery responsible for the most expensive wines in the world—Domaine de Romanée de la Conti, uses biodynamic principles, as does most of the cream of other Burgundian domaines with grand cru vineyards. Without question, Burgundy is the working heartland of the movement. She who has carried the torch with the most vivid ferocity is the empress of biodynamic viticulture herself—the controversial Madame Lalou Bize-Leroy. Domaine Leroy wines may retail for less than an average Domaine de la Romanée-Conti, but still, one bottle equates to the price of a good used car.

It should be noted that of the 3800 producers in Burgundy, only about five hundred are making really fine wines, with the rest relying on the reputations of their appellations.

I counsel the reader to entertain an open mind concerning biodynamism, and resist the urge to turn the page and skip this section. We will approach the subject objectively, and more from the scientific side rather than the metaphysical. Historically, biodynamics has it's roots in the philosophies of Plato and Goethe, but the prophet of the movement was Rudolph Steiner, who gave a series of lectures in 1924 when he mentioned and gave brief outlines of what is now known as the biodynamic preparations. The lectures were long on philosophy and short on practice. From those lectures devotees have formed the biodynamic movement.

Lets say that there are seven levels of consciousness, but we predominantly only function in the three densest—physicality being the first level. We rarely access, or are not aware of the four finer levels. That which we are not familiar with in our day to day lives we call "spiritual". Quantum mechanics, the physics of our era actually supports the notion of higher levels of consciousness.

There are those that vehemently adhere to the idea that we exist solely in a physical reality—everything is explainable by science. One must wonder however, why we cannot cure the common cold or arrest viruses—why when the top physicists on the planet get together every several years for their conferences still do not fully understand what gravity is. Physics is the basis of all science. Perhaps that gaping hole—the missing link in science and medicine is the connection with the unexplored and largely unaccepted realm of higher frequency consciousness.

Personally, I am not one to totally discount the possible effect of earth energies, nature spirits, lunar and astrological cycles on agriculture. But I want to see results.

The differences between organic and biodynamic viticulture vary both in philosophy and in the intensity of application. Organic practitioners may believe in using lunar cycles as planting guides, while the biodynamic crowd takes it as far as using astrology as a guide to help with pruning, spraying, and picking decisions. Organic vineyard owners may strive to improve the health of the soil, but biodynamic practitioners work at it aggressively, using compost seeded with homeopathic-like preparations. Organic horticulture promotes the use of natural fertilizers as soil amendments, which biodynamic philosophy eschews.

It is true, standard organic gardening practice shares the same kind of reasoning as orthodox NPK agriculture in that they will both add nitrogen and minerals to feed the plants. We now know that the urea-based inorganic fertilizers used for over eighty years by farmers are detrimental to the health of the soil. By reading the labels one can observe that some "organic" fertilizers are actually nitrate based as well, while others are simply mixtures of natural products like blood meal, kelp, rock phosphate, and bone meal.

The most fundamental biodynamic followers preach a strict non-additive dogma, in both the vineyard and the winery. In fact, the term "additives" has achieved a kind of four-letter-word status. They believe that by increasing the beneficial microbial content of the soil—with help from native plants, worms and insects—nutrient deficiencies will naturally adjust to where they need to be. It seems like a great idea, but one wonders how far we can take it. How long would it take for a soil acidity to change from 5.5 pH to 7.0 pH, and how deep? That is a big change. Adherents say no to added limestone, even though that is exactly what Eurasian *Vitis vinifera* vines often thrive in their native environments.

The philosophy is certainly a good model for growing native plants in their own environments, but the fact is, vinifera vines could be considered to be additives themselves in the new world. Like many imported, cultured plant species they would eventually adapt or perish if left on their own in our forests, deserts, or grasslands. We must intervene if they are to survive.

Vineyard managers following biodynamic principles claim that even though their vines are healthier, vigor is decreased, lessening labor-intensive summer green pruning rituals.

There have been incidences of biodynamic vineyards dramatically suffering from mildews, but generally they claim that pressure from diseases and fungus is decreased, particularly concerning *Botrytis cinerea.*

No matter how one chooses to look at it all, the bottom line is that when soil experts evaluate soils that have been farmed biodynamically they are inevitably impressed by the quality of the soils.

Preparations

The reader has probably heard of biodynamic preparations—particularly the one where a cow horn is filled with dung from a lactating bovine and buried over the winter (prep. 500). At first glance these practices do not strike one as merely medieval—that is far too modern. They seem to herald more from the era of Neolithic shamanism. It is not surprising that the knee-jerk reaction is to eject the entire idea like a stinky old herring tin.

One morning I woke up and a thought came to me that perhaps in that infamous horn there are powerful beneficial soil bacteria or fungi that are being cultured and interacting with local microbes under the ground where they will eventually be applied.

I contacted Alan Johnstone, preparations manager for Biodynamic Agriculture Australia Ltd. with two questions:

If one looks at a well made sample of preparation 500 under a microscope, what does one see? High population of fungal species? Bacteria? What about prep 501 under a microscope?

> *Yes, that is what you will see with the Horn Manure 500 and also to a lesser extent in the Horn Silica 501. However, it is not just the bacteria and fungi that give the preparations their punch. The cow manure in the cow horn is transformed during winter by the life forces that are in the soil during this time. Those life forces attract the myriads of fungi and bacteria you will see under the microscope as well as other soil organisms. The horn silica is finely ground silica. When buried under the soil during summer, these silica crystals are programmed by the forces of summer as per computers. Because they have been underground, they will have some bacteria and fungi evident under the microscope. The forces trapped in the horn manure are released into water during the 60 minutes of rhythmical stirring and then sprayed out with multiplying fungi and bacteria onto damp soil in the evening.. The water that is rhythmically stirred for horn silica has the 'summer program' transferred into the water which has a memory, before it is sprayed out into the atmosphere, bringing light and warmth to the photosynthesising parts of plants.*

Okay, so we are expected to take a leap of faith here, and perhaps that is why the biodynamic crowd has not ingratiated itself very well with the scientific community. Less than well understood "life forces" are accepted seemingly without question, and take precedence over microscopic observation. However, as expressed earlier, just because we do not understand something does not necessarily equate to its non-existence. I do find the comments concerning quartz crystals interesting, as it has been known for well over 100 years how quartz can hold electromagnetic energy, and yet the phenomenon is not fully understood.

Also, Alan mentions that water has a memory. The science of the remarkable crystalline structures of water, sometimes referred to as *clustered water* (referring to the gorgeous snowflake-like molecular structures), is a fascinating study, one that the orthodox scientific community has stubbornly been in denial about. In a nutshell, it turns out that water, much like wine actually comes in a myriad of different qualities.

In her book *Voodoo Vintners—Oregons Astonishing Biodynamic Winegrowers*, author Katherine Cole mentioned that Montinore Estate in northern Oregon had some success combating Phylloxera using biodynamic practices. Curious, I contacted Rudy Marchesi at Montinore:

I heard that you have had some success arresting the progress of Phylloxera in one of your vineyard blocks?

Working with/around the phylloxera here has been an interesting project, sometimes rewarding but also very frustrating at times. Phylloxera was discovered here in 1998, first in a vineyard block where we sold fruit to a California winery and the phylloxera had hitchhiked north on their picking bins. It gradually spread throughout the entire vineyard on tractor tires and cultivation equipment before we even realized it was there. It was in 2001 that I took over the vineyard management and started addressing the situation. Up until this time the vineyard had been farmed using chemical herbicides and a variety of non organic vineyard sprays and no soil cultivation or amendments had been employed. At this time "lenses" of phylloxera infestation were starting to show up around the entire Estate. It was then that I began the conversion to Organic/ Biodynamic with the intent of increasing the health and vitality of the soil and hopefully that of the weakened vines.

One of our best tools has been compost. Each year we make 300 to 500 tons of compost from the winery grape pomace, straw, and animal manure. These compost piles are inoculated with Biodynamic preparations and allowed to mature for 10+ months. We rotate applications around the vineyard based partially on the individual needs of each vineyard block but also ensuring that all of the vineyard receives compost at a minimum of once every three years. In experiments we have done we found that most vines weakened by phylloxera respond to compost treatments and rebound the following year.

In addition to the compost, we have applied an average of 6 Biodynamic preparation applications per year along with some special treatments on the trunks of particularly weakened vines.

Like most organic vineyards we grow cover crops in the rows adding nitrogen from legumes and carbon from stalky plants to provide food for the soil born fungi. We have also inoculated our entire vineyard with a strain of mycorrhizal fungi that works well with grapevines to help support the vine root systems.

All of this has helped to keep phylloxera in check but it is by no means a cure. At this time, 15 years after the discovery of phylloxera here, roughly 70% of our vineyards look and perform as if there were no phylloxera, but the other 30% have progressively weakened to the point where they are no longer economically viable to farm. Just this winter we pulled out 20 acres of Pinot Noir on thinner soils where the vines couldn't keep up with the damage caused by phylloxera. I feel satisfied that we have been able to extend the life of these vineyards for so long.

What mycorrhizal fungi strains are you working with?

I purchased our mycorrhizal stock from Mycorrhizal Applications in Grants Pass OR. The inoculant we applied has four different strains that work well with woody plants. I could not find specifics on their web site but they said when they get a chance they will email me the names, I'll pass it along.

What kind of cover crops have you been planting?

It changes a little every year depending on what we can get in organic seed but it always includes some stalky grains, i.e. annual rye, oats, triticale and a legume. I prefer to use winter peas. We use the stalky plants to provide carbon to feed the fungal populations and the legumes to provide nitrogen. We plant every other row so as not to risk erosion and alternate the rows every year. The cultivation for the seeds includes a deep ripping to break up any compaction from tractor traffic and to allow oxygen to enter the soil, encouraging oxygen loving strains of bacteria and fungi.

In summary, I think it is possible to grow own rooted vines in the presence of phylloxera given the right soil conditions, and employing farming practices that respect and work to improve the health and vitality of the soil. Certainly, for us, Organic and Biodynamic practices have proven effective and allowed us to keep farming in spite of phylloxera infestation.

Compost Basics

In practice, biodynamic viticulture involves predominantly the making of compost. This we can quantify.

When my friends ask me how it is that my vegetable garden does so well I point to my massive compost pile. It's as simple as that, but most gardeners are not willing to dedicate time and energy to make one. If they do, it is more often just a place to throw kitchen scraps, leaves and lawn clippings—which should do well, except that the pile is usually neglected and rarely stirred.

I had a pile like that once, until a friend that owned Yelm Earthworm & Castings Farm looked at it and was ruthlessly honest, "Mark, that is not a compost pile. That is a stinking mass of congealed anaerobic biofilm!" I was duly chastised, and since have endeavored to change my evil ways. As usual, I approached it formally, and poured a large concrete platform to make it on—a faux stone altar dedicated to the god of compost.

The most important thing to remember about making compost is that you are encouraging aerobic organisms to flourish in it by turning it regularly—introducing oxygen into the pile. This generates the heat necessary for specific types of bacteria to work, accelerating the process. Those that possess a tractor or backhoe with a bucket are at an extreme advantage here , because turning a large pile by hand can be very difficult.

Organic materials can be divided into two categories: "brown" and "green". Aged, brown materials are high in carbon, while fresh green materials are high in nitrogen. Achieving the proper balance between the two categories is the key to successful composting. This is referred to as the *carbon to nitrogen ratio* (C:N). The ideal C:N ratio for a beginning compost pile is in the 25:1—30:1 range.

Brown materials high in carbon include: leaves (40:1—80:1), sawdust (500:1), paper (170:1), wood chips, twigs, and branches.

Green materials high in nitrogen include: grass clippings (19:1), fresh weeds, kitchen scraps, and alfalfa meal. If one wants to make a bacterially dominated compost, green materials are favored. If fungal-dominated compost is needed, more brown materials are used. For vineyard use, we focus on fungal dominated compost.

Basic fungal dominated compost recipe
50% brown material
40% green material
10% alfalfa meal

Worm Castings

The creation of vermicompost is biologically a much simpler process than what occurs in a traditional thermal compost pile, which uses a more complex set of organisms to break down organic matter. Given the same basic materials to work with, the two different styles will produce composts yielding their own unique characteristics.

My personal favorite style of composting is to enlist Red Wiggler (*Eisenia fetida*) earthworms to work both in bins, and a large pile. During the warm summer months I nurture a population of worms in enclosed bins, making certain they are fed and happy. They love manure and low-acid vegetable scraps.

Later, during wine fermentation season, on a large concrete slab I will layer truckloads of good manure, grape pomace, grape stems, pressed white grapes, plant material, cardboard, kitchen scraps, and garden, vineyard, or forest soil with a bit of last years compost (adding indigenous microbes).

When the pile is deep enough, I dig a hole into the middle and seed it with the entire contents of the small worm bins I have been fussing over all summer. There may be 10-20 pounds of worms in the bins. Ten months later, the whole pile is teeming with worms, and has morphed into the most gorgeous, soft fine compost. Anything will grow in it, and it is far more potent than it appears, harboring a huge beneficial bacterial population. The beauty of a vermicompost pile is that if the worms are active, it really does not need to be turned. It certainly can be, especially shoveling or forking the unruly edges of the pile towards the center, or mixing up an anaerobic or moldy area. This makes working with a large pile practical for those without machinery to turn it.

Because worms are themselves an excellent food coveted by birds, moles, voles, mice and snakes, we protect them by raising them in bins or piles in areas designed to keep predators out.

The Greek philosopher Aristotle called earthworms, "The intestines of the soil". Millennium later Charles Darwin was fascinated by earthworms, and spent 39 years studying them. He wrote a book titled, *The Formation of Vegetable Mould Through the Action of Worms With Observations on Their Habits.*

Earthworms are members of the phylum *Annelida* and the class *Oligochaeta*, of which there are over six thousand known species. Earthworms are classified in the family *Lumbricidae*, which includes the genera of *Lumbricus, Eisenia, Dendrobaena*, and *Allobophora*. Even though hundreds of species are associated with these genera, we only use a few as composting worms.

Earthworms are some of the hardest working creatures on earth, helping to mix and aerate the soil, improving soil structure and water infiltration, modulate pH factors, increasing beneficial microbial activity, and making nutrients more available to plants by breaking down plant and animal material into castings (excrement).

Worms are capable of creating finished compost out of various materials very quickly—in as little as 60 days.

Earthworm castings have a neutral pH value (7 pH), regardless of the pH of the soil they are living in. They therefore either help neutralize acidic soils, or acidulate highly alkaline soils.

Castings have high levels of nitrogen, potassium, phosphorus, magnesium, and trace minerals—all in very plant-available forms.

Castings become food for other organisms, which release potassium, phosphorus, calcium, magnesium, iron, and plant available sulfur into the soil.

Since worm castings are about 65% organic matter, they help increase the humus content of the soil, which aids in water retention and helps combat compaction.

Mucus membranes produced by worms encase casting nutrients, causing them to be slowly released as food for plants.

The optimum carbon to nitrogen (C:N) ratio for plant food is 20:1. Tree leaves tend to have less than optimum C:N levels, such as 42:1 for oaks, and 90:1 for some pine trees. Worms, with a little help from their friends (other organisms) help break down the carbon in leaf litter, finally rendering it close to 20:1, a perfect C:N ratio for the plant's assimilation of nitrogen.

Composting worms digest most human pathogens. *Salmonella* and *E.coli.157* (to name a few) are digested and neutralized in the intestinal tract of composting worms. Earthworms break down the soil into smaller particles, mixing the soil as they work.

Nightcrawlers *Lumbricus terrestris*

Nightcrawlers are large common worms that have deep burrowing habits, making vertical tunnels as far as six feet into the ground. They feed at night, and get their food (such as leaf litter and mulch), from the surface, dragging it deep into their burrows to feed. Nightcrawlers can live as long as ten years, and are found in Europe, North America, and New Zealand. They are not particularly good for enclosed vermicomposting systems because they feed from the surface, do not like their burrows disturbed, and tend to roam at night--escaping the bin. Nightcrawlers are common however, frequently found, and welcomed in our outdoor compost piles and vineyard and garden soils.

Red Wigglers *Eisenia fetida*

Red Wigglers are the darling of the composting world, making them by far the most common worm used in controlled composting systems. They are shallow dwellers, have an upward migration habit, and prefer very rich compost, manure, and decaying plant material for food.

Red Wigglers can process large amounts of organic matter very rapidly, and in perfect conditions can eat 1/2 of their body weight in food each day. They are not fussy about their living conditions, tolerating fluctuations in temperature, acidity, and moisture levels better than many other worm species.

Contrary to what others have claimed, Red Wigglers can live in outdoor compost piles in temperate climates as long as they have enough oxygen, reasonable moisture levels, and providing they have the space to migrate downwards far enough to avoid high temperatures and freezing conditions. Some growers like to maintain an outdoor population of Red Wigglers as a back-up in the event problems occur in their contained worm bins. However, since they need a lot of rich organic matter to feed on, Red Wigglers will not survive long in ordinary vineyard soil. Their cocoons will normally hatch in 5-10 weeks, giving them the ability to be able to double their population in as little as 60 days. Red Wigglers prefer temperatures in the 75-85°range (23-29°C).

Blue Worms *Perionyx excavitus* and *Perionyx spenceriella*
Various species of Blue Worms are the choice for composting systems in warmer climates, as they do not tolerate cold temperatures well. They are voracious feeders, rendering them excellent for composting systems. Blue worms have an unusually good ability to feed on animal material as well as decaying plant material. Blue Worms are shallow dwellers and have good regenerative capabilities. While some do have a tendency to roam outside the bins at times, generally Blues are well behaved. One of the more common names is, "Indian Blue" worm. Some are native to Australia.

It should be mentioned that unless you live in an area where Red Wigglers or Blue worms live naturally, they must be purchased from a worm supplier. The different species of worms are not particularly competitive, and will feed side by side with few problems. Your indigenous nightcrawlers will have no problem cohabitating with composting worms. Since common names for worms are confusing, use the species names when ordering.

Compost Tea
The chemistry may be complex, but the concept is simple. Compost or worm castings, molasses and/or nutrients are placed into a container of water, and air is pumped into the bottom of the container, percolating up through the tea and soil. Aerobic bacteria, protozoa, and fungi grow and flourish in the presence of all of the oxygen. Compost tea is a brewed water extract of compost in which beneficial microbes and fungi are encouraged to multiply. Using compost tea is like using compost multiplied by 1000. One of the great things about compost tea is how little compost it takes to make a large batch of tea. The tea is concentrated, and is often diluted with water prior to application. It can be used for either a root fertilizer or a foliar spray. The benefits of compost tea on the roots and leaves of plants are many, and will be discussed later. It's enough to say that compost tea greatly improves the health of plants. Compost tea has no strong odor, only a faint pleasing earthy smell. Therefore, it may be brewed indoors as well as outdoors.

What is described in this section is a method for the creation of compost tea. While many roads may lead to Rome, this method is by far the most commonly used, being that it is easy, safe, reliable, inexpensive, and extremely effective. These techniques involve the culturing and preening of beneficial aerobic (oxygen loving) microbes, while in turn discouraging the growth of anaerobic (oxygen avoiding) organisms.

Compost tea is a microbial concentrate loaded with beneficial bacteria and fungi. When that huge microbial population is turned loose into your vineyard or garden, you are effectively re-introducing beneficial healthy life forms into your environment. These are some of the very same types of organisms that should have been there in the first place. Your vines will immediately respond favorably, as they will be receiving the nutrients they need naturally as a result of the microbes being there.

The plants initial positive response is only the beginning of a dramatic uptrend in their overall health. Eventually, not only will they be getting more (and more complex) nutrients, but the soil in the root zone will better retain moisture, have increased aeration, and the roots will be more protected from predation. The roots of any plant will grow considerably larger. Likewise, in the leaf zone the foliage will receive more nutrients and be better protected from diseases and pests.

Aerobic vs. Anaerobic

Why are aerobic compost teas the safest type? Compost tea is a general term that has been used loosely to describe different types of brewed and non-brewed products. Specifically, some of the different forms of compost tea are:

Aerated aerobic compost tea
Non-aerated compost tea
Anaerobic compost tea
Manure tea
Compost extract
Compost leachate
Fermented plant tea

All of the compost tea styles listed above are worthy of further studies, but we are concerned with only one type—Aerated aerobic compost tea.

Aerated compost tea is the style that viticulturists will find the most useful. Other styles should be considered experimental at best. Why? Generally speaking, aerobic or oxygen-loving organisms create healthy compost teas, while anaerobic organisms tend to make brews not beneficial for plant growth, and may contain human pathogens. Every bacterium has a necessary place in our world, have their own job to do, but not all are beneficial for the health of soil, plants, or inevitably, ourselves. Undesirable bacteria are usually anaerobic, and are considered to be pathogens.

Our goal in the creation of compost tea is to discourage the growth of pathogens, while encouraging the population of beneficial aerobic bacteria.

Anaerobic bacteria have important roles to play in our natural environment, and are identified by their notorious tendency to flourish in low-oxygen environments—a truly remarkable characteristic. Anaerobic bacteria are autotrophs. They actually do need oxygen, but glean it from chemically bound up forms. They get it indirectly, by "breathing" CO_2, NO_3, NO_2, and SO_4.

We can observe how oxygen is present in each of the compounds listed above. I used the term "breathing" very loosely, as anaerobic bacteria actually have very diverse ways they use to metabolize the oxygen.

In a compost pile or in a compost tea, the presence of anaerobic microbes can generally be identified by foul smells. For the purposes of this text, we are discouraging the growth of anaerobes in our teas. One should never use stinky compost or compost tea.

Organic gardeners often use the old "stick method", encouraged in some gardening publications. It is a very loose format; Compost, and/or plant material and whatever the gardener feels like is put into a barrel with water, stirred a few times and left for an unspecified period. I emphatically discourage this practice. Stirring a compost tea with a stick a few times does not add enough oxygen, and should be considered dangerous. Without plenty of oxygen, the brew will likely be dominated by anaerobic organisms.

In the making of compost teas, we are simply choosing to culture aerobic organisms because they perform functions favorable to our cause. Our goal is to provide first-class conditions for aerobic organisms to grow and flourish.

Aerobic bacteria are oxygen-loving organisms that tend to be more delicate than, and may be dominated by anaerobic bacteria—given a lack of oxygen. However, in the correct environment aerobics will easily dominate anaerobic populations.

Bacteria

Bacteria are the smallest, possibly most important workers in the soil building process. They increase soil structure, water-retention capacity, and create passageways for the diffusion of oxygen into, and carbon dioxide out of the soil. They also play an important role in recycling three important elements: sulfur, carbon, and nitrogen. Bacteria, by diverse ways, have the ability to retain nutrients (N, P, S, Ca, Fe, etc.) and provide those nutrients for plants, as well as serve to decompose plant-toxic materials and excess residues. Bacteria help build soils that have been damaged by compaction, over-tillage, inorganic fertilization, and toxic chemicals such as pesticides and fungicides. Bacteria are also a major food source for other, larger microbes.

In foliar compost tea applications, bacteria have a symbiotic relationship with the plants. Beneficial bacteria are applied in hordes, thereby dominating leaf surfaces, leaving no room for pathogens to grow or feed, while at the same time improving the plants intake of foliar nutrients. When microbes respire carbon dioxide, that causes the leaf stomates to open, allowing more nutrients in. In dry weather, the bacteria are less active, giving off less carbon dioxide, which causes the stomates to open less, effectively governing the plant's nutrient intake. Bacteria also hold and metabolize nutrients in various ways, many of which become available for the plants through the leaves.

Fungi

In 1885, German scientist Albert Bernard Frank discovered that pine seedlings grew better in sterile soil inoculated with forest fungi rather than in plain sterile soil. He realized that the trees actually benefit from the presence of fungus in the root zone. Today, the symbiotic relationships between plant roots and fungi is termed *mycorrhizae*. The presence of mycorrhizal fungi in our soils is paramount, as at least 90% of all plants form mycorrhizae.

Much like the unnamed bacteria, taxonomy does not have names for most of the fungi present in soil. Thousands of unclassified *species* exist in only one spoonful of compost tea.

The importance of beneficial fungi in soil structure also cannot be understated. Many of the roles fungi have in the development of high quality soils are similar to the roles played by beneficial bacteria.

Fungi help build aggregate soil structure, and create passageways for nutrients to move through, oxygen to flow into, and carbon dioxide to flow out of. Fungi are also some of the best workers we have to combat soil compaction because of their ability to continually break up the soil. They also have their own unique, powerful ways to decompose plant residue, plant toxic materials, and decaying microbes. Fungi also retain nutrients in the fungal biomass—particularly calcium.

Fungi commonly feed on more complex sugars, and food more difficult to digest than bacteria do. Bacteria, being opportunists, are very adept at snatching up the simple sugars, leaving the remaining food for the fungi. Therefore, fungi have developed many diverse, ingenious methods for finding, securing and digesting their food.

What mycorrhizal fungi contribute in their symbiotic relationships with plants is far too vast to be covered here. However, one of the obvious gifts fungi contribute is their unique capability to liberate and transport chemically locked up minerals to the plant. The most important mineral involved in this exchange is phosphorus, but fungi also help provide calcium, copper, magnesium, iron, and zinc in available forms that plants can use.

After a foliar application of compost tea, fungi may occupy only up to 25% of the leaf surfaces, but like bacteria, their presence tends to fend off undesirables, consuming plant exudates that disease causing organisms would otherwise use for food.

In brief, mycorrhizal fungi not only act as sentries, or watchdogs, attacking and feeding on parasites, but also provide essential nutrients that the plants would otherwise have difficulty getting.

Fungi help generate more acidity (lower pH) in the soil. Old growth forest soils contain some of the highest levels of fungal bio-mass, which encourages higher acidity and lower nitrogen levels. We can observe what kind of plants thrive in those conditions, namely: trees, shrubs, and perennials. When brewing a compost tea for the roots of those kind of plants, we ideally choose to make a brew that is fungal dominated.

An adequate amount of beneficial fungal bio-mass is needed in teas to help control many fungal diseases on the leaves, branches, and trunks of plants. In fact, fungal dominated tea is the tea of choice when there is pressure from fungal diseases such as powdery mildew and downy mildew.

Compost tea is made by pumping air into water into which compost and nutrients have been added. This can be accomplished in a myriad of ways, either by using a commercially available compost tea brewer or with equipment you have put together yourself. We have included a design for a small five gallon brewer, which is a good size for home vineyards.

5 gallon food-grade plastic bucket
Hydroponic air pump
20 feet clear vinyl food grade plastic tubing sized to the air pump
Diffuser—soaker hose tubing
Nylon paint strainer bag designed to fit over the top of a five gallon bucket

The air pump plugs into your house current so should not be immersed in water. The pump will sit next to the bucket. Each air pump has two or four outlets, from which you run 5 foot lengths of the tubing into the bottom of the bucket. The ends of the tubing are attached to your soaker-hose diffuser set-up. Air will be pumped into the bottom of the bucket and bubble up out of the diffusers. A compost tea brewer will be more efficient if it utilizes a high volume air pump. You can use a lot of creativity in making your diffuser set-ups. A 10 inch circle of ordinary garden soaker hose plumbed down to the vinyl aquarium hose works well.

Using Your Compost Tea Brewer

Place the diffuser in the bottom of the bucket and connect the tubing to the air pump.

Fill the bucket almost all the way with warm water. If you are using municipal water with chlorine, it is important to run the pump for one hour, aerating the water to remove the chlorine.

Place the clean nylon paint strainer bag into the bucket, securing it with the elastic band around the outside of the bucket top rim.

Into the open strainer bag carefully place your compost and nutrients, so as not to allow the entire bag to fall into the water.

Turn on the pump and let it run until the compost tea is brewed—from 24-72 hours.

Clean all equipment immediately after using it.

Brew in a warm, if not hot place. Ideal liquid temperature is about 78F/26C. It takes longer at lower temperatures. You must use good fully composted aerobic compost. Do not use stinky anaerobic compost. For vineyard applications we strive to make as fungal dominated teas as we can.

Ideally, your compost pile has a high fungal population. This is at times easier said than done. Fungal populations can be augmented by adding Canadian peat moss to the brewer, and/or rotting wood from forest stumps. Contrary to popular belief, peat moss contains soil fungi, but it does vary from bag to bag. If you do not believe me check it out under a microscope.

Digging rotten stump or log material from the forest will give you some superb fungus, particularly if it is from your local environment. Worm castings make powerful compost tea, but it tends to be bacterial dominated—not a bad thing. Adding plenty of stump material will render it more fungal.

For more detailed discussions, check out:
Compost Tea Making by Marc Remillard @compostteamaking.com

For most applications mix 1 part compost tea with 3 parts water before applying.

Fungal Compost Tea Recipe
Almost 5 gallons of clean chlorine-free water
1 ½ quarts (1.5 liter) fungal compost
2 Tablespoons (50 ml.) humic acid
2 Tablespoons (50 ml.) soluble cold water kelp
1 Tablespoon (25 ml.) fish hydrolysate (the expensive kind of fish fertilizer)
Extra ingredients: 1 liter rotten forest stump or log, powdered baby oatmeal, soybean meal, fruit pulp, glacial rock dust, rock phosphate

Effective Microorganisms EM•1®

In 1980, Dr. Teruo Higa, Professor of Horticulture at the University of Ryukyus, Japan began experimenting with microbes deemed beneficial for soil and plant health. What he found was a specific group of microbes that work very well as a team. These super-athletes are actually common microbes: lactic acid bacteria, phototrophic bacteria, particular strains of yeasts, fermentative fungi, and actimomycetes.

The EM•1® set of organisms do a great job out-competing pathogens, and exhibit an amazing ability to degrade dioxins and many other pollutants. Because of that, EM•1® products have a wide range of applications, beyond what is covered in this text. They are non-toxic to humans.

One of the great things about the product is that it is strong and does not require brewing. As long as it is relatively fresh and well stored, you just mix it 50:1 with water and apply it.

Here we are concerned with only our specific viticultural uses, as EM•1® microorganisms work in similar fashion, and in tandem with our beneficial aerobic compost tea microbes already described here.

My own work with an experimental 2 acre Pinot Noir vineyard is an example of how applications of compost tea and EM•1® may have helped arrest a sever *Botrytis cinerea* infection.

When I walked the vineyard for the first time in the spring of 2009 Botrytis was obvious, as well as mildew. The vineyard owner had never applied anything, and was reticent to spray synthetics, but he agreed to spray one application of sulfur, and several applications of either or both EM•1® and compost tea. That year the grapes shriveled with obvious Botrytis, but the following year we observed very little on the vines. After that he began applying one or two applications of synthetics (Rally and Rubicon), micronized sulfur, as well as several compost tea or EM•1® applications per year. All in all, that is not very much, and the vines are relatively healthy.

Most commercial vineyards spray *something* every 14 days or so during the growing season. Unfortunately, the 2 acre Pinot Noir project is an incomplete study, so no genuine conclusions can be drawn. We were amazed though, as to how little Botrytis there was in 2010 after only applying predominantly compost teas and EM•1® in 2009.

EM•1® contains yeasts and "fermentative fungi". What is still unclear to me, is if or how the product effects grape fermentations. We have observed vigorous spontaneous fermentations kicking off prior to yeast inoculation during cold soak at lower temperatures than I would expect, but that could be simply the nature of the yeasts in the vineyard itself. It's a viticulturally isolated vineyard. We have no control model to compare with. Due to this, I have yet to venture to try an indigenous fermentation from this vineyard. It is tempting, because the cold temperature wild ferments did smell pleasant and normal. So far we have worked with both Assmannshausen and RC212 yeasts, which did well.

For more information about EM•1® visit compostteamaking.com and select the TeraGanix corporation button.

The Lady Bonsai Becomes a Winegrower

She spent her Sunday working in her garden, preparing it for spring planting.

Now in repose, with a glass of Pinot Noir, she ruminates, surveying her work. She is glad they moved to Oregon. It is very nice here, and *dang* this wine is good. It better be. She was surprised at the price after walking over to finally buy a bottle from the winery next door; but didn't want to loose too much face after introducing herself as a neighbor. It is irritating when they spray who knows what over there, infringing on her organicness.

The vineyard is close enough to spit on, not that she would ever stoop to do such a vulgar thing. Her ex would though--the *beast*. When he left he very loudly proclaimed that she was a control freak. The corners of her mouth turn down into a mini-frown. It's not really about control, she just likes to have things her way--neat, tidy, and harmonious. Pruning is all about loving your plants, and encouraging them to grow the way you want them to. "You and those pathetic little bonsais", he had said. Well, who was he to talk? What about his apple trees, unceremoniously plopped into holes and then forever ignored? What would you call that? Survival of the fittest horticulture? He chooses to build a fence *after* the deer chewed the struggling trees down to the ground?

Why am I thinking about him anyway?

That was when the idea popped into her head. This wine was expensive. If they can grow grapevines over there why can't I? And then, looking over at the could-have-been orchard, she realized that not one, but two feel-good things could be achieved in one fell swoop: planting a nice orderly vineyard (certainly better than the vines next door), and having the pleasure of uprooting those dead little stumps of his! Much as the darkness of the night fades into dawn, she looses the frown in favor of a pugnacious little smirk.

Those magic moments!

She begins paying visits to the winery, but quickly realizes she doesn't connect well with the winemaker--another *prima dona*. The cellar master is a nice guy though; the solid steady type. The Lady Bonsai cleverly discerns when it's the most advantages time to just pop in--quitting time, when the wine flows remarkably freely. His highness himself is actually quite generous with the Pinot Gris or whatever is at hand. It's obviously an ongoing study and passion for him as he oftentimes has a bottle open from another winery somewhere else in the world. She slowly learns by osmosis, and is not shy about asking questions.

With little else going on in her life, she mentions the winery and crew a bit too often at work, bordering on name dropping. She never really considers that they, at the winery may talk about her as well.

The lady plants four rows, each with a different clone of Pinot Noir. Each row a total of 66 feet long between end posts with 12 vines spaced five feet apart. The rows, needing to be at least as wide as the six foot trellis height, are spaced eight feet apart. Seven foot (six ft. exposed) metal fence posts are driven in at ten foot intervals, with wooden training stakes in between the metal posts, one for each vine. The external bracing for each of the eight end posts is simple; a metal stake is driven into the ground at a 45 degree angle six feet out from the end post, and a 12 gauge wire with a fence tightener is run between the end post and the stake.

Near the 45 degree angled stake she plants a hybrid tea rose, one for each row. The roses, being sensitive to mildew, are like canaries deep in a mine, alerting the vigneron to potential problems before the vines become seriously infected.

She also plants fragrant honeysuckles on the north fence, with lavender, oregano and rosemary in the landscaping. The wine will take on the essence of the flowers, as in proximity they share a subtle relationship. The 48 vine vineyard is designed to give her 15-20 gallons of wine. It could yield more than that, but she is focused on quality. In fact, she wants a model vineyard, and within reason will go to extremes to achieve it.

Mycorrhizal fungi is applied to each baby vine as it is planted into the native soil, with a good layer of compost mulch on top before watering in. She also sets up a temporary drip irrigation system for the young vines. Eventually the established vines will never need irrigating.

The pasture grass had been eliminated prior to the beginning of the project, and replanted with a native wild grass blend purchased from a small company that specializes in wild grass seed.. Wild grasses are tough, have low nutrient needs, and are less invasive than lawn grass or weeds. For fun, she also plants a western wildflower mix.

There is little to do the first year except for the inevitable weeding around the plants and tying the young shoots to the training stakes to create straight trunks. However, the Lady Bonzai applies repeated applications of both aerobic compost teas, and EM1 (effective microorganisms) to the vines and the soils around them. She also sprays some on her strawberries and the wild blackberries nearby, because they can harbor *Botrytus cinerea*.

The following year, in February the single canes are pruned to two inches below the bottom wire, always leaving one inch of cane past the end bud she wants to grow. If one prunes too close to the bud it might suffer or die.

After the winter pruning is completed, she sprays copper-sulfate on the young vines to ward off fungal intrusions. She is fairly certain that both the compost teas and the EM1 applications will help to keep the mildews at bay, but she wants to make sure. She is grossed-out by mildew. Copper sulfate is listed as organic, as is micronized sulfur, which she will also use later in the season. The guys next door also use other products several times during the growing season, but she would like to avoid that because she wants her vines to be organically grown if possible.

However, after all of the work she has put into this vineyard project she is determined not to let the plants suffer or die.

When the shoots begin to grow in May she breaks off all of the lower shoots leaving three selected top shoots, two of which are destined to become fruiting canes in the following year—12 months into the future. The three shoots arising from each plant are tied to the wires in a loose vertical fan. Any small clusters of grapes that appear that year are removed, as all of the available energy the plants can muster needs to be focused on the growth of the vines and roots.

The third year or *third leaf* is the first year a small crop is expected. This year the lady chooses to dormant prune in early March when the buds are just beginning to swell. The technique is called *delayed dormant* pruning, and is used in cool climates where the buds and flowers are susceptible to frost damage.

The lady is cane pruning her vines. She chooses two of the three canes (last years shoots), to use for this years fruiting canes, cutting off the third (backup) cane. Each cane is carefully bent down, wrapped once around the bottom wire, and tied at the end with an ordinary wire twisty. The end of each cane is then pruned off so that it almost touches its neighbors fruiting cane tip.

Throughout the growing season shoots arise from each bud on the fruiting canes, and are tied to the trellis wires above. It is not even necessary to mention that the Lady Bonsai has the shoots tied up in immaculate vertical order, but her gentle fanaticism appears in her next acts of pruning. Through July and August she pinches off both the lateral shoots in the fruiting zone, and the tendrils growing off of her perfectly positioned verticals.

After the berries have fully set, some leaves are pulled off in the fruiting zone that are shading the grapes, allowing them to receive about 60% sunlight. At this stage the berries are not prone to sunburn as they are later after veraison begins. She pulls more leaves off of the east side of her rows than the west side, aware that the west side receives the hot afternoon sun.

Eventually the vertical shoots extend out past the top six foot wire. She hedges then off, making certain that each shoot has at least 11 leaves on it, since it takes 11 leaves to fully ripen one cluster of grapes. She would prefer to see 13 or even 15 leaves. The lady also removes all of the secondary clusters that are growing out of nodes above the primary clusters. The primary clusters are then all lined up like Napoleonic soldiers in the fruiting zone near the bottom wire. She is pleased.

In early September, at veraison, when the berries begin to turn color the lady strives to outdo herself. Wielding her trusty, pointed tip pruning shears she snips off the *auxiliary lobes* (commonly called wings or shoulders) from each offending cluster in the vineyard. The wings ripen slower than the rest of the cluster, bringing the overall sugar content down, and the malic acid levels up.

She is not sure if she has removed enough laterals from the upper part of the canopy, so in the evening she crouches down on the east side of a row to observe how much sunlight gets through the canopy. What she really wants to see is about 40% sun flecking. The next day, after work, the lady removes a few more laterals until she is satisfied.

A month later, not knowing exactly when to harvest, she waits until mid-October, when they are picking next door. By that time the daytime temperatures have dropped below 70 degrees F., so the fruit is not really ripening anyway.

She shouldn't have been surprised to find that her grapes were riper than the neighboring vineyard, considering the care she gave them and the fact that they are young vines, which tend to ripen early. The guys at the winery were nice enough to run them through their crusher-destemmer in between their own loads. It was amazing. The Fiat-sized machine processed her entire 270 pound harvest in less than two minutes. They measured and mixed in some SO2 for her (40 ppm). She wasn't too sure about that. It smelled nasty, but they showed her how it visibly arrested the oxidation, and assured her that the yeasts would easily consume that little bit of sulfur.

Two days later the cellar master measured the pH of the must, and showed her how to take a Brix reading with a hydrometer. The grapes had ripened to a high sugar content for Pinot Noir, at 24.2 Brix. In fact, they had probably over-ripened because the pH meter gave a reading of 3.55 pH.

He told her not to worry, did a quick calculation, and measured out some tartaric acid for her to acidulate her must down to 3.30 pH. He pointed out that the way she'd been growing her grapes suggested that they probably had low malates, so the pH wouldn't go up too much in the fermenter, or during MLF.

She wasn't really sure what he was talking about, but didn't let him know that. He knew anyway, but said that he was impressed by how great a job she had done; which was a completely honest statement. He likes feisty women, and finds the lady rather attractive, but didn't tell her that. She knew anyway.

After harvest the Lady Bonsai cleans up the vineyard and burns all of the debris. Later, after dormant pruning she will use the same burn pile to burn all of the pruned-off canes, and then she will put the ashes from the burn pile back into the vineyard, or into her compost pile.

Autumn is the time when the vineyard may need some added nutrition, She finishes up the season by applying compost tea one more time, making sure plenty gets on the ground around the plants. Considering the amount of vigor her vines had during the growing season she chooses not to fertilize with anything containing too much nitrogen. The compost tea will give the plant roots some good nutrition as they continue to grow after harvest. The vines have been under stress, and are happy to get a little food so their roots will grow before going into dormancy. They are then stronger, and more resistant to diseases and sub-freezing temperatures. Next year she will have enough compost to apply to the entire vineyard.

The Art of Vinification

Red Winemaking Simplified

{Pg.} Clean and prepare crushing and fermentation equipment.

{64} Perform a sensory evaluation of the fruit.

{64} Lightly crush and de-stem the grapes. Try to just barely pop the skins of the berries. Sort as you go, throwing out any unsound fruit.

{67} Immediately add 40 ppm SO2

{68}Tamp/flatten the surface, clean the fermenter, cover with a cloth, and put in a cool place.

{69} Begin gently pressing the cap three times daily to keep it wet.

{71} Two days later, following crush, test for sugars, and make adjustments if necessary.

{74} Also two days after crush, test for pH and acidity, and make adjustments if necessary.

{99} Three days after crush slowly raise the temperature of the must towards 69F/20C.

{99} Inoculate with hydrated yeast and RYN on the fourth day or let it ferment on it's own.

{101} Continue pressing the cap until you determine it is time to begin punching all the way through (day 6-7). Punchdown is the common term, and involves gently mixing the must (wine) three times per day.

{87} When the must has fermented down to 17-19 Brix (lag phase) add yeast nutrients if it is deemed necessary.

{102} Monitor the temperature of the fermentation, never allowing it to rise over 90F/32C. Target 86F/30C for a peak temperature (at about 12 Brix).

{103} When the must has fermented dry, to at least minus 1 Brix, the fermentation is complete. Use a high quality narrow-range hydrometer for this measurement. You may allow the must to rest for several days if necessary, but if so, clean the fermenter first.

{104} Collect, or press the must into juice and put into a temporary vessel.

{104} The next day rack the new wine into a barrel, carboy, or amphora—off of the sediment (gross lees), leaving the sediment on the bottom. Maintain at least 59F/15C

{105} Inoculate with a malolactic starter culture and maintain 70-74 F/21-23C degree temperature. Target 74F/23C

{107} Malolactic fermentation will take 2-3 months at 74F/23C degrees, or up to 6 months at 69F/20C. During that time, make sure the barrel is full, or topped.

{108, 111} If film/cellar yeast is observed clinging to the surface of the wine, treat with a strong SO2 solution in a spray bottle.

{111} When MLF is complete, rack into a clean barrel or carboy onto 50 ppm SO2.

{112, 135} Allow the wine to age in the barrel for at least 12-18 months at a cool temperature.

{124, 135} When it is time to bottle, first rack the wine into a temporary vessel onto a calculated amount of SO2. Wait at least two days, and then bottle.

{135} Allow your wine to age at least one year in the bottle before drinking.

The California Winemaker

After a long day in early October, a winemaker rests on the veranda outside the tasting room now closed for the season. A good thing too, as tasters would simply be in the way tomorrow. The veranda is cleverly situated, allowing a commanding view of the chateau-style vineyards surrounding the winery and house.

The sun is still shining on a vineyard block two thirds up onto a steep hillside, the leaves glittering with the breeze in the golden light. What a vineyard, south facing—the crown jewel of the winery. With the oldest vines on the property, the owners call it the A-1 block. He prefers to think of it as the Beethoven vineyard, the class and powerhouse of the estate; a masterpiece waiting to be made. The overture begins with the bass viols— slow, deep and steady. He can almost hear them tuning up, preparing to flow into immortal strains destined for the ears of the gods and, perhaps later, those of ordinary men.

He was up there this morning, tasting and taking samples. At 24.3 Brix and 3.51 pH the Beethoven block is technically ready to pick, but this year he is greedy and wants even more majesty. Greed could be considered an attribute to the vintner's portfolio, coupled with the ability to snatch up every bit of structure and fruit available. Besides, in the light of all eternity what is three days more hang time? The weather promises to be favorable; warm, but not too hot. The grapes won't over-ripen. They didn't taste quite ready.

At times he thinks of all the vineyard blocks as composers, each playing in a different mode, and offering a unique melody to enrich his blend. Looking towards the left, he notices that Rachmaninov, slightly east facing, is now in the shadows, awaiting the dawn.

Leaning forward he looks even further left toward the Jimi Hendrix block but cannot really see much of it, as it's almost out of sight. That was funny--a pun. He is too tired to be funny. Jimi is in fact, in the shadow of the mountains. He has never really observed this before, as to which block falls first to the shadows. Then he squints; is that a slight glow or…? In the last few moments of an extended journey Jimi, while passing back through the solar system figured out how to harness the energy of the sun itself. Chewing, looking up, the power cords to his amplifier are lying unplugged on the stage behind him—but still the vacuum tubes are glowing blue, volume on full and louder than ever as he plays towards eternity.

He's not worried about Jimi.

Tomorrow morning the crew will begin by picking the block next to the parking lot. They're young vines, planted when he first came here, seven years ago. It's been that long? The then new owners chose to plant a safe, ordinary, but reliable California Cab clone; undeniably fruity, and a good solid performer--John Phillip Sousa; that flag waving, love it or leave it, apple pie carrying Cabernet Sauvignon.

Why not start the fermentation season out with a bang? The crusher is set up, the fermenters are clean and Sousa is the opening act.

In an obscure corner of the estate is the Frank Zappa block, which won't be ready to pick for at least a week. Is it ever really ready? He never knows what to expect from that parcel. He's definitely thinking about using an aggressive yeast; one that can keep up with the high nutrient needs and the unusual mineral content, compounded by Franks tendency to go reductive. Some very interesting wine comes out of there, but no one in their right mind would want to have a steady diet of it. Well--maybe someone.

Still, the block is very important to the blend, adding that extra complexity and spice. He looks up at the wispy sunset guarded by puffy little clouds and hopes it doesn't rain on Frank.

The winemaker watches as the last crimson rays illuminate Aaron Copeland, slowly fading into the west. It's always a well balanced taste. At that moment he considers letting Aaron ferment on its own indigenous yeast; all natural, an American spirit.

Fermentation

Performing a Sensory Evaluation of the Fruit

After the bins of grapes arrive at the winery, the winemaker spends some time tasting the grapes and forming a game plan. There may be different varieties and clones from various parts of a vineyard, or from different vineyards. He or she may be accompanied by the cellar master, an owner or winery workers. They observe, taste and compare notes. What happened in the vineyard this year? How small are the berries? (small is good) How soft are they? Did they leave the wings/shoulders on the clusters? What is the general condition of the clusters? Is there much bird or wasp damage? How much raisining, mummies, and shot berries? How even is the ripening? How many unripe berries? How ripe are the stems? Is there visual mold? Can one smell mustiness or mold?

The grapes are assessed to determine if they have achieved full morphological ripeness. How is the perceived acid? What do the skins taste like? How tannic are they? Are the seeds brown and crunchy (ripe), or still soft and green? And last but not least: How do you like the taste?

Why perform this casual ritual? We are taught that we are supposed to have a previously devised plan of action to achieve certain goals. The winery has established markets for specific wines. Can one not simply follow standard procedures to produce a predictable product?

Sometimes, but a good winemaker is wise. A good winemaker is a bit of a chameleon. The best wine will be made if the grapes are allowed to express what they are; not what anyone thinks they *should* be. They can be encouraged, courted, cajoled, or nudged; but one should never use force.

Too often the nouveau winery uses young vine Cabernet Sauvignon to produce a "Reserve" vin de guard style wine for long aging that turns out to be nothing more than a coarse vulgar beast. Young-vine fruit is better served to make simple, lively, fruit forward wines. Adolescent vines make adolescent wines. Wines made for long aging need to be from grapes sourced from old vines.

Experienced winemakers may take it even one step further, and endeavor to make wines that honor where the grapes were grown—expressing the terroir of the vineyard itself. Or, a vintner may choose to make a wine that has varietal expression—classy, austere Mourvedre; silky, perfumey Cabernet Franc; or tarry, dense Syrah.

The sensory evaluation ritual resides squarely in the artistic realm, having occurred prior to lab testing for sugars, pH, titratable acidity, and YAN numbers. At that point the winemaker starts to think about how these particular grapes will be handled in the winery, and begins to visualize a potential finished wine. Later, when the numbers come in, he or she will figure out how to go about doing it.

Crush

The ultimate tool for crushing the grapes, at least in terms of gentleness is in fact...the foot. Somehow the foot stomping action macerates the skins well but avoids cracking the seeds open. However, this rather sensual experience can only be performed practically in shallow fermenters, and smaller quantities. If you do choose to stomp, don't overcrush.

Home winemakers that are de-stemming several hundred pounds by hand should consider leaving some of the berries as they are. The de-stemming process frees up enough juice to soak the berries, and get the ferment started.

A difficult problem for the stomper is how to get rid of the stems. In days of yore our ancestors used a kind of small hand-held rake with short wooden teeth, stripping the berries from the stems cluster by cluster...a tedious chore at best.

Many wines made in those olden days were fermented with the stems, now termed *whole cluster* fermentation. This can add a higher concentration of tannins to the wine, which can certainly help preserve it, but can also impart levels of bitterness that may be considered undesirable by modern drinkers. If the choice is to use the stems in the fermenter, make certain they are ripe. Ripe stems (depending on the varietal and clonal selection), will begin to lignify, and turn brown. Tannic varieties like Cabernet Sauvignon will typically always have harsh tasting stems.

Others add back or allow some stems into the fermenter, adding tannic structure for wines intended for longer aging. The stems tend to absorb pigments, rendering a wine with a lighter color, but they do serve to modulate and cool down a fermentation.

Stems impart tannins, which, as mentioned are often green and aggressive if the wood is not fully lignified and ripe, but can enhance character and add substance to the wine. Stems help aerate the must, keep the temperature down, and promote a gentle lowering of the temperature towards the end of fermentation. Wines made with the inclusion of stems are less prone to oxidation. However, including stems in less-than-stellar years provides poor quality tannins, absorbs color, and causes the wine to loose alcohol and acidity.

If it is decided that a portion of the stems are to be retained, try using whole pristine bunches from old vines that are kept intact. Those clusters can be placed in the middle of the fermenter, promoting a long intra-cellular fermentation, which releases an element of fruitiness and fine tannins into the mix. The technique is still used with discretion by some of the best Burgundian domains. After fermentation with whole clusters, un-crushed berries still containing sugars will often finish fermentation in tank or barrel when the juice is liberated by the press.

Most wines today are made from completely de-stemmed grapes. The modern tool designed to perform both crushing and de-stemming operations may not be as romantic as treading by foot, but much more efficient. The machine can cost from $400 to $40,000+, and is called a crusher de-stemmer. Even the most humblest hand-crank models can deal with a surprising amount of grapes in short order. However, inexpensive machines with hard plastic or aluminum non-adjustable rollers are not recommended for quality winemaking. They tend to over-crush, which releases harsh seed tannins and bitter vegetal tasting phenols from the grapes. Home winemakers will make better wine de-stemming by hand.

Most good crusher de-stemmers have two opposing star-shaped soft rubber rollers that can be adjusted to fine tune the intensity of the crush. Each batch of grapes from different vineyards or varieties will behave uniquely in the crusher, requiring specific roller adjustments. The general idea is to just barely pop all of the berries open. As mentioned, over-crushing can result in harsh tannins, unpleasant phenols, and rapid, hot fermentations. Under-crushing, leaving many whole un-popped grapes may yield a wine with less body, structure and color, but with a pronounced fruitiness.

Some vintners choose to do a whole berry or partial whole berry fermentation, for various reasons. One aim would be to endeavor to accentuate the fresh fruitiness of the wine, yielding a drink-now style. Or, when working with tannic varieties, like Nebbiolo, Petite Verdot, Tannat, or Cabernet Sauvignon, some vintners prefer to handle them gently, particularly if the fruit came from old vines. Others welcome mature old-vine tannins in the fermenter as part of structure building tools. Pinot noir producers often favor whole berry fermentations due to the delicate nature of the varietal. As the reader may have discerned, there are many options for crush levels.

Many vintners have eliminated the crusher, and use only a de-stemmer machine in the process. A good de-stemmer machine can be adjusted to just barely pop the berries, or leave them whole. Burgundian producers typically de-stem first, then sort through the individual whole berries as they move by on a conveyor belt toward the fermenter.

As the grape clusters are loaded into the hopper of the crusher de-stemmer machine, throw out all brown leaves, moldy clusters, mummies, raisins, and unripe or unsound fruit. In the French language the sorting process is called either *triage*, *tri*, or *rapiage* (depending on the region). Triage is beginning to be used as the term in English. One way or another, the old rule of thumb is very simple; if you wouldn't eat it, don't put it into your wine.

Tech Talk

What is "free" SO2 ?

Crystalline potassium metabisulfite powder may be inexpensive, but it's certainly not free. We keep our powder dry, cool, dark, sealed and purchase a fresh supply every year. Potassium metabisulfite powder ($K_2S_2O_5$) is only 57.6 percent sulfur dioxide (SO_2). One gram of potassium metabisulfite powder produces 576 milligrams of sulfur dioxide. The bisulfate salts rapidly ionize under the acidic conditions in wine, releasing sulfur dioxide. Much of this SO_2 binds with over 50 different compounds, becoming largely unavailable to the wine. This *bound* or *combined* SO_2 usually consists of over 50% of the total SO_2, so is considered inefficient. However, under certain conditions some of the bound SO_2 may unbind and become *free* SO_2. Therefore, the bound SO_2 functions as a kind of reserve. The free SO_2 typically constitutes at least 30% of the remaining total. A small percentage of the free SO_2 is *molecular*, or active, and is the part that does most of the work. Unfortunately, molecular SO_2 is not readily measurable, but free SO_2 can be measured in the winery or in a lab. Bound SO_2 can be measured in a lab or with a special meter in a winery.

Lets take a snapshot of the some of the benefits of sulfur dioxide in wine.

SO_2:

Inhibits oxidation in musts and wine

Immobilizes undesirable bacteria prior to fermentation, giving the yeasts time to dominate

Binds with and de-activates acetaldehyde, an unwanted by-product of fermentation

Allows yeasts to utilize the sugars efficiently, and with more oxygen ensuring a complete fermentation.

Encourages the release of variety-specific flavor compounds, called flavonoid polyphenols from the grapes

Reduces oxidation, stabilizes color, and inhibits spoilage bacteria during the cellaring process

Inhibits CO_2 producing bacteria and yeasts in the bottle, and scavenges oxygen from the head space--the air between the wine and the cork

SO2

Why do winemakers add potassium metabisulfite at various stages to their wines?

We all agree that "sulfites" are compounds we would prefer to consume in only the smallest of quantities, but choosing not to add SO2 to your wine may not be a realistic option. To assume that sulfur dioxide functions merely as a "preservative" in wine is not only an over-simplistic viewpoint, but a gross understatement.

A "sulfite free" wine is an oxymoron, as sulfur compounds are naturally present on vines and grapes. The skin of the grape is covered with fine platelets of wax, and dotted with *peristomata*. Like tiny volcanoes, the peristomata exude a sweet sap, accompanied by high concentrations of silicon, calcium, phosphorus, sulfur, and chlorine. Nestled around the peristomata are found small colonies of wild yeasts.

The relationship between sulfur compounds and wine is chemically extremely complex. When potassium metabisulfite is added to a wine, some of it reacts with other chemical components to become bound SO2, the remainder functions as free SO2. The free SO2 is actively available in the wine as an antioxidant and exhibits anti-microbial properties. Free SO2 in wine is measurable, and diminishes with time. Some of the bound SO2 then becomes unbound and acts as free SO2, functioning as a partial reserve. However, much of the bound SO2 remains fixed and perpetually unavailable.

Parts per million (ppm) is another way of describing milligrams per liter. A tenth of a gram (0.1 gram, or 100 milligrams) of a substance dissolved in a liter of liquid equals 100 ppm.

When 40 ppm (parts per million) of SO2 is added to the grapes when they are crushed, the must becomes more resistant to oxidation. Contrary to popular belief, 40 ppm at crush does not kill the bacteria nor the wild yeasts already present. Since bacteria tend to be more sensitive to sulfur than yeasts, the SO2 added at that point merely slows them down, allowing the yeasts to multiply and dominate the fermentation.

SO2 Levels Continually Diminish

During the entire winemaking process, right up until it is poured into a glass, wine tends to consume sulfur compounds. The SO2 added immediately after the grapes are crushed is chemically metabolized by the hungry, active yeasts during the fermentation process. Then, after about three weeks, at the end of primary fermentation there may be very little SO2 left in the wine. At that point there is typically less than 10 ppm SO2 present. That is just about how much sulfur was naturally present on the grapes in the vineyard. Also, the yeasts not only metabolize sulfur during fermentation, but actually produce some of their own, up to 5 ppm.

Several months into the future, after malolactic fermentation is complete, the winemaker once again adds 40-60 ppm of SO2 to the wine. Six months later into the cellaring process the free SO2 level may have dropped to below 20 ppm. Also, every time the wine is racked it interacts with oxygen and typically looses 5-10 ppm free SO2. Finally, depending on the acidity of the wine, it may be brought up to about 35 ppm free SO2 at bottling time. One year later, if the same wine were opened and tested, it would contain less than 35 ppm.

A wine's pH has a dramatic effect on the way SO2 functions. At lower pH levels, less total SO2 is needed to get the same level of free SO2. Also, SO2 is much more effective at lower pH (higher acid) levels. This is a good reason to create wines with textbook levels of acidity. Contrary to this paradigm, lower acid/high pH wines are very much in vogue in the US and Australia. These wines tend to be susceptible to microbial spoilage, and more and more of them end up being pumped through sterile filters to remove unwanted bacteria and yeasts. Recently, winemakers have been aware that unwelcome bacteria are mutating, tenaciously developing resistances to SO2 and ending up in even the best of wines, feeding on residual sugars and creating CO2 in the bottle.

The most common undesirable early fermenting cold tolerant bacteria present in musts is *Kloeckera apiculata*. The Kloekera genera tend to be some of the first microbes to multiply in the pre-fermentation stage, as well as various strains of *Lactobacillus* and *Pediococcus*. As stated earlier, bacteria are fortunately more sensitive to sulfur than yeasts.

Another undesirable--*Brettanomyces* is an aerobic yeast that is responsible for making great Belgian-style ales, but has a dubious reputation as an interloper in wine.

Some claim that Brett, in modest doses, contributes character to a wine, while others would prefer to keep it's population to a minimum. Regardless of ones ideology, all of the microbes mentioned above and many more are always present in a wine. The question is: How many? Perhaps the winemaker is a warrior, or even a hero, relentlessly endeavoring to hold billions of foes at bay. Should this discussion frighten the burgeoning winecrafter? Perhaps. Professionals do loose sleep worrying about the effect of these persistent bogeymen.

The protective power of the sulfite you add is directly governed by the wine's pH. At any sulfur dioxide level, the wine receives less and less protection as the pH rises.

When the crushing or de-stemming process begins, the winemaker has already prepared an SO2 solution, which will be added in stages as the grapes are being crushed for a large fermenter, or—for smaller fermenters— added and mixed in immediately after a fermenter has been filled. Potassium meta-bisulfite powder is carefully measured, mixed with hot water into solution and thoroughly blended into the grape must. Once the powder has been mixed with water it becomes unstable and gives off Sulfur Dioxide gas, or SO2.

Most winemakers add 30-50 ppm of SO2 to the freshly crushed grape must, which immediately retards oxidation, and slows down the growth of unwanted bacteria. However, 40 ppm (a standard) is not enough SO2 to inhibit the generation of yeasts, which are less sensitive to sulfur than bacteria tend to be. The winemaker thus creates a medium in which yeasts can dominate, and is fanatical about limiting bacterial growth during primary fermentation. Please refer to the charts on pages 134-140 to determine SO2 quantities.

If the grapes have been sourced from an organic vineyard, experienced winemakers may add less SO2—perhaps only 25-35 ppm of SO2 at crush. Why? Winegrapes raised using organic methods oftentimes arrive at the winery already accompanied with quite a bit of sulfur. This is due to the high amounts of sulfur typically used in organic vineyards. Since organic vineyards are inhibited from using synthetic products, their choices of fungicidal products are limited. Check with the vineyard beforehand to determine what their spray program is for mildews.

After the SO2 has been added, and mixed in well, the grape mass is tamped down, and the surface flattened to reduce oxidation. The fermenter is cleaned, and a sheet is fastened to the top, or the lid closed to protect the must from fruit flies. The wine-to-be is moved to a cool place where pre-fermentation maceration, more commonly known as *cold soak* can occur for several days.

Pre-Fermentation Maceration

Cold soaking has become a standard procedure for the majority of quality wines worldwide. The simple technique gently extracts more flavors and color from the grape skins prior to the onset of fermentation. The liquid temperatures in the fermenters are ideally held well below 57F/14C degrees for typically 3 to 6 days.

Phenols Basics

Phenols are a large and complex group of compounds of particular importance affecting the flavor and character of red wines. Phenols in wine are divided into two distinct groups: flavonoids, and non-flavonoids. Flavonoids are derived primarily from the skins, seeds, and stems of the grapes. They commonly constitute more than 84% of the phenolic content of a red wine. The most common flavonoids in red wine are anthocyanins.

The Websters dictionary definition of a Phenol as "an alcohol-soluble aromatic compound" is over simplistic, as we find that some phenols, such as some anthocyanins, are actually water soluble. In fact, the water soluble anthocyanins are largely responsible for extracting blue colors from the grape skins, while red color extraction is mostly the result of the alcohol-soluble malvin, one of the predominant anthocyanins in red wines.

Since cold soak occurs prior to the yeast fermentation, there is, as yet no alcohol present in the must. The grape skins do however, begin to soften, and break up, or *macerate*. Due to the water soluble nature of some anthocyanins, more of the color blue is extracted during cold soak, along with a host of both flavonoids and non-flavonoids. Wines that have been through a pre-fermentation maceration therefore are darker in color—more purple than red.

During cold soak, it is important to keep the cap wet --using the punch down tool—three times per day. This begins what is called *cap management*, a fancy term for the (sometimes fun) grunt-work tasks termed *press-down* and *punch-down*. The punch-down tool is used for both, and has a long stainless steel tubular shaft, a tee handle, and a piece of stainless steel sheet metal the size of a dinner plate welded 90 degrees onto the business end. Amateur winemakers working with small quantities can devise simple tools from kitchen utensils. Press down can be performed using the bottom of a clean glass or stainless steel cake pan, and punch down with a potato masher, or simply with the hands.

Never allow aluminum to contact wine or must.

Press Down

The grapes congregate at the top of the fermenter, to form the *cap*, a surface too hard for the flat of the tool to penetrate deep into. For the first few days, the tool is used to press-down, or just submerge the grapes enough to fully, but gently wet them (about 2"/5cm). Each time, the surface is again tamped down and flattened to reduce the surface area before cleaning up and putting the cloth or cover back on. The idea is to allow the berries to begin to macerate, while inhibiting unwanted microbial spoilage bacteria from finding purchase in the must.

Home winemakers—Listen up. None of the authors of books or on-line amateur winemaking sources are aware of the press-down discipline. It is a matter of simple ignorance, where the two worlds, amateur and professional have not connected.

No matter what they-all say, do not mix the must vigorously at this stage (except to mix in acid or water). The simple fact that home winemakers are oftentimes dealing with small 100-200 lb. batches means that they are physically bigger than their wine. It would be like if a winery hired a huge ogre to perform press downs. The 2 ton fermenters barely come up to his knees. Sure, he is strong enough to brutally mix the must, but he mustn't.

As tempting as it may be, do not be the ogre. Press down—gently. Just keep the cap wet and allow the grape mass to soak in its own juice. Keep it as cold as you can. You might put the fermenter on a Harbor Freight roll-away cart and move it outside. Since there is more oxygen associated with smaller fermenters, a 3 day soak should be the maximum duration. If the must begins to smell *different*, you are sensing volatile acidity (VA), and it is time for yeasts and higher temperatures. Do not delay.

Towards the end of cold soak, the ambient room temperature is adjusted to at least 69F/20C to allow the must to gradually warm up. A one ton fermenter can take over 24 hours to do so.

Two days after the crush during cold soak, the juice is tested for it's pH value, titratable acidity, sugars, and possibly YAN numbers. By that time, the skins have softened enough to allow for more accurate readings--pH readings taken before that time will be inaccurate.

In the USA and Australia, winemakers use either the Brix scale and/or Specific Gravity to test for sugars. In France the Baumé scale is used, and in Germany, the Oeschle scale, which is related to Specific Gravity.

One way or another, the idea is the same. How much sugar is in the grape juice?

Hydrometer

The most reliable tool for determining the sugar content of unfermented must is the hydrometer, sometimes termed a saccharometer. Another tool used to quickly check sugars is a hand-held refractometer. Please don't be fooled by those who love their gadgets, as the refractometer may be a very common, useful tool in the vineyard, but due to calibration and quality variations, it is not as consistently accurate in the winery compared to a quality hydrometer.

What is a quality hydrometer? One that costs over $10. Those common, triple-scale $6 hydrometers are notoriously inaccurate, and cannot be relied upon to give accurate measurements within plus or minus 1 Brix of the true reading. We need accuracy within 2/10 of a Brix, particularly for the initial Brix reading for total sugars—O.S.G. (original specific gravity), and for the final measurement to determine the end of the fermentation process. Consider purchasing a good full-range (0-30 Brix) hydrometer—or better yet--a narrow range (20-30 Brix) hydrometer for the initial reading, and another narrow range (-2 to +2 Brix) for the final reading. A full range hydrometer (even a cheap one) can be used for all of the measurements in between those two values—because those readings are always just general guidelines due to practical inaccuracy; the presence of alcohols in the must skew the readings. You will also need a narrow cylindrical hydrometer jar tall enough for the job. Some of the better hydrometers are longer than others.

How does a hydrometer work? The beauty of a hydrometer is in its simplicity; It is a piece of sealed glassware with a weight on the bottom. When placed in water it floats in and out of the water. If you mix sugar into the water, the water becomes heavier—and the hydrometer floats higher out of the water.

A paper tube with numbers on it has been captured inside the glass tube. The number that is level with the surface of the water is your reading (the *meniscus* level). The only practical difference between a hydrometer calibrated in Baumé, Brix, Oeschle, or Specific Gravity is how far apart the numbers on the paper tube are.

Hydrometer Temperature correction

Before we are all bored to tears discussing the intricacies of hydrometers, we must mention temperature corrections. Hydrometers are calibrated to be accurate at a specific temperatures (The temperature is stated on the tool). Modern hydrometers are usually calibrated at 20C., while the older cheap ones are usually at 60F. You can adjust the temperature of your sample to match the hydrometer, or add .25 degrees Brix to the reading for each 9 degrees F. if the temperature of the must is higher than the calibrated temperature; if the actual temperature is below, deduct .25 Brix from the reading for each 9 degrees F.

When you use a hydrometer make sure the sample in your cylinder has no particulate matter in it. Strain if necessary. Insert the hydrometer carefully into the liquid and give it a little spin to dislodge bubbles before taking your reading at the meniscus level.

The beauty of the Brix scale is it is, for all practical purposes the same as % sugar; If you get a Brix reading of 15 Brix in unfermented apple juice, the juice contains 15% sugars.

The optimal range for wine grapes is from 23-25 Brix, but good wines are made from as low as 20 Brix (some Burgundys), and as high as 27 Brix (some Zinfandels). A wine must starting at 23 Brix will yield a wine a tad higher than 12%, and a must that is initially 25 Brix will make a wine at about 13.7% .

Styles, varietals and opinions vary as to how much alcohol is optimal in a wine. 14% alcohol in a finished Pinot Noir can overpower the delicacy of the wine, while a late harvest Zinfandel at 16% is considered acceptable, because we expect to taste the alcohol in a wine-style that expresses Port-like characteristics.

Sugar Adjustments

What does one do if the sugars in a must are lower or higher than optimal? (23-25 Brix). Adjustments can be made.

Raising Sugar Levels---Chaptalization

Add 1.5 ounces of cane sugar per gallon for every point of Brix short of the ideal (23 Brix).

Mix the sugar fully into solution in a small amount of must before adding to the fermenter. Some vintners chaptalize at the end of the yeasts' lag phase, which will usually occur about 3 Brix shy of the original reading. Others feel that chaptalization is best performed when the must has fermented down to 8-10 Brix. I recommend slowly bleeding the sugar in twice—the larger dose at the lag phase, and the remainder at or above 8 Brix.

The process of adding sugar to unfermented wine in order to increase the final alcohol level is known as chaptalization after the French chemist Jean-Antoine Chaptal, who advocated the technique in 1801.

Today, cane sugar is always used. Do not use beet sugar or dextrose (corn sugar). It should be noted that in California chaptalization is technically illegal (rarely necessary), but grape concentrate may be added (legal bulk-wine loophole). Do not over-chaptalize as it tends to generisize the flavor. Target 23 Brix.

Since we are discussing chaptalization, we should mention a more advanced technique used by the Burgundians. A very slight addition of sugar may be added towards the end of fermentation of Pinot Noir (6-8 Brix); not to add alcohol, but to extend the fermentation, allowing more time for the skins to be in contact with the juice.

Reducing Sugar Levels
Target 23-24.5 Brix

The current fad in the US and Australia leans towards higher alcohol wines. However, there are many technical and sensory reasons disfavoring the production of higher alcohol levels in wines. One may think that chemically, high alcohol in a wine should contribute to increased longevity, but that is not the case. Alcohols upset the integration of tannins and color compounds—so important for longevity and creating subtle aromatic nuances in red wines. High alcohol is actually an impediment to finer flavors in wine. Bottled world-class wines generally weigh in at about 12% to 13.5% alcohol.

Saignée

In old French medicine, *saignée* means "bleeding" or "bloodletting". In winemaking, the term is commonly used in both French and English to describe the technique of drawing juice off of a fermenter prior to the onset of fermentation—for various reasons.

Immediately after red grapes have been crushed, the juice is white, but quickly begins to color as the skins macerate. (The exceptions are teinturier varieties such as Regent, Marechal Foch, Leon Millot and Alicante Bouschet--which have pinkish juice.)

The juice is primarily sugar water. The flavor of wine originates from the skins.

If a winemaker wants to make a more concentrated wine, juice may be removed at that time from the fermenter to increase the skin to juice ratio. This will also serve to decrease the sugar content of the must. This method will make the best wine.

If the winemaker times it right (by color), a rosé can be made of the residue.

Rosé Simple
With water, dilute the saignée juice down to 22 Brix

Acidulate with tartaric acid to 3.2 pH

Put juice in a carboy or closed tank (plus airlock) with head space to allow for fermentation. Inoculate with a low-temperature rosé yeast, or a white-wine type yeast like EC-118 with Go-Ferm or add nutrients.

Ferment at 56-60 F. for several months.

Tip: If you want your rosé to have a bit more fresh acid taste, add a touch (be careful) of ascorbic acid (vitamin C) at bottling (not before). Not dietary Vitamin C, due to the sugar content. On that note, if you want a sparkling rosé, add a measured amount of sugar at bottling and use the appropriate closures. Do not use citric acid.

Amelioration

Waterback

After the saignée juice has been removed from the fermenter, water can be added back to replace it. This technique is called waterbacking, and will reduce the sugar content of the must. How much water is added back is at the discretion of the winemaker. It could be more or less than the volume of saignée juice. One way or another, every gallon of water added back to the fermenter should be acidulated with 23 grams of tartaric acid to make up the difference between the pH of the water and the pH of the must, or 6 grams tartaric acid per liter of water.

Direct Dilution

The most common method used to decrease the sugar content of must is direct dilution—or simply adding acidulated water. Obviously the technique waters down the wine—in both flavor and in concentration.

Calculate how much juice is in the undiluted must------14 pounds per gallon is typical. If you bought 1000 pounds of grapes -with stems- there is about 71 gallons of juice there. However, if you are working with a variety with very large grapes, and/or thin skins (Cinsault. Grenache, Counoisse etc.), one can figure it at 13, or even 12 pounds per gallon.

Convert gallons to liters------1 gallon = 3.785 liters

OB= The original Brix of must.
L1 = Volume (in liters) of the juice in the undiluted must that will become wine.
DB=The desired Brix you want the must to be diluted to.
L2 = Volume (in liters) of the juice in the diluted must that will become wine
Y = Volume (in liters) of acidulated water needed to dilute the must to the desired Brix level (DB)

Equation 1: $(L1 \times OB) / DB = L2$
Equation 2: $L2 - L1 = Y$

Some publications suggest adding the water in stages after performing the initial calculation—checking the Brix as you go. That is certainly a wise idea in theory, but it assumes there is no juice trapped inside the grapes. If you are doing a whole berry, partial whole berry, or barely popped berry fermentation the initial Brix reading will be correct, but once you start to add water you will be working with a blind hydrometer. The reading will be inaccurately skewed towards the low side. Also, when working in larger vats, getting anything fully mixed into the must is dubious at best.

Reducing sugars in a must is also a good time to add acid, if necessary. The tartaric acid can be fully mixed into the water prior to waterbacking.

Make sure you account for the acidity of the water itself. To adjust it from 8.5 pH to 3.4 pH add about 23 grams per gallon/6 grams per liter of tartaric acid

Hot water helps to fully dissolve the acid. Use non-chlorinated well or spring water, not distilled water. If you have to, you can boil tap water and let the chlorine gas off.

pH/TA

Two days after crush (not before) the pH of the must is measured, as well as the titratable acidity (TA). Why? The skins are higher pH than the pulp. Some winemakers run some of the must through a blender, pulverizing the grapes before taking the pH and TA readings. They claim they get accurate readings without having to wait for the skins to macerate for the two day period.

All wineries know the TA of the musts, whether the titration is done in house or by a lab. However, between pH and TA, it is the pH that is most important to know. When you find yourself in a group with winemakers, they are usually talking pH. There are however, differing philosophies regarding viewing the expression of acids. Winemakers emerging out of some colleges use the more "scientific", international Specific Gravity as a gauge for sugars, and prefer to use TA as their standard reference for acids. Before we get into a primer on the nature of pH and acidity in wines, we should discuss the devices themselves.

pH Meters

Home winemakers—if you purchase one expensive piece of equipment consider it being a better pH meter—your wines will improve. If you know the pH, you can get by without knowing the TA of your wines. Litmus paper-type tests are not accurate enough—particularly for red wines.

The functionality of a pH meter is directly related to it's price. You get what you pay for.

Amateurs can try to struggle with meters that cost less than $150 but it is not recommended. The tool may work okay out of the package, but if it does not have a detachable probe, when it begins to malfunction it must be discarded. Lower-end pH meters are good for soil testing, where the difference between 5.10 pH and 5.40 pH is considered a finite measurement. We need accuracy plus or minus 0.01 pH (the better meter specs). From a winemakers perspective, the difference between a wine at 3.51 pH compared to the same wine at 3.56 pH is important.

The literature accompanying many of the cheaper meters claim accuracy better than +\-0.02 pH, or worse +/-0.05 pH. First of all, that is not accurate enough. Secondly—we weren't born yesterday—the sales department is making claims based on the theoretical performance of the device right out of the box. When accuracy wanes due to calibration, residue, etc., readings will be unreliable.

One must ask oneself why one should pay $400 for a meter when a $200 unit claims the same accuracy specs? The answer is two-fold—reliability and stability. High quality meters dial-in to a reading quickly, with minimal wandering, and you can rely on the reading. Anyone who has used a lesser meter knows how they can wander.

We can roughly place pH meters in three categories of quality by price: $0-150, $150-300, and $300 +

Potential winery owners—splurge for a high-range device. You will be glad you did. Meters in the $150-300 range work fine, but are less stable, and fussier.

The electronic circuitry in a pH meter is not rocket science. The delicate glass probe is the key element. When the probe wears out—get another one. Unless it has been abused, the electronics in the meter itself are probably still fine. The separate stainless steel thermometer probe (if it has one) is tough, and very usable, as it's probably the most accurate liquid thermometer in the winery.

Acidity Basics

Grapes grown in warmer climates tend to have lower acidity than the same grapes grown in cooler climates. In general, warmer climates result in high sugar and low acids whereas cooler climates result in low sugar and high acids. In California and Washington State, where grapes tend to ripen well, it is common for high pH/low acid grapes to arrive at the wineries ready to be fermented.

All of the great wines of the world tend to have good natural acidity. The vines happen to be growing where the grapes ripen well enough, but with balanced higher acids. The resulting wines have the potential to be multi-dimensional in flavor. The natural higher acidity of the grapes set the groundwork. World-class Cabernet Sauvignon grapes in Bordeaux may be pulled off the vines at 22 Brix, and 3.20 pH. If Washington State grapes are harvested at those numbers the resulting wine can easily be thin, lean and herbaceous tasting.

Viticultural areas where the grapes ripen easily, those with acidic soils, or not enough stress on the vines, tend to produce wines that are full bodied but single dimensional in character. There are of course, superb exceptions. However, the vast majority of California, Washington, and Australian wines fit into that category. Over ripening, high pH, and low acids are synonymous with flat, dull, single dimensional wines. If we, as winemakers must resort to adding oodles of tartaric acid to a wine because the pH is high, we must acquiesce to the reality that it will be, at best, that style of wine. It has been called the international style—jammy, deeply colored, and heavily oaked. It is in fact a very popular easy-to-drink style (for those who like that much oak). So who are we to judge what consumers should like and what they should disdain? Wine is to be enjoyed, irregardless of the preferences of the elite. And yet, our goal here is to endeavor to produce multi-dimensional wines.

From a marketing perspective, new world wineries seeking to produce wines more in the minerally, acidic European styles struggle with local consumers preferences towards easier to drink low-acid wines. Purchasing a wine in a tasting room that has been well crafted to cellar for a few years, but tastes more acidic and tannic *now* does-not-compute for most new world consumers. On behalf of the consumer, it is difficult to ascertain how well, or *if* a young, rough wine will improve with age.

Very young wines typically have a grainy astringency we refer to as "green" tannins. These tannins may evolve in different ways.

If a wine has insufficient exposure to oxygen during aging, they will eventually form into "dry" tannins, which leave a course, grainy impression all over the tongue and cheeks. The dry tannins dominate the taste, interfering with other flavors. Dry tannins are unstable and are associated with poor aging potential.

In more balanced wines, careful exposure to oxygen transforms the green tannins into aggressive, sheetlike, grippy "hard" tannins that are perceived wholly on the top of the tongue, covering the entire palate to the back of the throat. These are desirable tannins that are generally stable, and tend to resolve and age gracefully.

Oak tannins are perceived as a fine-grained "parching" astringency on the top of the tongue slightly back from the tip. They contain eugenol, an anesthetic which causes a numbing in the center of that region on the tongue, surrounded by an aggressive parching sensation.

There is a kind of semi-misnomer that has been passed around wine lover's circles and publications for 30 odd years concerning the nature of acidity in Washington State wine grapes. The idea is that the grapes grown on the eastern side of the Cascade range can ripen with high sugars but retain high acidity due to the cold desert-like night time temperatures.

Well--it all sounds good in theory, and is certainly true in some winegrowing regions, but in reality, for those of us working in the trenches in Washington--by the time the flavors come together what we actually receive is predominantly high pH fruit. As an example, we consider it normal to get Bordeaux cultivars ready to process at 3.50-3.70 pH and higher, and Rhone varieties even more so. Looming over our heads is the semi-justified fear that less-ripened Cabernet Sauvignon will end up tasting weedy and herbaceous—a death knell for a finished wine. So what do we do? We allow the grapes to over-ripen, and we add acid. Therefore, Washington State wines are known to be good, clean, straight-forward, simple, full-bodied wines that rarely retail for over $100. It seems as if the intent of many new-world winemakers has been to produce products that are so soft and fluffy that they offend no one's senses--politically correct wines.

Yes, we live in a world blissfully immersed in mediocrity--but one can only hope. Perhaps it is futile, this yearning for a better world—the baby-boomers dream--but we cling to it with a gnarled, grasping, forlorn tenacity. Maybe it is indeed time for a change of attitude.

"I Shall Fear No Tannin"--Winemaker Randall Grahm

Sophisticated Phenols

In the wild, grapes turn red to attract birds so they will eat the grapes and spread the seeds around--a survival technique. Prior to the seeds being ripe (sprout-able), the grapes produce pyrazines to repel the birds. Pyrazines are the source of the dreaded "bell pepper" flavors associated with less-than-ripe Merlot, Cabernet Sauvignon, and other varieties. Years ago enologists postulated that the remedy for bell pepper was extended hang time in the vineyard. The idea was that when the grapes hang on the vines after they have technically ripened the flavors soften and become richer, yielding a wine that is easy to drink sooner. Today we are not so sure how wise the technique is.

Like being afraid of the bogeyman, I must admit to having endeavored to avoid vegetal characteristics in wine without ever really experiencing much of the phenomenon. Recent studies at UC Davis indicate that hang time actually has a negligent effect on pyrazines. But old habits die hard. A quirk in human nature is that we tend to overreact to a negative, then cling on it.

Optimum ripeness is a difficult thing to define, or determine, especially in practice when one is making the decision when to pick an entire vineyard block. Brix is far from being a reliable indicator, nor is acidity as to determining full morphological ripeness. New world winemakers often have the luxury to be able to allow the clusters to hang out there until they begin to raisin. The pH goes up, sugars stabilize and some flavors increase a tad due to dehydration. This has been considered an asset by many. Not necessarily so today.

It turns out that field oxidation associated with extended hang time deprives wine of depth, complexity, and longevity in favor of early drinking bombs. The chemistry occurring inside of the grapes is complex, not fully understood and therefore much debated. There are older and newer models of thinking based on extensive studies and experience.

On older model is the solution based model. Wine is a solution. A comfortable, simple way of looking at it. Alcohol and water extract flavors dissolve in the wine, acids and sugars are added or detracted, the sugars are eaten by yeasts, become alcohol, and voila! We have wine. It is, at its worst, a test tube way of looking at wine. However, on behalf of the solution model, it is one that helped pull California wine out of the gutters of the 1960's, to make sound, reliable products.

Current models focus more on what is going on at the molecular level in wine.

Tannins are already present in the ripe berry skins and seeds as polymers. A polymer is a large molecule composed of many repeating subunits, known as monomers. When grapes are crushed, polymers encounter the acidic grape juice, which break them down into monomers. Perhaps at that point the monomers feel insecure, so like teenagers they stubbornly cluster together in groups as similarly dressed, but distinctly unique individuals.

These groups, or aggregates, collect into colloids, tiny beads of various sizes and compositions. An analogy would be an exposed aggregate concrete patio, with all of those rainbow-colored little pea-gravel stones poking up, half exposed to the sunlight. The entire patio is like one big molecule in a droplet of wine, but unlike the concrete, they are not fixed in place. Like teenagers, they are destined to change.

The evolution or progression of the tannins journey into a finished wine is extremely complex, but eventually, over months and years they reassemble and form into permanent chains. First though, they cluster together in groups—the smaller the better. The smaller the groups are, the more surface area is exposed, so the more aromatic expression the wine will have—eventually. Getting them into small groups is the key, to avoid early polymerization into larger groups.

We are concerned with managing tannins progression over time, as phenols rearrange themselves into colloids and polymers during gradual exposure to oxygen.

The role oxygen plays in the evolution of a wine is very important. The extensive work with oxygen done by Dr. Vern Singleton at UC Davis years ago has as yet to be fully digested and implemented by the enological community. Singleton illustrated oxygen's power to elaborate and refine structure.

Wine structure does not yield itself well to analysis. Wine can contain thousands of different phenolic compounds. Imagine the complexity when they all form into unique configurations. We can begin to understand why wines can express a seemingly unlimited variety of aromas and tastes.

When phenols find themselves in water (or aqueous solution like grape must) they try to escape by either evaporating, or they aggregate into groups driven by water molecules to form colloidal structures. Other, more volatile phenolics may then join the party too, and bind with the little groups. The phenomenon diminishes the overall initial aroma impact, and is termed *aromatic integration.* This is eventually good wine—wine with structure. When the colloids are small the texture is fine and the flavors blend together into a single voice.

These colloids want to form into larger groups, or polymers. What is interesting is how color anthocyanins in wine serve to govern the length of the polymers--keeping them small. It turns out that deeply colored wines tend to handle tannins more gracefully. Therefore, we encourage the extraction of color compounds in our wines. Monomeric anthocyanins (color) are highly reactive with oxygen-rich tannins so are therefore readily incorporated into these chains. However, since anthocyanins themselves cannot form into polymers they terminate the polymer chains, serving to shorten them and create finer tannic structures.

That is very important.

Yes, over-ripened grapes tend to be deeply colored initially, but there is a rub. They are already oxidized. The tannins in those grapes have polymerized, forming long, large tannin chains. The color is unstable, resulting in wines that are either plain (carefully handled), or with harsh, unyielding tannic flavors that will rarely resolve in the bottle. The tannins have already formed into a polymeric state while the grapes were still on the vine. We don't want that. We want to receive grapes with tannins still in a monomeric state so that—with the help of oxygen--they can resolve and age gradually and gracefully. Also, grapes submitted to extended hang time may have lost as much as 90% of their reductive (antioxidative) strength due to field oxidation, reducing the wines cellaring longevity by a decade. That kind of wine can fall apart in the carafe or bottle rapidly when served. There is no inherent strength to the structure.

From the skins and the seeds a young wine has extracted monomeric anthocyanins and unpolymerized tannins such as quercetin, catechin, epicatichin, and gallic acid. These soluble building blocks gather into copigmentation colloids, like tiny beads. In this stage they are perceived as a graininess on the tongue, commonly known as tannin vert or green tannins. But green tannins can evolve over time into more sophisticated flavors and aromas.

Winemaking decisions throughout the process has profound consequences on the nature and stability of these colloids; the texture on the palate, the exotic aromas, and the aging characteristics are all products of evolved tannins—enlightened tannins if you will. In a well-aged great wine the tannin chains are short, and the colloid groups are small. We perceive these as subtle flavors, and superb aromas.

As mentioned, a key to refined structure is a good concentration of red anthocyanin pigments.

Wine lovers are aware of quercetin as being a healthy component of wine, but recent studies illustrate the importance of the flavanoid in color extraction as well. It turns out that quercetin is the multi-talented renaissance man of flavanoids, performing multiple functions. First, the plant produces quercetin as a UV protectant for clusters that are exposed to the sun early in the season. Later, during fermentation quercetin becomes an important cofactor, pairing with anthocyanin color molecules. Contrary to previous notions, without tannin cofactors (in this case quercetin) the color molecules impart very little color into the wine. Tannins and color ensemble well.

Acids

As a group, the acids in wine are responsible for enhancing refreshing fruitiness flavors, and modifying the perception of other taste, and mouth-feel sensations. Acids also add a particularly noticeable balance in the reduction of perceived sweetness in a wine.

During fermentation and aging, acids are instrumental in the formations of esters, which contribute to the fresh, fruity fragrance of wines. In fact, the influence of acidity, in favoring reductive reactions, favors the aging process and the development of a desirable bottle bouquet.

The low pH produced by wine acids has a beneficial antimicrobial effect, as at lower pH values most bacteria struggle to grow. Also, the role of acids in maintaining a low pH is crucial to the color stability of red wines. As the pH rises, anthocyanins decolorize and may eventually turn blue. Higher pH/lower acid wines are much more likely to become oxidized and lose their fresh aroma and bright color.

In wine chemistry, acidity is customarily divided into two categories: volatile and fixed. To avoid going into unnecessary detail, it must be pointed out that acetic acid is, by far the predominant volatile acid found in wine. So much so in fact, that volatile acidity in wine is usually measured in terms of it's presence alone. However, by volume acetic acid levels are typically low (below 0.55 g), and for good reason. Acetic acid above those levels can give the wine a bitter, hard taste. Many attribute a vinegary odor to acetic acid, but it is actually more likely due to presence of ethyl acetate.

During fermentation, activity by yeast cells naturally produce a small amount of acetic acid. If the wine is improperly exposed to oxygen, Acetobacter bacteria will convert the ethanol into acetic acid. This process is known as the "acetification" of wine and is the primary process behind wine degradation into vinegar.

The most important acids in wine are the fixed acids. Finished wines contain predominantly tartaric acid—the fixed acid specific to grapes and to wine. It is interesting that grapes are the only temperate fruit to contain tartaric acid, rarely found elsewhere in nature. It is the strongest major wine acid (it liberates the most H+ ions), and the pH of wine depends on a large extent to it's richness in tartaric acid. Of the major wine acids, it is the one most resistant to the decomposing action of bacteria. Therefore, through most of the winemaking process tartaric acid levels remain stable, until towards the end, when potassium bi-tartrate salts crystallize and precipitate, ending up on the bottom of the vessel or bottle. Wooden barrels used for red wine storage will have a hard layer of rose-colored potassium bi-tartrate acid crystals stubbornly adhered to the oak interiors.

In practical terms, when we want to raise the acidity/lower the pH of a red wine-to-be, it is tartaric acid that we add to the fermenter.

Malic acid derives it's name from the Latin malum, or "apple", due to the green apple flavor it most readily projects. Malic acid is very important in wine, and occasionally, in some musts may actually be the predominant acid at the onset of fermentation. That changes as the fermentation progresses; because malic acid is fragile, easily metabolized by yeasts (who consume up to 30% of it), and later by bacteria, who metabolize more of it during malolactic fermentation. Unripe grapes contain higher levels of malic acid than ripe grapes. In fact, vineyards often use malic acid levels to determine when the grapes are ripe--but not always--sometimes even morphologically ripe fruit can contain high levels of malic acid due to excessive leaf shading in the vineyard.

Citric acid is the other fixed acid that is important in grapes, but at typically small volumes. Citric acid is unstable and quickly metabolized during fermentation.

Other important acids in grapes that do not originate in the grapes but are a product of fermentations are Succinic acid, and Lactic acid.

It should be noted that there are so many lesser acids and acid reactions in wine that chemistry volumes have been written concerning them, but for the practical winemaker, understanding the main wine acids is of primary importance.

Although titratable acididty and pH are related, they represent different ways of measuring the acidity of wine.

> An important thing to remember is that during the winemaking process the wine pH naturally increases, and in turn the titratable acidity decreases .

pH

pH(potential hydrogen) has been described as a measure of the strength of the acids in a solution. A pH of 7.0 is neutral, above 7.0 is alkaline, and below 7.0 is acid.

Good quality crushed red grapes are acidic---usually from 3.10 to 3.80 pH, while finished quality red wines will be typically in the 3.40 to 3.80 pH range. You will see pH values often described as units, which appear as tenths. A change from 3.60 to 3.70 would be an increase of 0.10 (one) unit. Since winemakers work in values smaller than units, they usually express the actual numbers, such as 3.63 pH, or 3.68 pH.

pH numbers are inverse to both total and titratable acidity numbers. A wine with a lower pH is more acidic than a wine with a high pH.

Why is it important for us to track the pH of a wine? pH expresses the strength or power of the acids in wine.

Lower pH in wine:

Increases microbial stability through increased inhibition of bacterial growth

SO2 becomes more effective as an antimicrobial agent

Enhances production of fruity esters during yeast fermentation

Favors the more desirable types of lactic acid bacteria

Increases aging potential

TA--Titratable Acidity

Titratable acidity is determined by standard laboratory titration procedures. "Titratable acidity" is not the same as "total acidity", which is defined as the equivalent number of protons that the organic acids would possess if they were not dissociated.

Titratable acidity is a measure of the hydrogen ions required to obtain a specific pH end point, and is always lower than total acidity.

The titration method advocated by the Office International de la Vigne et du Vin (OIV), and used in France, titrates to the endpoints pH 7. Whilst the method advocated by the Association of Official Analytical Chemists (AOAC), used in the United States, titrates to the endpoint pH 8.2.

Obviously, the difference between the French and US standards can lead to some confusion. Adding to the confusion is the tendency for sources to refer to both total acidity and titratable acidty as "TA". For the purposes of this text, we shall be only referring to titratable acidity as "TA". We will however refer to both total acidity and titratable acidity specifically.

In general, our perception of acidity in a wine is better gauged by the total acidity than pH. Although there has been some debate concerning the issue, most sources (based on studies), agree that total acidity relates more to our sense of taste than pH values in a wine. The taste effect of dissociated ions is about 10 times that of the undissociated acid molecules, but one can practically ignore the effect of pH because only about 1% of the acidity in most wines consist of the dissociated ions.

Accurate Original pH and TA

The original TA and pH readings will be more accurate if one waits for two days after crush to take the measurements. The skin of the grape is much higher pH than the pulp (juice). In two days, the skins will soften, and macerate enough to integrate with the juice better. You can observe the color of the must darken daily. If the pH is taken immediately after crush, the reading will indicate a lower pH and a higher TA than the true reading.

Another technique is to run a random selection of grapes through a blender before taking a reading. That allows the vintner to get an instant reading. The trick is to select enough grapes from more and less ripened clusters to get as close an average as possible.

Tech Talk

Acids

All acids that are dissolved in wine tend to separate into two parts: a hydrogen ion (H+), which is characteristic of all acids, and an anion (A-), which is different for each particular acid. Many of the effects of acids depend on the concentration of the hydrogen ion. In wines some of these effects include inhibiting unwanted microbes from growing, as well as maintaining the color and stability of red wine.

pH is defined as the negative logarithm of the hydrogen ion (H+) concentration, expressed in gram-atoms per liter. Since the atomic weight of hydrogen is 1.008, then 1 gram-atom per liter is equal to 1.008 grams of hydrogen ion per liter of solution:

$$pH = -\log [H+]$$

If the [H+] is 0.001 (1 X 10-3) gram-atoms/liter, then the pH = 3.0. The pH increases one unit for each 10-fold decrease in hydrogen ion concentration. Therefore, a wine with a pH of 4.0 has only 1/10 of the hydrogen ion of a wine with a pH of 3.0

Water is very weakly dissociated; about 1 in 10,000,000 atoms are dissociated. The reciprocal of the logarithm of that number is 7. A pH of 6.0 would be 10 times as acidic as pH 7.0, while a pH 5.0 would be 100 times as acidic as pH 7.0. Since grape wines have pH levels between 3.0 – 4.0, they are from 1,000 to 10,000 times as acidic as water.

Determining TA by Titrating with a pH Meter

Titration is a process where you determine the concentration of an unknown substance in a liquid. In our case, we are looking for the amount of acid in must or wine by slowly adding a small amount of a reagent (sodium hydroxide - NaOH) to the wine until an 8.20 pH endpoint is reached.

Equipment needed:
pH meter calibrated to 7.0 pH
Small beaker
10 cc/ml syringe
Sodium hydroxide (NaOH) solution at 0.2N concentration

Procedure:
Transfer 15ml/cc of strained must or wine to the beaker
Fill the 10cc syringe with the 0.2N sodium hydroxide titrate solution
Hold the pH meter's probe in the wine
Add the titrate solution 0.5 ml at a time while continuously swirling the beaker
Stop adding titrate solution when the pH reading is 8.20 pH
Record number of ml of titrate solution used
Use the formula below:
TA in g/l (expressed as tartaric acid) = 1.5 x ml of NaOH used

Tips: Remember to calibrate the pH meter to 7.0 pH. Strain the must to clarify. For accuracy the wine and the reagent should be at the same temperature. For best accuracy use a fresh (this seasons) reagent solution. Make certain you purchase the NaOH solution at 0.2N concentration.

Note: Popular titration procedures involving using color changes as an indicator are not accurate for red wines. However, if you do not have the basic lab equipment, one can purchase inexpensive kits that will provide you with some sodium hydroxide, a beaker, and a syringe. The kits are assembled for the color change technique, but the same equipment can be used with a pH meter. Once you have the lab gear, all you will need is the sodium hydroxide solution.

Adjusting Acidity in the Must.

Acidulation Simplified

If the original pH of the must is above (roughly) 3.45 pH, you will need to add tartaric acid to adjust the pH down to (roughly) 0.28 units **below** where you would like the finished wine to be. You shoot for lower than the ideal because during fermentation and MLF the pH will naturally rise about 0.28 pH units. Example: Desired pH of finished wine – 3.50 Original pH of must – 3.52 Acidulate to equal 0.30 units down to 3.32 pH.

Formula for acidulating musts with tartaric acid.

1 g/L (0.13 oz/gallon) of tartaric acid for every 0.10 unit of pH short of the ideal (units to change).

Or, if you prefer to acidulate using TA numbers: 1 gram of tartaric acid per liter of wine raises the TA by 0.1 gram per ml.

The calculation should be based on the volume of finished wine, not on the original volume of must. For quality, small thick-skinned wine grapes yields will average about 14 pounds per gallon, or 7.2 gallons per 100 pounds of grapes.

This formula is easier if you work in, or convert to liters first. Mix the tartaric acid into solution completely before adding to the must. Heating the liquid will help.

Remember to add only 2/3 of the acid during cold soak, and later, make a pH assessment at about 10 Brix to see if you should add the remainder.

Home winemakers: Never use "acid blend" from the home-brew shop. Do not use citric or malic acid. We are not making blackberry wine. Assume that the guy behind the counter is not a winemaking consultant. Purchase tartaric acid from a professional winery supply, and have it shipped to you. It will be far more economical and it will keep indefinably if stored dry.

Discussion of Acidulation Techniques

Lowering the pH of the must is a very common procedure in wineries in the new world. Here the soil types tend to be more acidic, yielding lower acid grapes than in France or Spain, where limestone based vineyard soils predominate.

In Bordeaux for example, Cabernet Sauvignon can achieve full morphological ripeness at only 22 Brix and 3.20 pH, and yield superb wines. In California and Washington, if we harvest Cabernet Sauvignon to those numbers, the resulting wines will usually be thin, weedy, and herbaceous. Here, even if the Brix numbers are still modest—say 23 Brix, the pH is more often higher than the ideal by the time the fruit is fully ripe.

So what does one do? We add tartaric acid.

So begins the dance with the acid queen--an elusive, unpredictable, but powerful entity.

It is advisable to engage in the dance as early as possible in the winemaking process. Acid added to the wine after MLF has negative impacts on the flavor, and is unstable—precipitating out and dropping to the bottom of the vessel or bottle. Acidulating during fermentation helps the acid integrate into the wine. The technical reasons for this remain speculative, but the good tasters unanimously agree.

What pH should a finished wine be? (see chart below)

There is, unfortunately no simple answer to the question. Here the winemaker is an artist, and draws on experience, and knowledge of history—regional, local, and specific vineyard typicalities, varietal characteristics, and stylistic choices. We continue to mention the difference between Bordeaux and the new world. A common tendency for the nouveau California winemaker is to endeavor to recreate a Bordeaux by using the French formula—with local grapes. The resulting wines are often disappointing. It is much wiser to seek to express what your environment has to offer. In practice that means targeting higher pH numbers in Washington and California than is typical in Bordeaux using the same varieties. The same caveat can be applied to Rhone varieties, but possibly to a lesser degree.

Oregon Pinot Noir is a unique issue (as always with Pinot), in that the ripening numbers do not differ quite as much from those of Burgundy, even though the climates and soils are different; one a marine west coast climate with acidic soils, and the other a continental climate with limestone.

The eastern half of the US presents the winemaker with difficult choices to make. French Hybrids, like Marechal Foch, Leon Millot, and selected American varieties may oftentimes have high pH *and* high TA.

Therefore, it is important for winemakers to be aware of what works well in their region, and more immediate local. Networking with fellow local artisans is time well spent.

One of the most important things to remember is that most batches of wine react to the introduction of tartaric acid uniquely. Yes, we have an acidulation formula, but wine musts do not accept the acid in a linear fashion. Therefore, I recommend adding 2/3 of the calculated amount early during cold soak, and possibly more later during fermentation at about 10 Brix. The pH reading will not necessarily be accurate at that point, but by the time the skins have softened, the original introduction of acid will have integrated in enough to where you will have an idea about how the must is accepting the acid. Let's face it; the dance involves shooting from the hip to a certain degree, as you finesse the must towards your target points. Don't over acidulate.

Even though it may seem boring to make wine with the same variety from the same vineyard block every year, eventually the winemaker can tune in to the idiosyncrasies of that vineyard block. This leads to an important point; you will find that the grapes from a specific vineyard block will react to the addition of tartaric acid in a predictable pattern year after year.

pH Gain During Primary Fermentation (about 0.15 pH units)
During fermentation the yeasts will first consume the citric acid as an appetizer, then metabolize up to 30% of the malic acid. This causes a rise in the pH that can range from 0.10 – 0.30 units. If you have no previous data to work from, a ballpark figure would be a gain of about 0.15 units or, say from 3.45 to 3.60 pH.

pH Gain During MLF (about 0.12 pH units)
Another consideration when determining the target points is the conversion factor associated with malolactic fermentaion (MLF). We are jumping forward here, as MLF will be discussed more in detail later, but it needs to be taken into account during the calculation of the final pH end point of the finished wine. Put simply, during MLF, the pH rises—typically from 0.10 -- 0.15 units. If you have no previous data to work from, a ballpark figure would be a gain of about 0.12 units or, say from 3.60 to 3.72 pH

I would prefer to avoid generalizations, but if you have no other point of reference to navigate from, here are some basic guidelines for good **finished** wine pH numbers for western USA:

Cabernet Sauvignon	3.60	Mourvedre	3.55
Merlot	3.65	Grenache	3.70
Cabernet Franc	3.55	Counoisse	3.45
Malbec	3.55	Tempranillo	3.65
Petite Verdot	3.50	Sangiovese	3.55
Pinot Noir	3.50	Petite Sirah	3.55
Syrah	3.70	Zinfandel	3.70

Example #1 Normal Acid Adjustment

We will use the above conversion factors in our example.

Lets say that you are working with Syrah from a vineyard you have sourced from before. It tests out at 3.78 pH. Reviewing your notes, you determine that the average primary yeast fermentation conversion factor for the Syrah from that vineyard is 0.15 pH units.

You also determine that the MLF conversion factor for that vineyard has been averaging 0.12 pH units.

You prefer Syrah a little on the fleshy (higher pH) side, so you set the final end point target (finished wine) at 3.70 pH. So right there you can determine a theoretical target point for your acid adjustment.

That is—3.70 minus 0.15 minus 0.12 = **3.43** pH (target)

The original pH of the must is 3.78 pH. So you need to add enough acid to adjust the pH from 3.78 to a theoretical 3.43 pH. (0.35 units to change).

The temporary target you are shooting for at the end of primary fermentation is 3.58 pH (Due to 0.15 pH gain during fermentation). Later, after the Syrah is in a barrel, it will go through malolactic fermentation and change from 3.58 to 3.70 pH (the 0.12 MLF conversion factor).

Example #2 Extreme Acid Adjustment—Reality Check

Lets say you bring in some over-ripe Merlot that is 27 Brix and 4.00 pH. You were hoping to make a structural, dense but approachable Merlot with good acidity at about 3.60 pH with some aging ability. Get real. If you try to muscle that out of those grapes you will end up with an unbalanced wine no-one will want to drink. Bringing the pH from 4.00 to 3.60 (finished wine) is too radical a change. It would be wiser to alter your strategy, and make a soft, low-acid drink-now style wine you can offer for a discount in your tasting room, or drink up with friends. Figure on a finished wine at, say 3.80 pH.

Over-ripened grapes have less malic acid, so the conversion factors for the Merlot will be slimmer—say 0.12 during primary fermentation, and 0.10 later during MLF.

3.80 minus 0.12 minus 0.10 = 3.58 pH

So you need to acidulate the Merlot from 4.00 pH to 3.58 pH. (0.42 units to change)

Your target at the end of primary fermentation is 3.70 pH.

Example #3 Finesse Acid Adjustment

Okay. You are disappointed that the Merlot was over-ripe but when the old-vine Cabernet Sauvignon arrives a week later it's beautiful, tastes ripe and the numbers are fairly good. The sugars are at 24.4 Brix and by the time the flavors came together in the vineyard the pH ended up at 3.56 pH. You would like to make a reserve-style Cab that has some aging ability. You were thinking about blending in a little Petite Verdot later to add structure and some acid, but those grapes have not been picked yet. Your target pH for the finished wine is 3.57 pH. We shall use the average conversion numbers for convenience.

3.57 minus 0.15 minus 0.12 = 3.30 pH

So you need to acidulate the Cabernet Sauvignon from 3.56 to 3.30 pH (0.26 units to change)

Your target at the end of primary fermentation is 3.45 pH

Formula for acidulating musts with tartaric acid

1 g/L (0.13 oz/gallon) of tartaric acid for every 0.1 unit of pH short of the ideal
(units to change)

This formula is easier if you work in, or convert to liters first. Mix it into solution completely before adding to the must. Heating the liquid will help. Remember to add only 2/3 of the acid during cold soak, and later, make a pH assessment at about 10 Brix to see if you should add the remainder.

De-acidification

Frankly, chemically lowering the acidity of a must is something we should never have to deal with concerning quality winemaking. But those with northern home vineyards are faced with the harsh reality of potentially under-ripe fruit. Many publications spend an undo amount of time discussing techniques involving the additions of calcium carbonate, Acidex, and other agents to fully adjust a wines pH to the ideal point. This is unwise, as it yields unbalanced wines susceptible to many problems we shall not spend time discussing. We should remind the reader that we are making wine. Wine is food--not a chemistry experiment. De-acidifying a wine should be done with finesse, and not be considered purely a chemical adjustment.

What we would rather do is to start the natural de-acidification chain reaction in the wine by first using calcium carbonate to nudge the pH up to 3.00 pH, fermenting, encouraging MLF to occur, followed later by the precipitation of acid salts during cold stabilization.

Lets say that your Pinot Noir ripened to a miserable 2.90 pH. You suspect the pH is low when you picked, so only add 10 ppm SO2 at crush. Add calcium carbonate or Acidex targeting 3.00 pH. Ferment with an acid reducing yeast like Anchor Exotics, but do not allow the must to rise above 86F/30C degrees. Wild ML bacteria is inhibited above 86F/30C. You will be inoculating with an ML bacteria, but every bit helps here. After yeast fermentation, inoculate with a ML culture that is acid tolerant like the OSU-2 strain. After ML has occurred, eventually chill the wine to below 32F/0C if possible to cold stabilize for several weeks (outside?). Rack the wine off of the acid crystals, and you may have managed to bring it up to about 3.35 pH or so, a reasonable target pH for a finished Pinot Noir.

2.5 grams of calcium carbonate per gallon of wine will lower the TA by about 0.1%

Carbonic Maceration

The famous, fun, fruity, easy drinking Beaujolais Nouveau is created using a unique process termed carbonic maceration. We shall not be discussing the technique in detail here, but we will outline the basics, because we are in fact introducing a modest variant of it when we ferment with whole berries or whole clusters.

In Beaujolais France, the carbonic maceration procedure involves placing whole pristine Gamay clusters into a closed fermenter, and allowing them to ferment without oxygen.

Inside the berries fermentation proceeds without yeast intervention, rather by an intracellular bacterial fermentation. This fermentation can produce--at best 2.5% alcohol, at which time the cells are terminated by the alcohol and the lack of oxygen. Carbon dioxide is formed, as well as some glycerol, succinic acid, and various other compounds. Malic acid levels are reduced dramatically. Carbon dioxide surrounds the berries--thus we have *carbonic maceration*. Naturally, due to the intracellular fermentation, some of the berries pop open, release some juice, and a native yeast fermentation begins. At some point shortly thereafter, the grapes are pressed, and the wine pumped into a tank where the fermentation finishes.

Then, at midnight on the third Thursday of November the wine is released, and in a kind of feeding frenzy, massive quantities of it are consumed and shipped out in haste. It is a pagan event unlike any other in the world of wine.

As mentioned, when we ferment using some whole berries or whole clusters we are encouraging some intracellular fermentation to occur.

Think about it. During cold soak, we are not introducing oxygen into the must (except mixing in acid or water). Any whole berries below the surface of the cap will begin, and may complete an intracellular fermentation before the yeasts begin to feed (after the lag phase).

How will this improve our wine? It can help the wine gain in complexity, fruitiness, reduce malic acid levels, and prolong the fermentation.

Yeast Nutrients

Yeast need a reliable source of nitrogen in forms that they can assimilate in order to successfully complete fermentation. YAN, or *yeast assimilable nitrogen* is a measurement of the primary organic and inorganic sources of nitrogen that can be assimilated by yeast. The amount of YAN that winemakers will find in their grape musts depends on a number of components including grape variety, ripeness, health of the vineyard, rootstock, vineyard soils, and viticultural practices as well as the climate conditions of particular vintages.

Unless a winery has the equipment to test for the YAN numbers of a must, they are provided by a wine lab. One can generally shoot for a target YAN of 250 ppm (250 mg/L).

Yeast need more than just nitrogen to flourish. Like us, they benefit from a complex set of vitamins (especially thiamine), minerals and amino acids.

Say No to DAP

Old-school winemakers used predominantly di-ammonium phosphate (DAP) as a cheap source of nitrogen for the yeast. DAP is inorganic nitrogen, a food-grade equivalent of agricultural (lawn) fertilizer (actually used in wine in some countries). Today, the use of DAP by itself is considered passé. An analogy would be like trying to make your house plants survive indefinitely on Miracle Grow alone. The plants are not really healthy. The soil harbors no micro flora or fauna, and is saturated by inorganic nitrogen ammonium salts. The plants survive only until their next shot in the arm--so to speak.

DAP can cause runaway fermentations that fail to ferment to dryness due to lack of other essential micronutrients. DAP may actually be responsible for many stuck fermentations.

Or, a ferment with DAP may finish to dryness, but leave leftover micronutrients in the must, which become food for unwelcome microbes—in particular Brettanomyces yeast. Therefore, over-nutritional additions are unwise, but quite common in wineries with seemingly good technology. Many of the universities are still preaching full nutrient programs for musts, based on old models of conventional farming, which produce grapes with typically fewer on-board natural nutrients.

Thus we have products such as Lallemand's Fermaid K, or Red Star's Superfood, which contain both DAP as well as vitamins and minerals. They are two very similar products, but Fermaid K contains more DAP than Superfood does. The wine industry terms these products *complex yeast nutrients*, or CYN. They work. The idea however, is not to use DAP at all.

Even though DAP by itself should be considered junk-food for yeast, it is wise to keep some on hand in the wine first-aid kit in case a fermentation goes reductive and begins to produce H2S. If stored in a sealed container, it keeps better than CYN products, which should be purchased fresh every season.

Ideally the vineyard ecology is healthy enough where the grapes contain enough of their own nutrients for a complete fermentation---but in practice, the grapes may often need a little help keeping the yeasts happy. I am recommending yeast nutrients that do not contain DAP.

AEB's Fermoplus DAP Free is a CYN specially formulated for organic wines and to reduce high alcohol perception in wines. Also Laffort's Nutristart Organiq, Lallemand's Fermaid O, and Rouge Noblesse. Keep your eyes and ears open. There are always new nutritional products being developed. It is wise to follow the manufacturers specific guidelines for their products.

Home winemakers: The info I am providing here is cutting edge. Do not expect to find a "DAP free" nutrient product at your local brew shop. Remember—the shops and amateur online suppliers all get their products from only one distributor in the US. That is why (if you haven't noticed) they all carry exactly the same products. Circumvent them and start purchasing chemicals, yeast and nutrients from a winery supply outfit. {Resources--page 130}

The old-school winemakers also had the tendency to add DAP at the same time as they introduced the yeast into the musts. Not so today. The inorganic nitrogen, such as the ammonium salts in DAP shock the yeast, and are toxic at higher levels. It should never be added during inoculation when the biomass of the newly rehydrated yeast is low.

Many winemakers split up the dosage of CYN with the first addition being made at the end of the lag phase, when the yeasts enter their period of exponential growth and alcoholic fermentation begins. In most musts this occurs from 6 to 24 hours after yeast inoculation. A second dosage is then often added around a third of the way through sugar fermentation and again before the sugar levels hit 12 Brix. This is because as the fermentation progresses yeast cells are no longer able to bring the nitrogen into the cell due to the increasing toxicity of ethanol surrounding the cells. This leaves the nitrogen unused and available for spoilage organisms that may come afterward.

Nutrients added towards the end of fermentation (below 12 brix) should not contain nitrogen but should contain polysaccharides, either in the form of yeast hulls or granulated cellulose. At high ethanol levels, yeasts loose the ability to ingest ammonium ions. This is why it's really important to make any nitrogen additions before the fermentation is past the halfway point.

The addition of nutrients as described above will work for any yeast type, including wild indigenous yeast fermentations.

Say Yes to YRN

Another nutrient regimen that is very popular is the use of *yeast rehydration nutrients* (YRN) such as Lallemand's product Go-Ferm, or similar products (Fermoplus Energy GLU) formulated by various companies. YRN is added along with the yeasts during yeast rehydration. Go-Ferm is officially rated an organic product by Swiss standards, being mostly comprised of yeast hulls.

It gives the yeasts a very natural source of nutrients which, in some musts will be sufficient for the entire fermentation. In other words, sometimes Go-Ferm is the only nutrient added to a must.

Many pro winemakers however, will use YRN at inoculation, as well as some CYN later at the lag phase (6-24 hours after inoculation) and at 1/3 sugar depletion (about 12-14 Brix).

Home winemakers: Lallemand's Go-Ferm brand YRN is available from some home brew suppliers.

Note: YRN type products are not designed to work with indigenous yeast fermentations.

If YRN is added directly to a must, the nutrients will be gobbled up by undesirable competitive organisms. Use YRN products only with yeast rehydration.

Yeast need plenty of nutrients if:
YAN number is low
Grapes are in rough shape
Grapes are over-ripe
High pH must
Low TA must
High Brix must
Yeast type is nutrient hungry

At the risk of being repetitive, it is not wise, for many reasons to over-add nutrients to a must.

Nutrients Simplified

I recommend always using a YRN rehydration product with commercial yeasts.
Use a CYN with natural, indigenous yeasts.
For high brix, and/or high pH musts use both a YRN and a CYN

If you are using just a CYN (like Fermoplus DAP Free or Fermaid O), an average addition is: 2-3 pounds for every 1000 gallons of must (25-40 grams/HL). Follow the product's guidelines.

For wineries working with YAN numbers, a high (225 mgN/L) number indicates the need for less nutrients, while a low (125 mgN/L) number indicates the need for more.

Examples are two extremes:
23 Brix must testing at 225 mgN/L may only need Go-Ferm as a nutrient.
26 Brix must testing at 125 mgN/L may require a fuller nutrient program, such as:
YRN at inoculation—10-20g/hl CYN at end of lag phase--10-20g/hL CYN at 1/3 sugar depletion (about 12 -14Brix)

Yeast

Yeast consume sugars, nutrients, metabolize acids, and produce carbon dioxide, alcohol, and a host of flavor related compounds. Yeast are facultative anaerobes--meaning that they can function in both the presence and absence of oxygen. In ideal conditions (fermenting wine or beer) yeast reproduce rapidly, and can reach extremely high populations at the height of a fermentation.

By far the most common yeast associated with wine and beer is *Saccharomyces cerevisiae.*

Commercial yeast has been selected, cultured, dehydrated, and packed in foil packages. Winemakers rehydrate the dry yeast before adding it to the grape must. (page 99)

Upon entering the must, the yeast begin to produce an enzyme that triggers an intricate series of reactions. Sugar molecules are split in two, half becoming ethyl alcohol, and half carbon dioxide.

Yeast do not divide in two, but sprout vegetatively; 3 or 4 small buds form on the mother cell, then split off to form other cells. The process creates heat. Needing air to multiply, yeast finds it in open vats. The buildup of CO2 soon blankets the wine. No longer able to reproduce, the yeast shift from their aerobic (oxygen requiring) mode to their anaerobic (alcohol producing) mode. Enologists refer to the first mode as the *lag* phase, the second as the exponential or *log* (logarithmic) phase, the third as the *stationary* phase, and finally, the rarely mentioned *decline* or death phase.

In Taxonomy, yeast is defined as a single-cell eukaryotic microorganism that usually divides by budding. By far, the most predominant yeast found in fermenting must is *Saccharomyces cerevisiae.*

S. cerevisiae is now used as a model eukaryotic organism in research activities in hundreds of laboratories worldwide. It can grow and function both aerobically and anaerobically. As mentioned earlier, studies of *S. cerevisiae* genetics eventually led to the mapping of the human genome.

S. cerevisiae has an unusually large amount of genes in it's makeup (over 6000), and is largely diploid in nature. Each cell contains two copies of most genes. Although typical in plants and animals, diploidy is uncommon in microbes. *S. cerevisiae* is unique among yeasts in that it has the ability to feed in the presence of high levels of alcohol. Wines can, at times exceed 18% alcohol by volume.

One of the most unusual characteristics of *S. cerevisiae* is that this yeast has no known habitat on our planet. It is known to exist under the bark of oak trees in France, and in the intestinal tracts of some fruit flies and possibly other insects, but the trees and insects are hosts, not homes for the yeast.

Somehow, *S. cerevisiae* is closely associated with man, as it has been found only in areas near to human civilization. Attempts to find this species of yeast in regions remote from human activities have been unsuccessful. Closely related species such as *S. paradoxus* and *S. bayanus* are however, found in some remote regions.

In wine making, the yeast cells are generally present on the grapes, and later in the fermentation for a mere few weeks in the year. Attempts to find them in the vineyard either several weeks before or soon after harvest generally have been unsuccessful. Recent evidence suggests that the yeast are brought to the vineyard when the grapes are nearly ripe by insects which possibly transport them from their nests or hives.

Yeast are known to exist in barely detectable colonies on the skin of the grape. On the surface of the grape there are tiny bumps, like little volcanoes, called *peristomata* which exude a sweet, nutrient-rich liquid. Surrounding the stomata are found high concentrations of silicon, calcium, phosphorus, chlorine, and sulfur. Also around the stomata are found yeast cells nestled on the wax platelets covering the skin—of various genus and species.

We shall begin our journey through the vast territory of yeast chronologically, beginning with the oldest style of fermenting wine.

Indigenous Fermentation

Indigenous, native, spontaneous, wild, or feral yeast fermentation all refers to the same practice: the use of the yeast populations that are already on the grapes to ferment a wine. No yeast is added to the grape must in the fermenter. The practice is very popular in Europe—in some areas predominant, but far less common in new world wineries, where there remains a stubborn resistance to it.

The Resistance

I find myself talking with another winemaker at a trade show. He seems like a cool guy—kind of a taller techy—not the more typical compact, physical, self-assured, mercurial type of winemaker.

At one point, I venture to ask, "Do you ever play around with native yeast?"

A loaded question.

He moves his shoulders in an odd way. "Oh no, I wouldn't recommend that at all. Too much chance of a stuck fermentation."

That jibes me. I wasn't looking for a recommendation, rather seeking to discuss techniques with a colleague. The bane of the male ego.

But why do they always say exactly the same thing?

So I am compelled to press on, "But all of the finest wines in the world--hundreds of them--are fermented on their own yeast."

He squirms, "I don't know about that."

"Well what about the Burgundians? The most expensive wines in the world."

I am assuming he already knows they almost unanimously use indigenous yeasts on the top flight cuvées.

"Well—this isn't Burgundy."

They always say that as well!

"What about the Bordeaux first growths, and the right bank wines—from St. Emillion and Pomeral? What about Chateau Petrus?"

I notice the beginnings of a glazed look in his eyes.

"Well—we're not in France."

Oh. Thanks for pointing that out. I look around just to make sure. For a moment I feel relieved, as I'm not particularly in the mood to be sneered at or insulted by French taxi drivers. I realize it would be redundant to press further into Europe by mentioning the best Spanish wines, or the Italians--Antinori's Tuscans and Angelo Gaya's Barbarescos.

But—why do they always say the same things?

An odd paranoid thought suddenly popped in: Maybe this guy was brainwashed by one of the universities, or worse—big brother implanted a chip in him to ensure uniform thought patterns! Resistance is futile. Curious, I press on, "The most sought after California wines are made on their own yeast."

The glazing thickens. I almost think he's going to state in monotone, "We're not in California," but the fact is—we are in California!

"That's not true."

An even more irrational thought came to mind: Maybe this guy standing before me is actually a clone—while the real winemaker's body is reclining in some cryogenics facility somewhere in western Utah. I take a few breaths to slow down my heart rate, and continue in a more reasonable tone, "Well, I am talking about the California cult wines—you know, the ones consumers are all standing in line to get. It's hard to keep track of what is popular this year, but the fact is, they are generally made on their own yeast."

"I've heard too many horror stories," he replied.

They always say that too.

Perhaps resistance *is* futile. So after that, I let it rest.

The conversation ended shortly thereafter—regrettably. I would prefer to make friends than enemies, or at least maintain contact with colleagues. But the fact is: I had become an antagonist. I challenged a belief system which, typical of belief systems do not originate from, and are rarely backed up by observable science.

If we are discussing observations and potential ramifications of the data gathered from those observations there really is little need for emotions or personal issues to enter the picture. The truth is though—they too often do. The Achilles heel of science. But it takes two to tango. The guy pushed one of my buttons and I went on the aggressive.

The resistance harbored by new world winemakers towards spontaneous fermentations seem to spawn from a fear of lack of control, which appears to be culturally ingrained in us. If we do not understand, cannot classify, or think we cannot maintain a modicum of control over a biological process we tend to avoid engaging in it.

Therefore, the fears that are expressed tend to be either grossly exaggerated realities or partially fabricated ones. Personal issues affecting science. Negative ideas keep getting passed around until they become considered truth. It is certainly true that indigenous fermentations are known to get stuck—but not nearly as commonly as the pictures painted by the naysayers. We must remember that cultured commercial yeast fermentations occasionally struggle to ferment to dryness as well.

It's often claimed that there are not enough yeast yet in new world vineyards to support strong fermentations, and yet healthy, successful natural fermentations are the norm.

So how do multiple yeast species remarkably appear in a fermenter in sufficient numbers? The question is still debated amongst ampelographers and enologists, concerning both new and old world wines. There is so much we do not understand about the relationship between grapes, vines, and yeasts, that we must be compelled to keep our minds open and continue to experiment and observe.

Modern wine-making and baking sometimes involves the use of wild strains, and it is apparent that such strains, in contrast to the commercial yeast now also used in all of these industries, are still evolving.

Yeast, like most microbes, can mutate and evolve rapidly—responding to environmental conditions.

In contrast, a pure strain of yeast is one that has been selected because it has desirable characteristics for a particular style of fermentation. The yeast companies then endeavor to maintain those cultures as pure as possible. Those yeast strains, as good as they can be, are not allowed to evolve—and for good reason.

Tech Talk

The maintenance of the strict genetic identity of strains in a pure culture is complex. Although the term "pure culture" denotes that it has been derived from a single cell, this does not imply that the culture is genetically uniform. Even under closely controlled conditions, a yeast strain reveals *genetic drift*—slow but distinct changes after many generations.

A significant number of wineries worldwide do not inoculate, yet their fermentations nevertheless proceed and are carried out predominantly by *S. cerevisiae*. Studies point to over 10% spontaneous fermentations annually occurring in quality California wines. Due to both the traditional and burgeoning popularity of spontaneous fermentations, many studies have been performed at universities and private facilities worldwide. We shall discuss and summarize some of what ampelographers and enologists have learned so far.

An older model that should be mentioned is the idea that wild yeast fermentations originate from yeast cells lingering in the winery. The idea has less merit today, especially considering the cleanliness of wineries, closed-tank fermenters, and outdoor closed fermentations, not to mention the fact that *S. cerevisae* does not travel independently through the air. However, the predominant species found lingering in winery environments is, in fact *S. cerevisiae*.

Tech Talk

Yeast exhibit characteristics of both the animal and vegetable kingdoms. Years ago, taxonomists debated as how to classify them. Today yeasts are defined as: Unicellular ascomycetous or basidiomycetous fungi whose vegetative growth results predominantly from budding or fission, and which do not form their sexual states within or upon a fruiting body. Of the over 100 yeast genera representing over 700 species, only about 15 are associated with wine-making.

The wine yeast *Saccharomyces cerevisiae* is found in extremely low populations on healthy, undamaged grape berries. By far, the most predominant species found on the surface of grapes are *Kloeckera apiculata*, and *Hanseniaspora uvarum*, two species undesirable in the fermentation of wine. Fortunately, both *K. apiculata* and *H. uvarum* are oxidative microbes, their growth greatly inhibited in the presence of the typical 40-50 ppm of SO2 winemakers add to the must during crush or de-stemming.

Interesting Phenomenon

The number of fermentary-type yeast obtained from a bunch of grapes picked from the vine is few and irregular. When several healthy, ripe grapes are crushed and encouraged to ferment on their own in a lab, fermentation may not occur. The yeast important to fermentation are scattered throughout the vineyard. A mystery is how quickly they multiply between the time they are picked, and the time they arrive at the chateau-style winery thirty minutes later, and even more so by the time the crushing or de-stemming has been performed. According to enologist Dr. Emile Peynaud, the number of yeast per cubic millimeter are typically: 1-160—grapes on the vine, 2-280—arriving at the winery, 460-6400—immediately after crush. How can the yeast multiply double in the picking baskets in a few minutes, and why? One way or another, there is a questionable population of yeast on the grapes on the vine to begin a fermentation, but by the time they get into the winery they are in full swing.

Life Cycle of Yeasts During Indigenous Fermentations

During an indigenous fermentation, various yeast genus and species can be involved. Typically, the non-Saccharomyces, and non-cerevisiae yeasts are the first to become active, closely followed and finished up by the *Saccharomyces cerevisiae* strains. The process involves a progressive growth pattern of indigenous yeasts, with the final stages invariably being dominated by the more alcohol-tolerant strains of *S. cerevisiae*.

Each native yeast prefers a slightly different pH range to be active in. The first to perform is the yeast that prefers the highest acidity. As the ferment proceeds, and as malic acid is metabolized by the yeast, the pH of the must goes up, and different yeasts become active--kind of like a relay race, with the baton being passed from yeast to yeast. Finally, our star swimmer--*S. cerevisiae* seizes the baton and finishes the fermentation in glory immersed in a pool of declining resources and threatening alcohol levels. Why the yeasts are willing to cooperate as well as they do in a typical natural fermentation is somewhat speculative.

Most of the early-bird yeasts will not function above alcohol levels more than 3%, but they may begin respiration at relatively low temperatures. Following cold soak, as the must warms it is not unusual to observe indigenous yeast activity beginning at 61F/16C degrees.

This is important, because it should be noted that many fermentations (even those using commercial strains) have undergone a brief spontaneous fermentation prior to yeast inoculation. Oftentimes there is considerable native activity occurring by the time the winemaker adds yeast to the fermenter. Some winemakers welcome it. How much native activity a winemaker is willing to allow borders on stylistic choices, and is considered a technique.

A common misnomer has been passed around the home winemaking community: yeast and bacteria are killed by the introduction of 40-50 ppm SO2 during crush. Not so. Concentrations of 40-50 ppm of SO2 is considered an inhibitor of bacteria, and to a lesser degree—yeasts. In reality, all fermentations involving grape skins harbor multiple species of yeasts and bacteria either in active or hibernating states.

One way or another, due to the complex nature of compounds produced by multiple yeast strains, the resulting wine will typically express more complexity of flavors. Most winemakers are aware how every strain of yeast adds it's signature flavor profile to a wine, whether it is a pure commercial yeast or native strain. Another factor may well be partly due to the consequence of higher concentrations of glycerol and other polyols produced by indigenous yeasts. Also, the extended lag phase before the onset of vigorous fermentation allows for the reaction of oxygen with anthocyanins and other phenols in the absence of ethanol, which is thought to enhance color stability in red wines as well as accelerating phenol polymerization.

In contrast, a fermentation using a pure yeast strain—like a commercially produced yeast, is theoretically a fermentation of only that single strain. One can perceive why the wine from that fermenter would tend to be simpler in flavor profiles, but possible more focused. Some winemakers feel that wines from indigenous fermentations taste more of the microbes themselves, while commercial yeast wines are cleaner, and tend to express more terroir and varietal flavors.

Commercial Yeast
The selection of commercial yeast over the years has been performed in many ways:

Natural Selection
A naturally selected yeast is one that has been gleaned from a famous vineyard, fermentation, or even from the vineyard soil (as with D21). As an example, the Bordeaux yeast BDX was selected from Bordeaux, and is recommend for Bordeaux varieties, like Cabernet Sauvignon, Merlot, etc. A Syrah yeast, D80 was selected from Cote Rôtie in France. On the other side of the Rhone river, the Syrah yeast was selected from Hermitage, while D254 came from a Languedoc vineyard.

The first natural yeast selection was performed in 1883 by Emil Christian Hansen of the Carlsberg Brewery in Denmark when he isolated a pure culture derived from a single yeast cell. Several years later, in 1890, Muller-Thurgau from Geisenheim introduced the concept of inoculating wine fermentations with pure yeast starter cultures. In 1965, the first two active dried yeast strains were produced for a California bulk winery. These two "all purpose" strains, Montrachet and Pasteur Champagne, were offered worldwide with limited commercial success, but are still used by amateur winemakers today.

Selecting a yeast involves a detailed study of it's physiological characteristics: alcohol tolerance, nutrient needs, temperature range and tolerance, high glycerol or low acetic acid formation, aroma profiles, fermentation of malic acid, flocculation characteristics, and so on. In fact, an advantage in choosing to use a commercial yeast instead of allowing spontaneous fermentation is that the winemaker can select a yeast for a particular situation based on the known characteristics of the strain. Important characteristics for those of us on the west coast of the US are: alcohol tolerance, and nutrient needs of a yeast. When we routinely have grapes arrive at our wineries at over 25 Brix we need to know the nutrient needs of a yeast strain, because the riper the grapes get, the more of their own nutrients are depleted. However, avoid the urge to choose not to use a yeast just because it has high or moderate nutrient needs. Some very good yeast strains are greedy feeders.

Genetically Selected Yeasts ("Cellar" selections)
The techniques used to select yeasts based on favorable genetic characteristics are varied, technical, and beyond the scope of this text. Traditional techniques such as: clonal selection of variants, mutation & selection, hybridization, and rare-mating have been done for many years.

Intra-strain selection has been used for decades to obtain improved yeast strains. Many excellent commercial yeast products available on the market fall into this category.

A notable yeast type winemakers should be aware of are the so-called "killer", or *zymocidal* yeasts. These strains have proven to be very useful due to their ability to dominate a fermentation. Lallemand's yeast selection chart rates the competitive factor as either: sensitive, neutral, or active.

A common inoculation technique used by winemakers who want both the wild yeast complexity, and a clean, dry completed fermentation is to first allow spontaneous fermentation in the must, followed by the addition of a commercial yeast at about 17 to 20 brix. A zymocidal yeast works well in this situation. Of course, there are some who feel that this inoculation regimen is instigating nothing short of a cat fight, but we must remember that microbes exist in a dog-eat-dog reality anyway. In practice, many winemakers observe wild yeast fermentations beginning to occur when they inoculate with a commercial yeast anyway. This is very common, in particular for winemakers who use a modified pre-fermentation maceration (cold soak), where the must temperature gradually becomes warmer during the cold soak period.

Exotic Yeast Blends

For those that are as yet unwilling to go totally native, a few yeast companies are producing products that combine both selected wild yeasts and *Saccharomyces cerevisiae*. The idea is to approximate flavors similar to indigenous fermentations, but with more control.

From the South African Anchor company "Anchor Exotics" *Saccharomyces cerevisiae* and *Saccharomyces paradoxus* is good for reducing malic acid levels prior to MLF.

Christian Hansen's "Melody" is a blend of *Saccharomyces cerevisiae* with wild yeasts such as *Kluyveromyces thermotolerans*, *Torulaspora delbrueckii*, and *Pichia kluyveri*.

The German SIHA yeast company's "Pure Nature" is a wild yeast (they don't disclose the species), and a *Saccharomyces cerevisiae* in two separate packs. The wild yeast is rehydrated and added first followed later by the *Saccharomyces cerevisiae* yeast.

GMO Yeast

Many folks are alarmed by the idea of GMO yeast. Since I concur, I investigated.

Genetically modified yeasts differ from traditionally genetically selected yeasts in that GM yeasts are transgenic.

The first move to release a commercialized GM yeast to market was made in 2005. A transgenic wine yeast, ML01, was given the green light from regulatory authorities in the USA, Canada and Moldova. The parental strain of ML01 is the common Prise de Mousse S92 yeast.

ML01 is unique in that it carries genes that enable it to perform yeast fermentations, as well as malolactic fermentation (MLF), in which grape-derived malic acid is deacidified (decarboxylated) to lactic acid.

From a microbiological perspective, this proposes quite a dramatic change in the fermentation process. Typically, MLF occurs later, primarily due to the bacteria *Oenococcus oeni*, whether by an induced selected strain or by allowing it to occur due to the varied indigenous fauna. (page 105)

Today, the developers involved in creating GM yeasts are purportedly aware of the qualities of finer wines, and claim to be striving to develop yeasts for that sector. This new focus is in contrast to some zymologists 30 years ago, who worked to create products specifically for the lucrative bulk wine industry. The attitudes however, are tenacious, and still persist. Why would one want MLF to occur in tandem with the yeast fermentation? Or more accurately; why would we want the yeasts to perform MLF by supplanting the *Oenococcus oeni* bacteria? The reasoning seems to be that ML fermentations could be safer and swifter. The developer claims ML01 was a pet project because he got headaches from red wines. Somehow, it all doesn't add up.

In practice, quality winemakers do not necessarily want yeast fermentations or MLF to happen quickly. Some (but not all) winemakers want the processes to be long and drawn out.

The bottom line is—the idea of ML01 has all the hallmarks of a jug wine yeast.

A second commercially-available GM wine yeast, ECMo01, received clearance from the American and Canadian regulatory bodies in 2006. ECMo01 was engineered to reduce the risk of ethyl carbamate (a potential carcinogen) production during fermentation. Ethyl carbamate is typically produced at such low levels (if at all) in winemaking that it is generally not a concern. Nonetheless, in some fortified wines and in some wine-producing regions, it can make an appearance. Interestingly, this yeast is cis ("self") cloned; it carries no foreign DNA and therefore is not transgenic. Nevertheless, because it was generated using techniques that involve manipulation of DNA in vitro, the regulations of most countries require it to be classed as a GMO. ECMo01 is also clearly a bulk and fortified wine yeast. But one must ask why anyone would go to the trouble and expense to genetically engineer a yeast to avoid a rarely occurring pathogen? Fishy.

Wines made with GM yeasts are not as yet (2014) required to be labeled as such. While no winemakers from the USA and Canada have admitted to using ML01 or ECMo01, it is common knowledge that these GM yeasts have been used, albeit on a very limited scale. The general wise counsel is to be wary of jug, boxed, and cheap fortified wines.

In spite of my personal resistance to the practical application of GMO products in general, I must admit to being rather fascinated by what the yeast developers are doing. After reading through some of the articles concerning related studies performed by the various disciplines associated with GM yeast research, I came to the conclusion that this is not necessarily an evil cadre of scientists lusting to dominate mankind. We need not call in James Bond--yet. The geneticists and microbiologists are merely doing what they love to do. Lets face it—genetic manipulation is very sophisticated, cutting edge science. The projects they are receiving funding to work on may certainly be questionable in the opinions of many (and the sources of the funding), but the science itself will continue, in hopefully less potentially dangerous forms.

As the reader is probably aware, the European Union will not allow the use of GMO yeasts within EU member countries. Please do not overly alarmed. Frankly, I cannot imagine how any quality winemaker would even consider using a GMO yeast—for many reasons. We are all aware of the environmental concerns; but what do you think would happen to the sales of wine from a winery that consumers found out had used a GMO yeast? We can presume that it would not be the wisest career move by the winemaker or winery.

Since 2008, information concerning ML01 and ECMo01 has thinned dramatically. They seemed to have fallen off the edge of the earth. The company distributing GM yeasts is (or was) Springer Oenologie, Lesaffre Group of North America. As of 2014 neither GM yeasts appear on their (public) product list. Hopefully, by now it's a dead horse.

What Yeast Shall I Use?

There are so many commercial yeast products available, and so little time to try them all. There are over 200 active dry wine yeast strains available. A good starting point is to check out natural selections of regional strains—Bordeaux yeasts for Bordeaux varieties (Merlot, Cabernet Sauvignon, Cabernet Franc, Malbec, and Petite Verdot), Rhone yeasts for those cultivars (Syrah, Grenache, Mourvedre), Burgundy types for Pinot Noir, and so on. If you are willing to purchase the yeast in 500 gram packages your choices become far greater. You can actually get Merlot specific yeasts, like MT and Cepage Merlot, or Cabernet Franc yeasts like F33. GRE is a great Grenache yeast. Syrah yeasts are many: D21, D80, L2226, D254, SYRAH, and L2056. There are Spanish yeasts for Tempranillo--VRB, and Ribera. For Pinot Noir--Assmannshausen, BGY, RC212, and more.

However, one should avoid limiting the choice to regional types. Many great cellar selections are not particularly regional specific. When choosing a wine yeast, always pay attention to the basic characteristics of the yeast as published by the producer. Important factors are: alcohol tolerance, nitrogen needs, and temperature range. You may also take note of the fermentation speed and, as mentioned above, the competitive factor. Ignore the nonsensical fluffy descriptions of yeast flavor profile characteristics dreamed up by the sales departments.

I must not forget to mention that there are specifically white wine yeasts, and red wine yeasts. White wine is generally fermented at lower temperatures than red wine, so those yeasts have been selected to do just that. For red wine--use red wine yeast.

Now, no matter what some naysayers claim, different yeast selections do impart into the wine their own unique characteristics. Winemakers know this, and use it to great advantage by oftentimes using several yeast types in different fermenters to ferment the same grape variety. As an example, lets say that eventually, in the cellar there will be barrels of Syrah from the same vineyard with various yeast types marked on the barrels. One barrel has wine in it fermented with D80, another with D21, another with L2226, another indigenous, and so on. They all taste different. Eventually the barrels may end up being blended together in the same tank. The idea is that the finished wine will gain in complexity due to the various yeast types used, as well as fermentation disciplines, not to mention different barrel types (French, Hungarian, American, old, new etc). The technique is standard procedure in wineries—blending for complexity.

Fermentation Begins

Let us pause, reconnoiter and review as to where we are in the winemaking process:

The crushed grapes have now been cold-soaking in the fermenter for a few days.

We have performed an analysis of the pH, TA, sugar level, and possibly the YAN number.

Based on those numbers, and sensory perceptions we have refined our game plan as to the style of wine we shall produce.

We have made adjustments for sugars and acids that we deemed necessary.

Yeast and nutrient regimens have been outlined.

End of Cold Soak

Towards the end of cold soak, the ambient room temperature is adjusted to at least 69F/20C to allow the must to gradually warm up. A one ton fermenter can take over 24 hours to do so.

Yeast Fermentation

If you have chosen to allow the must to ferment on its own yeast, you should begin to observe, smell, and hear fermentation activity by the time it warms it up to 69/20 degrees, or shortly thereafter. Or, if you have chosen to add yeast, it is time to perform the yeast rehydration and inoculation ritual.

Yeast Rehydration & Inoculation

The process is similar to getting a child up in the morning. They are hibernating and dehydrated, so you wake them up by giving them some water while keeping them warm. They arise and begin to feel better so you feed them a good breakfast before sending them off to school. So we first hydrate the yeasts for a specific time period, and feed them before putting them into the wine.

Research shows that the yeast cell wall is very fragile during the first few minutes of rehydration. Some of the components of the yeast are going from a dry crystalline form to a gel-like state. They will go through this transformation successfully if rehydrated carefully.

The quality of the water you use for yeast rehydration is very important. Chlorinated, fluoridated city water is taboo for obvious reasons. Distilled water should not be used either, because the yeasts need the minerals naturally present in well water or spring water. Properly filtered water is acceptable. Water at 250 ppm hardness is optimum. Artesian, or good well water is superb.

If in doubt, always follow the manufacturers directions for rehydration of their particular yeast or YRN product.

Recommended: If you are using a YRN type of product (such as Go-Ferm), the yeast hydration procedure is generally as follows:

--For musts up to 25 Brix--per gallon of must:
1 gram yeast
1.25 grams YRN
25 ml 110F/43C water

--For musts over 25 Brix—per gallon of must:
1.2 grams yeast
1.5 grams YRN
30 ml 110F/43C water

Sterilize all equipment
Use a stainless steel stock pot with a lid, or a food grade plastic bucket with a lid.
Slowly mix the YRN into the 110F/43C water until dissolved. Allow it to cool to exactly 104F/40C
Slowly mix the yeast into the 104F/40C solution.
Wait exactly 20 minutes, then stir again gently.
Using a thermometer, begin to add grape juice from must to be fermented to the yeast slurry.
Stop when the temperature is at 90F/32C—wait 10 minutes.
Add more juice until the temperature is at 80F/26C---wait 10 minutes.
If the must temperature in the fermenter is above 65F/18C you may add the yeast slurry to the fermenter. If the must temperature is below 65F/18C, perform one more 10 minute temperature step down before inoculating the must in the fermenter.

If you are **not** using a YRN type of product, the yeast hydration procedure is as follows:

For musts under 25 Brix---per gallon of must:

1 gram of yeast

10 ml 102F/39C water

For musts over 25 Brix---per gallon of must:

1.2 grams of yeast

12 ml 102F/39C water

Slowly mix the yeast into the 102F/39C water.

Wait exactly 20 minutes, then stir again gently.

Using a thermometer, begin to add juice from must to be fermented to the yeast slurry.

Stop when the temperature is at 90F/32C—wait 10 minutes.

Add more juice until the temperature is at 80F/26C---wait 10 minutes.

If the must temperature in the fermenter is above 65F/18C you may add the yeast slurry to the fermenter.

If the must temperature is below 65F/18C, perform one more 10 minute temperature step down before inoculating the must in the fermenter.

Thermometer tip

Invest ($10-20) in a chefs-style digital thermometer with a long 8" stainless steel probe. A digital thermometer will give you a quick reading accurate in 10ths. Those big stainless steel dial thermometers sold at the home brew shops may look official but are a poor excuse for an instrument. The floating dairy thermometers are also not accurate enough--they are calibrated in too great a range.

The only temperature measurement that is important is the liquid temperature of the must or wine. **Do not rely on the ambient room thermostat to give you a must temperature.**

Discussion

The reasoning behind the temperature step-down process is to avoid shocking the yeasts. Technically, the yeast companies recommend less than 15F-18F maximum drop in temperature in any step (depending on the company). I am recommending only 10F/8C steps. Pushing the parameter to the maximum should be considered an unnecessary use of force, which I abhor.

This is a good time to demonstrate to the yeasts how much we care about them, and appreciate their willingness to help us craft a superb wine. Providing them with some healthy nutrients in the near future would also be a display of gratitude on our part.

Following the final step down, some winemakers will wait for up to 45 minutes (max) for the yeasts to populate in the rehydration vessel before inoculating the must with it. That way, the winemaker has conjured up a powerful starter to boost the onset of fermentation. If the yeast threatens to foam up out of the container—use it then.

Before adding the yeast slurry to the must, wet the cap by pressing down. After spreading the yeast over the surface of the must, wet the cap again. While the yeast begins to populate it is important to keep them wet. Do not violently mix the yeast into the must.

The old technique for creating a starter for an indigenous fermentation is still quite viable. Several days prior to picking, a few of the ripest, healthiest clusters were picked, crushed, sulfited, put in a warm place and nurtured to begin a mini-fermentation (say—10 gallons). By the time the grapes from the vineyard proper was placed into vats the pre-fermentation batch was active and used to inoculate. We can use the same method during the cold soak period.

Punch Down

Typically, about 3-4 days following yeast inoculation, the cap will become too dry for the press down technique to work. Fermentation is obvious—the cap rises, odd aromas waft into the room, accompanied by a soft, insidious, percussive snap-crackle-and pop symphony. It is undeniably the most exciting phase of the winemaking process. Ventilate the room at this stage.

The cap has become so hard that one needs to lean into it with the tool to punch through the first time. In a one ton fermenter the cap may be 12 inches thick, and breaks off in blocks like chunks of ice. Those chunks need to be plunged deep into the liquid below, wetting and breaking them up. As the fermentation proceeds, the cap will—from that point become softer until it finally surrenders, falling—drowning beneath the surface.

Punch downs can be scheduled to be performed 2-4 times per day. Three times is a standard, until the must is below 10 Brix, then perhaps twice per day. Over-punching is not recommended, as it can bring out harsh unmanageable tannins into the wine.

If one is punching down multiple fermenters with different yeasts, the tool should be rinsed between fermenters so as not to mix up the yeasts (until the sugars drop below 12 Brix).

After punching a fermenter, the cap is carefully tamped flat, using the same technique as in press down mode.

Pump Over

Other types of cap management techniques and equipment are used by commercial wineries during fermentation; pump over, submerged cap, pneumatic punch, rotary fermenters, and others. For the most part, the equipment is used to make consumer level wines. Pump over techniques however, are synonymous with high quality wines. In fact, many Burgundian domaines pump over, but there is no set rule as to how often or when. Some perform the operation early to help the indigenous yeasts respire and populate, some throughout the fermentation, and others just toward the end of fermentation. The common theme is that pump overs are often performed in conjunction with manual punch downs in any given day.

Many will pump over once in the morning, followed by a manual punch at noon, and another in the evening. Pump overs require special equipment, but the concept is simple; fermenting juice from the bottom of the tank is gently pumped up and distributed on to the cap. Wineries that use the technique are usually working with fermenters over 2 tons in capacity. Home winemakers, and boutique wineries working in smaller fermenters still manually punch; and some of the best wines are made in this way.

Fermentation Temperatures

Ideally, temperatures are taken and recorded every day during fermentation, as well as Brix and pH numbers at least every other day. That way the winemaker can monitor and track the fermentation.

Towards the end of the 3 week process, the recorded fermentation log begins to look something like a stock chart; but here sugar is the commodity and yeasts are the buyers and sellers. Here we can use the pH, temperature, and Brix numbers as indicators to help determine where our market is headed, possibly even engaging in a little market manipulation--and loving it!

Fermentation kinetics are very important, and influenced by many factors: sugar levels, temperature, yeast type and health, available nutrients, infused oxygen, and fermenter size. Fermentation generates it's own heat, which can rapidly rise far above ambient room temperature. Unassisted, the temperature peak will usually occur when the sugar levels have dropped to about 10-13 Brix (depending on original Brix).

The ability to control, or influence the temperature of a fermenter is a valuable asset. Warming can be influenced by ambient room temperature control, or special heater inserts, but cooling is more difficult. Some stainless steel fermenters have glycol cooling jackets. Prudent home winemakers will have a few frozen gallons of water ready in plastic water bottles. Milk jugs are not advised, as Lactobacillus could be lingering on the outside of the containers.

Ideally, the temperature of a vat will, over a weeks time gradually rise to the desired target point, and then slowly decrease, elegantly finishing the fermentation at about 70F/21C. In reality, many fermentations do not behave to that level of perfection, and can be in fact quite unruly, especially for those winemakers who do not have hands-on experience with the basic given parameters: vat size, sugar levels, and ambient temperatures.

Temperature kinetics have a major influence on the style of wine that will be produced. I shall divide stylistic types into three loose temperature ranges:

Low temperature fermentations that peak out up to a high temperature of 79F/26C tend to yield easy-to-drink, single dimensional, grape-juicy wines that have been popular with the American consumer market. Due to the long skin contact time, low temp ferment wines can have good color profiles.

Medium temperature fermentations that peak at from 81F/27C to 86F/30C are by far the most popular in quality wineries worldwide. In fact, unless you have previous predilections, 86F/30C is a good magic number to shoot for.

High temperature fermentations that peak out at as much as 90F/32C have been popular in old-world wines that are destined for long aging in bottle. The chemistry is complex, but in brief--high temp fermentations tend to extract more of those particular anthocyanins and tannins that contribute to structural, cellar-worthy wines.

When the fermentation is nearing completion (3 Brix), the ambient temperature in the room should be kept at 69F/20C to help the yeasts finish up with the last bits of sugar. By this time, the cap may have sunk, and the must needs to be kept covered and protected from fruit flies. Punch downs at that point are unnecessary. Clean the inside walls of the fermenter with paper towels soaked in SO2 solution, put a clean cover on and let the fermentation finish up undisturbed, except for checking the sugars each day.

Sugars

The predominant sugars in grapes are fructose and glucose, in roughly equal amounts. The yeasts—since they have to convert the fructose into glucose before they can eat it--opportunists that they are—gobble up the glucose first. Towards the end of the fermentation the last, toughest, most alcohol tolerant individuals consume the final bits of fructose. Then, a minuscule amount of sugars are left, which are predominantly the exotic pentose sugars---arabinose, rhamnose, ribose, xylose, and hexose etc. The yeasts either do not know quite what to do with them, or they frankly don't care.

Fermentation Completed

On the hydrometer, you want to see the must ferment down dry—to -1 to -2 Brix, or .997 SG to .993 SG. Yes, that is below zero on the Brix scale, and below 1.0 on the Specific Gravity scale. Whether it is calibrated in the Brix or Specific Gravity scales, it is recommended to have a narrow-range hydrometer for this measurement.

The importance of the must fermenting to dryness cannot be underscored enough. An excess of residual sugar becomes potential food for spoilage organisms. Wineries send out samples to a lab where the actual residual sugar level is determined. The measurement requires a fairly sophisticated piece of equipment. Wineries want the residual sugar in a wine to be less than 0.2%.

Oak in the Fermenter?

There has been a bit of a buzz lately concerning the idea of putting oak chips or staves in the fermenter. The idea is that the oak helps to extract color from some anthocyanins.

During a fermentation, the winemaker may want a more complete extraction of the anthocyanin pigments which are not soluble in an aqueous solution. Anthocyanins are positively charged, so they tend to repel each other and resist aggregating into colloids. What is needed here are uncharged cofactors, which layer between anthocyanins, creating kind of a sandwich.

Untoasted oak is a source of gallic acid, a powerful cofactor, and can be added to a fermenter. Gallic acid is delicate, and is functional only in properly slow-cured oak. Gallic acid is also a powerful antioxidant that can impart supplemental reductive vigor to wines that have lost their energy due to field oxidation during extended hang time. It should be pointed out that poorly cured oak can contain TCA, which will ruin a wine. If you do choose to use this technique, purchase untoasted oak products only from reputable coopers.

Contrary to the popular buzz, toasted oak does not enhance color extraction, either in the fermenter or later in the barrel. It can't. The toasting process polymerizes the small molecules into large chains that will not help anthocyanins form colloidal structures. Toasted oak contributes no copigmentation cofactors or antioxidative tannins to fermentations.

Extended Maceration

This is an advanced technique used by wineries seeking to make a wine suitable for cellaring, with plenty of phenolic structure. Following fermentation, the must is left to rest in the fermenter for up to four weeks. During that period, the winemaker tastes it every day. The must gradually becomes more and more tannic, until one day, the winemaker determines that the tannins have suddenly softened and smoothed out.

On that day, and no later, the juice is removed from the skins and becomes wine. If the juice is not removed from the skins promptly—from that point it would become exponentially tannic and undrinkable.

The extended maceration phenomena has been studied extensively, and attempts have been made to create testing procedures for determining that magic point—that day when the wine has to be secured, and rescued from tannic oblivion. Once again, this is very complex chemistry, but as of this writing, human sensitivity and experience are still the most reliable indicators as to determining when the wine is ready.

Pressing

In wineries, the free-run juice is drained out of a lower port on the fermenter, or a tall screen is inserted into the vat and the wine pumped out into a temporary tank.

The pomace that is left on the bottom of the vat—skins, seeds, and spent yeast, is transferred into a wine press. In the latter part of the 20th century, wineries favored bladder presses and tank presses, due to their ability to gently extract the tannins from the pomace. The current trend in quality wineries is reverting back to the old vertical basket press, albeit in newer stainless steel formats. Some vintners feel they have better control with the basket presses, are less fearful of tannins, and welcome the extra oxygen infused into the wine when it is most famished for it.

The press wine, particularly the hard press can be of a lesser quality than the free run wine; the pH is higher, and the wine may have more strong unpleasant vegetal characteristics, and harsher seed phenolics. The press wine is often separated, due to taste, high pH, or practical reasons.

If the free run wine is already high pH, why compound the problem by mixing the even higher pH press wine in with it? Press wines often end up in marked barrels or carboys. Wineries are always looking for ways to use it. In days of yore, French chateaus would traditionally provide the picking crews with lunch—soup, loaves of fresh bread, big chunks of hard cheese, and carafes of press wine from the previous year. We can assume that the pickers rarely complained.

Some wineries do not even bother to press, and throw the pomice away.

However, some consider the press wine an integral part of the potential character of the finished wine. If the wine in general has good minerality, reasonable acidity, and the press wine tastes good, the flavors will integrate well if the press and free run wines are blended together soon after pressing. The higher oxygen level in the press wine helps color anthocyanins to work with flavonoids to form stable phenolic structures.

Always press slowly and gently, particularly when in the hard press part of the cycle.

Home winemakers: The basket press—that charming wooden and brightly painted metal device that more than any other object we associate with winemaking--an icon that proudly rests all year in the front corner of your garage as a testament that you are, in fact a winemaker.

The stark, harsh truth is that you do not really need it if you are fermenting less than 800 pounds at a time. It is an expensive tool. Your funds would be better served used to buy a good pH meter.　Beware of older wooden basket presses, as the wooden parts can harbor spoilage organisms, in particular *Brettanomyaces,* which, once embedded in the wood is very difficult if not impossible to remove.

On behalf of the wooden basket press, it is an excellent tool for making apple juice.

Home winemakers can bucket the juice + pomace out of the fermenter and pour it through a large stainless steel colander that fits securely on a bucket. Using your body weight, the pomace can be pressed with your hands in the colander for each load. Yes, you would extract more wine out of it with a press, but not much. If you only fermented 200 pounds of grapes, you might get an additional four bottles of press wine out of it. Is the investment, storage, maintenance, and set-up of a $350 press really worth four bottles of hard-press wine per year?

Double transfer from fermenter to tank to barrel

Once the liquid from the must has been removed from the fermenter it receives congratulations, a little diploma, and officially becomes wine. The wine is typically allowed to settle in a holding tank for from 4 hours to 4 days. I recommend 24 hours, or the next day. The wine is then racked or pumped into barrels, tanks, or carboys that are clean and ready for malolactic fermentation.

The reason for the double transfer is to secure fine sediment, termed *lees*, that will settle to the bottom of the barrels and provide nutrients for the bacteria responsible for our next step-- malolactic fermention (MLF).

When we transfer out of the holding tank into the barrels we are leaving behind the *gross lees*, heavier sediment particles that harbor unpleasant flavor compounds. Since the wine has been in the holding tank for a mere 24 hours, it has still not clarified. It will do so later as it is resting in the barrels, leaving the desired pinkish fine lees on the bottom of the containers. In glass carboys, one can observe how the wine gradually clarifies as the particles flocculate, forming a visible layer of lees on the bottom.

Malolactic Fermentation

Malolactic fermentation (MLF) is a bacterial fermentation that occurs naturally in red wines. As a result of the life cycle of the ML bacteria, the wine benefits in several ways. Harsh tasting malic acids are consumed, and replaced in part by more supple tasting lactic acids. The wine softens, the pH rises, the flavors become more complex, and the potential bouquet of the wine is enhanced. MLF also renders the wine microbiologically stable--The wine becomes less prone to spoilage organisms.

Today, the primary ML bacteria is *Oenococcus oeni*—formerly termed *Leuconostoc oenos*.

Much like our star yeast *S. cerevisiae*, *Oenococcus oeni* is a wine-specific microbe, has an unusually large amount of genes in its makeup (a remarkable number of which mirror human genetics), and the species also has no known habitat on our planet. The ramifications of the mathematical odds that two microbes from unrelated families would share such similarities is almost unfathomable. Certainly something to chew on. One way or another, in our production of wine they are partners in crime so to speak, or players on the same stage.

Act One-- *Saccharomyces cerevisiae*.

Act Two--Enter *Oenococcus oeni*

ML bacteria are always naturally present in the must during the yeast fermentation, and begin to metabolize malic acid in the fermenter while the yeasts are struggling to finish up. Contrary to some sources, it is best when making age-able wines not to inoculate the primary fermenter with ML bacterial culture. I prefer to wait, to discourage competition between the two actors.

The two prima donas tend to fight when they find each other both on stage together. To ensure that the primary (yeast) fermentation finishes consuming sugars completely, we would like the yeast to have their day in the shade in relative peace.

After the yeast fermentation is completed, and the wine is secured in tanks, barrels or carboys, the warm (70-74F) wine is often inoculated with a selected bacterial culture, and ML-specific nutrients may be added as well. The wine is then kept warm (74F/23C) for several months to encourage the bacteria to flourish.

Perhaps that is confusing. I mentioned that the wine has naturally occurring ML bacteria in it, but I also refer to inoculating with a special ML bacterial culture! Yes and yes—both are true. We shall discuss the nature of natural MLF a little further down the road, but for now we are concerned with the practical aspects of MLF procedures.

It should be noted that barrels that have been used for MLF previously typically harbor the beneficial bacteria. The old rule of thumb suggests that when putting new wine into such a barrel it is not necessary to inoculate with a culture. The barrel already has *Oenococcus oeni* in it.

After the primary yeast fermentation has completed there is very little free SO2 in the wine— typically about 5 ppm (almost nothing). The yeasts have done an admirable job of metabolizing it. We do not add SO2 at this point in the process. Why? Our star ML bacteria are very sensitive to sulfur, and we are endeavoring to create an environment that is conducive for them to flourish.

Add Oak?

This is a good time to add the oak-of-your-choice to the wine if it is going into carboys, tanks, or neutral barrels. One cup of chips per 5 gallons is maximum. I prefer less, if any, since oak chips, if overdone can express an obnoxious, in-your-face kind of characteristic. Contrary to popular dogma, cubes, spirals, or staves do not necessarily taste better than quality chips. In fact, the interior of the thicker oak adjuncts, being less toasted, can have a detrimental affect on the wine. Yes, a barrel is thick as well, but they are used for years—leaching out some less-desirable untoasted compounds.

When working in carboys, it is wise to add the oak first, then transfer the wine onto it. Since the wood is more alkaline, a slight foaming reaction can occur when the two are put together.

Not all oak chips are of the same quality. Barring the high price of chips on the retail market, it is wise to be willing to buy expensive chips from a quality manufacturer. Some cooperages toast and market their own chips.

The pH of the wine is determined, and slight acidic adjustments can be made if necessary prior to ML.

Remember that the wine will gain in pH during MLF—perhaps 0.13 pH or so. Traditional wisdom maintains that tartaric acid added at this point is irritating to the ML bacteria (a simplified way to state it). This is certainly true, but winemakers working in the trenches have found that as long as the acid adjustments are minor the ML bacteria tolerate it with few complaints.

So—hopefully you won't have to add acid. But if you must, keep your acid adjustments less than--say 0.8 pH. Once again, here is the acidulation formula:

1 g/L (0.13 oz/gallon) of tartaric acid for every 0.1 unit of pH short of the ideal (units to change).

The winemaker now has the wine in barrels, tanks or carboys---the acid has been adjusted, and the wine up to temperature.

MLF Temperature

The magic number is 74F/23C for the liquid temperature for most cultures. Your trusty digital thermometer is indispensable here. Below 69F/20C MLF slows dramatically, and above 86F/30C the ML bacteria can suffer and die. At 69F/20C MLF can take twice as long (4 months?) than it will at 74F/23C (2 months?).

How do you maintain a stable liquid temperature during MLF?

The best way is to put the wine in a room with temperature control, and adjust the thermostat until the liquid temperature in the wine is where you want it. The higher the wine is in the room obviously will contribute to energy efficiency. In a winery, when barrels are double or triple stacked, the elevated barrels complete MLF earlier than the ones on the floor (unless they are rotated).

Home winemakers—you can be creative with light bulbs, small ceramic space heaters, blankets and sleeping bags. Carboys can be arranged on 2" x 12" boards that are set on 16" x 8" concrete blocks, with a space heater underneath—all covered with sleeping bags. Or find a place in the house you can heat—a bathroom, closet, or cabinet. At this point in our discussion I must be honest; temperature control during MLF is somehow an Achilles heel of amateur winemakers. The lack of temperature control during MLF is one of the reasons why homemade wines suffer in comparison to their commercial counterparts. Home winemakers—you can do this!

When the temperature of the wine changes it increases or diminishes in volume. If you fill a barrel or carboy completely with the wine at 69F/20C, then warm it up to 74F/23C it will flow out through the airlock and make a mess. Leave the levels about 2"/5cm low until the temperature has stabilized—then top up with wine.

However, before you top up the barrels you may consider inoculating with an ML culture and adding a nutrient.

MLF Cultures

Strains of *Oenococcus oeni* have been selected, packaged and marketed since the 1980's.

Today there are two distinctive types: traditional cultures, and direct inoculate style products. Unless you are dealing with large volumes of wine, and love to perform lab work, always choose the **direct inoculate** style product. They are a bit more costly, but far easier to use—you just dump it in. Traditional ML inoculates can result in a strong culture, but they require a 3-step culturing process than can take several days to accomplish.

Direct inoculate ML cultures are selected and marketed by various companies, and come in different types; the most notable being cultures for lower original Brix/pH wines, and others for higher original Brix/pH wines. Take note; I said higher **original** Brix/pH wines. When the grapes arrived from the vineyard with high Brix and high pH, we assume that their nutrient needs are greater—and that caveat carries over into ML bacterial nutrient needs. Some ML cultures are also selected for high alcohol tolerance, like Christian Hansen CH16.

MLF Nutrients

Nutrients are not absolutely necessary to add during MLF, as it usually proceeds and finishes without them. Excess nutrients can become food for spoilage organisms. Low Brix, low pH wines may not need nutrients during MLF. High Brix, high pH wines however, may benefit from the addition of special ML nutrients.

ML bacteria are more functional in lower alcohol musts than in higher ones, and MLF usually takes longer to finish in high alcohol musts. Specific polyphenolics in red wines from high maturity grapes also have an inhibitory effect on malolactic fermentations. Once again, ML nutrients vary in nature; in particular those for high Brix wines, and others for normal Brix wines.

The absolute low pH limit for MLF is about 2.90 pH. Below that pH, ML organisms may struggle to begin.

During MLF an airlock is secured in the bung to release CO_2, and it can be observed doing just that. In a barrel one can remove the bung and put ones ear over the hole and hear the crackle of fermentation. These are two important indicators as to how the MLF is proceeding.

MLF is an anaerobic fermentation. The wine is never racked during MLF, as gross oxidation is kept to a minimum. However, fine, steady micro oxygenation through the sides of the barrel or amphora is encouraged. Containers are judiciously topped up, keeping the head-space between the surface of the wine and the bung to an absolute minimum. Some spoilage organisms are aerobic, and can populate using the little oxygen there is in the head space, particularly in containiers where the level of the wine is low. This is another discipline all winemakers need to follow.

Always keep the barrels or carboys topped-up to the maximum.

Arresting Film Yeasts

Not necessarily the scariest, but certainly the most common, irritating spoilage organism plaguing wines during the entire cellaring process is the infamous *film* yeast, or *cellar* yeast.

Winemakers use the common terms, because cellar yeast can actually be one or more of three different species of two genus—*Candida* being the most common. It appears as a white, greasy, chunky film clinging to the surface of the wine. If left to have its way in the wine, it can affect the flavor to the point of ruin. Once it is in a barrel or carboy it's usually going to be there for the duration of the cellaring process, in greater or lesser amounts. The good news is that it is relatively easy to control. Diligence is imperative. Cellar yeasts are aerobic, so the importance of keeping the container topped up is paramount.

The official technique for the temporary arrest of cellar yeast is as follows: The cellar yeast is floating on the top of the wine, and populating a little further down near the surface where it can get some oxygen. Use your handy spray bottle that already has a strong SO_2 solution in it—say a good spoonful of potassium or sodium metabisulfite powder in a liter or quart of warm water. Adjust the nozzle to a cone pattern, and spray hard directly down through the cellar yeast film into the wine, soaking the bunghole and coating the upper inside surface of the barrel, or neck of the carboy.

Top up and replace the bung and airlock with a new sterilized set. The operation can be performed every time you top up, or more often if the problem is persistent.

The obvious question, and a very valid one comes to mind: ML bacteria are not fond of SO_2, and yet here we are spraying some into the wine? Don't worry--It's not actually very much SO_2—mathematically. Also, this is not a normal situation folks. This is war, in which casualties are an ugly and unfortunate reality. If one is diligent, ruthless, and takes no prisoners (except for studying to form possible strategies) cellar yeast will not affect the taste of a wine.

Indigenous MLF

Prior to the 1980's MLF was always natural—inoculant products had as yet to appear on the scene. For those that consider wild yeast fermentations scary, natural MLF might be even more frightening, because the bacterium that may or may not be involved are not only from different species, but varying genus as well. Because of the lack of control with natural MLF, American and Australian universities prior to the 1980's adamantly discouraged allowing the wine to go through MLF. They preached centrifuging, filtering, and judicious sulfuring (up to 300 ppm) to create safe, reliable wine products (I'm getting a headache just writing about it). They deemed MLF "filthy" winemaking; warm wine sitting around for months on its sludge, without any protection from sulfur?—old world mumbo jumbo!

Meanwhile, a growing number of winemakers, privy to how fine wines were actually made, ignored the professors, and began working with MLF anyway. Eventually critical mass prevailed, which spurned extensive studies of the process in both the US and down under. We must point out that many studies had already been performed by European institutions (particularly the University of Bordeaux), but perhaps due to language barriers (we're being generous), or more likely a kind of self imposed secular, scholarly isolationism—tinted with near-sighted arrogance—the European studies were patently ignored.

At that time (circa 1980), yeast-producing companies, being product and profit driven responded, began marketing selected ML *Oenococcus oeni* inoculums, and eventually developed related nutrient products. The practice of MLF then became far more acceptable, because it was then associated with a modicum of control. Today, more winemakers travel, and with the advent of the internet, wine technology is far more international in scope.

It must be pointed out that many home winemakers are aware of how carboys of wine can go through MLF naturally in the warm summer months—even those that had been previously sulfured. Observable fermentation in the summer. This is an important point; unless red wine is sterile filtered or heavily sulfured deep into headacheville, the wine will always eventually go through MLF anyway.

Today there is a quiet growing trend amongst winemakers on the west coast of the US to allow spontaneous MLF to occur. It should be mentioned that some Burgundian producers have always allowed their best wines to undergo indigenous MLF. How effective is feral MLF?

To date the jury is still out, but the proponents claim the practice gives the wine more complexity of flavors. We do know that natural MLF can take longer to play out than ML fermentations using selected cultures. Tip: Wild ML bacteria are inhibited by primary yeast fermentations whose peak temperatures are above 86F/30C.

Topping

During MLF the barrels or carboys are kept topped-up with wine that is also going through MLF, or has no SO2 in it. Home winemakers can use boiled water if necessary. In wineries they use slick systems with modified beer kegs, nitrogen as a propellant, and triggered stainless steel applicator wands.

It should be noted that the failure to maintain topping levels is another typical problem with amateur winemakers, much of which may be due to the lack of easily available topping wine.

Negligent topping levels can seriously impact or ruin a wine. A simple technique for home wine-makers is to collect and use screw-top wine bottles to hold some of the topping wine. After the bottles are sterilized, filled, capped, and rinsed—you can back off on the screw caps just enough to allow CO2 to escape. The bottles are kept warm and stored upright. Always smell the contents of a bottle before using it. It may smell slightly of sulfides, but that is natural; it should smell like the wine in the carboys. Remember, your nose is the most sensitive analytical instrument you possess. After topping, if there is wine left in a bottle it may be consumed (I am always asked that question), but resist judging it too harshly—it is far from ready. Essentially, you are "barrel sampling".

Batonnage

Stirring the fine lees during MLF, or *batonnage* is a technique used with white wines, and occasionally with reds in France. In the US, a few Pinot Noir producers do perform batonnage, claiming it reduces incidences of Hydrogen sulfide production.

Some cutting edge winemakers are now performing batonnage with more tannic red varieties as well. The technique should be used only after the wine has been in barrel for more than six months. Why? Immediately after fermentation, when the wine has been transferred into barrels, it is extremely hungry for oxygen. Barrels slowly infuse oxygen into the wine, but at that point, tannic wines can consume as much as thirty times what a barrel can give. If the lees are stirred too early, they can scavenge oxygen and absorb precious anthocyanins, bleeding color and hampering the phenolic structure building process. In common speak, the result can be harsh, dry tannins—adhering to the top of the tongue.

Later on however, when the oxygen needs of the wine have diminished, lees stirring can help coat, soften and tame aggressive tannins. This generally means stirring the lees after MLF, during the cellaring process. Some winemakers actually save some of the lees and add it back after MLF.

Some Burgundian producers do not even rack after MLF, but leave the wine on its lees throughout the cellaring process. That minimalist technique may generally be considered viable only for Pinot Noir.

It should be mentioned that racking during MLF is counterproductive, serving only to oxidize (not oxidate) the wine.

Low-tech indicators one can use to determine the end of MLF are as already mentioned: the sound in a barrel has ceased, and the airlock is no longer bubbling. Carboys can be given a little twist to see if bubbles come up from the bottom. pH readings taken every two weeks during MLF (and recorded) should show a slow rise at first, a faster rise a month in—with the ascent gradually tapering off to the end. As long as the liquid temperature has remained stable, when the pH stops rising and stabilizes for two weeks MLF is probably done. Home winemakers might wait another two weeks, or a month and call it good. Wineries, after observing that MLF has most likely completed will send samples off to a lab. Lab report results will be accurate.

Home winemakers can purchase paper chromatography kits to help in determining the rough amounts of malic and lactic acids present. The lack of malic acid is assessed in relation to the presence of lactic acid; there should be very little malic acid left, but there should now be lactic acid that was produced by the ML bacteria. The results obtained are modestly reasonable, but not entirely definitive. The analyst is trying to determine the amount of the two acids based on the spread of spotting on a piece of Whatman paper. If our earlier advice was not heeded, and "acid blend" was used to acidulate instead of tartaric acid, paper chromatography results will be completely inaccurate. ML bacteria only metabolize natural malic acid; they will not eat added malic acid (in "acid blend").

The SC-50 MLF Analyzer by Vinmetrica is an option for home winemakers or small wineries. The electronic device comes in a kit that will take five tests, and must be plugged into one of their other electronic testing products, like the SC-100 SO2 analyzer.

Whether using a lab or in-house chromatography, at that point the winemaker is merely reassuring oneself that what he or she has already observed is, in fact correct. Wineries are reluctant to make the effort and the expense of sending samples to a lab until they are fairly sure MLF has completed.

A winery is filled with groups of barrels that may be each going through MLF at their own speeds. Only a neurotic winemaker would repeatedly send samples to a lab for each and every barrel, unless there was a perceived problem with a barrel. In practice, one sample is often sent in for a group of barrels. Has MLF completed in those six barrels of Merlot from that vineyard we crushed on that day that was fermented in that vat? Therefore, in reality the vast majority of barrels are assumed to have completed MLF. Once again, in practice what does a winery actually do? They wait. They wait until they are confident that all of the barrels in a group are done. Then they can perform the racking procedure en-masse.

When MLF has completed, rack the wine off of most of the sediment, onto (add) 40-60 ppm SO2 (see chart on page 138), and prepare the wine for aging in the cellar.

Cellar Yeast

What is that greasy white scum that is floating on the top of the wine in the carboy, clinging to the neck of the glass like a sinister creature?

Professional winemakers refer to the annoying substance as *cellar* yeast, or *film* yeast.

The reason it is not refereed to as a single yeast is because it actually can be one or more of several kinds. The first thing to remember is that any cellar yeast tends to be aerobic. They like air. So always keep all of your barrels and carboys topped up as high as is practical. There are some other conditions that encourage the growth of cellar yeasts: Low topping levels, oxygen/air, high pH, dirty airlocks, high temperatures, low SO2 levels, old wine. When you observe cellar yeast---act immediately, as it can eventually ruin the wine.

Here is what to do. You need:

Common spray bottle [you know the kind with the squeeze trigger]
1 pint of hot tap water
1 heaping teaspoon of either potassium meta busulfite, or sodium meta bisulfite powder

Mix the sulfite powder with the water. Put the solution in the spray bottle and give the carboy with the offending substance in it a healthy squirt directly down into the carboy. You will observe how the SO2 solution penetrates an inch into the wine. One or two applications usually takes care of it, but you may have to perform the operation again later.

Barrels

The art of making water-tight barrels is surprisingly old, considering the skill necessary to do so. The Romans used amphorae to store and ship wine, but when they arrived in southern Gaul they found the inhabitants had not mastered the art of creating the elegantly-shaped fired-clay 6 gallon vessels.

The Celts were barrel makers, so at some point in the nebulous mists of the past the bond between wine and oak was forged. Oak has certainly not been the only wood coopers have used to craft wine barrels out of, but it is by far the most popular. Only in the last 60 years or so has the flavor of oak been showcased such as it is today, as winemakers covet their precious inventory of expensive French barriques or nutty American barrels.

Today the marriage of fine oak aromas and wine is considered synonymous with quality wines. It may therefore be somewhat of a surprise that, even though the characteristic has always been known; years ago some old world producers went to considerable lengths to avoid it. When new pipes were introduced into the port lodges, mediocre table wine was first made in them for several years before they were finally dedicated to vintage port.

The popularity of the 225-228 liter/60 gallon wooden barrel is undeniable. A new barrel infuses nutty, seductive aromas into a wine until it's fourth year of use; but even after the pleasant nose of the wood has dissipated, the vessel still improves the character of wines stored in it due to the evaporative quality of the wood itself. Subtle exchanges of oxygen through the staves, the gaps in the staves, and head of the barrel enhance the character of the wine, and cause it to age faster than the same wine stored in a sterile tank such as glass or stainless steel. The slow, steady oxygenation of the wine continues until it is bottled. This is the most important function of a barrel--it breaths—both in and out. In comes a gradual steady flow of fine oxygen, and out goes funky smelling gases.

Gradual, low level exposure of oxygen to the wine is important for a variety of reasons. Color is intensified by interactions between anthocyanins and tannins in barrels with untoasted oak heads, and eventually some of the short-chain tannins are softened by polymerization, causing them to precipitate out of the wine. Also, untoasted oak contains gallic acid, a powerful cofactor, and as an antioxidant can impart supplemental reductive vigor to wines that have lost their energy due to field oxidation during extended hang time.

The rate of oxygen that a wine receives when stored in a standard 225L/60 gal. barrel depends on the particular barrel (depending on the thickness and porosity of the staves), but averages about 1 ml. of oxygen per liter of wine per month.

Evaporation concentrates the flavors in a wine. Water is a small molecule, with a molecular weight of 18. With a molecular weight of 46, ethanol molecules are also small, but more volatile. Both diffuse into the wood as a solution and then escape as vapor. The rate of loss is faster at higher cellar temperatures and the relative loss is affected by the humidity of the cellar as well--the balance point being about 65% relative humidity. Drier than this, water escapes faster and the alcohol content of the wine rises. If the cellar is more humid than 65%, the alcohol in the wine will slowly decrease.

As water molecules leave the barrel, the level of wine in the vessel decreases, forcing the cellar master to dogmatically add more wine to it—topping up. In the course of a year, as much as 3 gallons of topping wine are needed for a single 60 gallon barrel. Therefore, the wine gradually becomes more and more concentrated as the water escapes.

Barrels contribute to the flavor of wine in many ways:

Controlled oxygenation. Oxygen gradually entering the barrels contribute to softening of the tannins, increased color and wine stability, and production of various aroma compounds by oxidative processes.

Gassing off. Unwanted gases naturally escape out through the wood.

Barrels add reductive strength (antioxidative power) to the wine.

Evaporation. Concentration of flavors due to the loss of water and alcohol molecules.

The extraction of aromas, flavors and tannins from the oak which enhance the complexity and intensity of the wine. In general, the European species *Quercus petraea* contributes sweetness, while *Quercus robur* can help add tannic structure to a wine.

Over 200 volatile extractable components of oak have so far been identified, falling largely into the broad class of volatile phenolics, which derive mainly from oak lignin. The most important compounds from oak lignin are vanillin (vanilla), eugenol (spicy & clove-like), and guaiacol and its derivatives (smoky).

The amounts and effectiveness of these compounds extracted from the wood into wine depend on differing factors:

The time the wine spends in the barrel

The type of oak (French, American etc.)

The forest the oak is sourced from (discussed below)

The growth ring density (fine to course grain)

The method and duration of drying the staves (kiln or air dried)

Toast level (light, medium, medium+, heavy toast)

Toasted heads or no toasted heads

The method of toasting (wood or gas fire)

Size of barrel (smaller barrels = faster oak extraction rate, large barrels=slower)

Barrel shape (some feel Burgundy barrels differ in flavor vs. Bordeaux barriques)

Previous use of barrel. Depending on the oak used, a barrel will give off from 60%--80% of it's flavor the first year of use, and is finally considered "neutral" (no flavor left) after its fourth year.

During the course of the first summer of barreling, the aroma of the wine begins to alter and becomes bouquet. It intensifies as time goes on, and reaches its optimum after several years in the bottle. The development of the bouquet is associated with reductive characteristics, intensifying in the bottle in the absence of oxygen. The bouquet has its origins in both the essences of the skins, and in the phenolic compounds of premium wine grapes.

Controlling the oxidation process in a wine depends on the choice of wood grain for the barrels it will be held in.

Contrary to a popular held notion, fine grained wood is more porous than wide grain wood, and therefore promotes more dramatic changes between the wine and the cellar atmosphere.

The study of the chemical composition of oak demonstrates the complex relationship between the grain and the quality of the wood. In fact, studies have shown that wide-grained woods are richer in extractable compounds and tannins while poorer in aromatic compounds than tight grained oak. In general, very tight grained (VTG) barrels are recommended for aging wines for more than 14 months, while tight grained (TG) barrels are recommended for more than 12 months. Wider grained barrels give off flavors faster, and are recommended for white wines or reds to be cellared for 8-12 months.

Air Drying

Wood seasoning plays a major role in the enhancement of oak flavors in barrels. Quality oak staves are often seasoned for two years with full exposure to rain, which washes away some of the harshest tannins. Also, in the presence of the open air, certain strains of fungi develop, the influence of which positively affect the phenolic profile of the wood, converting lignin into vanillin far more effectively than kiln-drying.

In western France, *Aureobasidium pullunans* represents 80% of the fungi, with *Trichoderma harzanium*, and *T. koningii* constituting the secondary species.

Awareness of the typical procession and development of the fungi on staves is wise when considering purchasing barrels made from wood older than two years. For the first 20 months, the three species listed above dominate, with their mycelia covering the surfaces, aided in part by their resistance to phenolic substances leaching out of the wood, which are toxic to other competitive species. After 20 months many more fungal species begin to appear, rendering the situation far more complex. From that point the decomposition of the wood is accelerated.

Cooperages will take orders for barrels made from wood seasoned longer than the standard 24 month period, but studies conducted by University of Bordeaux in concert with Tonnellerie Demptos point to the likelihood that the three original fungal species do an admiral, if not optimal job in the two year period.

This is certainly not definitive, as there are winemakers that swear by older wood who, worldwide place orders for thousands of barrels per year made from 30 month, three year, and even four year wood. The bottom line is—the finest wines in the world are aged in older wood.

There are certainly French tonnellerie (cooperages) who are crossovers—making barrels for both Burgundy and Bordeaux (especially in the US), but they really can be divided into two general camps. Barrels made in eastern France tend to favor wood from forests that work well with Syrah, Grenache and Pinot Noir in nearby Burgundy. Nearer to Bordeaux, in southwestern France more barrels are made for the Merlot, Cabernet Sauvignon, and Cabernet Franc market.

The two barrel shapes are different: The 228 liter Burgundy barrel is shorter and fatter, while the classic 225 liter Bordeaux barrique is long and thin. It should be pointed out that the standard 60 gallon American oak barrel shape is unique to itself. Wineries usually favor one shape, especially if they are in the habit of double-stacking barrels on racks. American oak barrels can be ordered to be made in their traditional shape, or either French shape to facilitate even stackage.

If you visit cooperage websites you may notice that other larger barrel sizes are available, like the 300 liter hogshead, and larger puncheons. Big barrels are used for a variety of reasons; barrel fermenting white wines, and for the long, slow extraction of oak flavors into red wines.

Home winemakers—smaller French oak barrels in many sizes can be ordered from Radoux USA, and Sirugue USA offers a 114 liter Feuillette, made from French oak aged for 24 months.

Allain Fouquet will ship a 30 gallon French oak barrel out of Napa. Artisan Barrels offers a full range from 20 liter to their fully-branded 112 liter Hungarian oak barrel, and Tonnellerie Rousseau offers a deluxe French Burgundy-shaped 114 liter barrel with both painted hoops and chestnut hoops. A&K sells a 113 liter American oak barrel. The Barrel Mill in Minnesota makes barrels in 5, 10, 15, and 30 gallon sizes. Kelvin Cooperage out of Kentucky makes a 30 gallon barrel, and World Cooperage offers a nice 27 gallon American oak piece they call the "Octave" barrel. (see resources--page 130)

Important: The smaller the barrel, the more oak flavor will be imparted into the wine due to the ratio between the volume of wine and the surface area of the barrels interior. The first year of use, I would not leave any wine in a five gallon/20 liter barrel for more than one month. For a first-year 30 gallon/110 liter barrel I would leave a wine in it for six months maximum. If you like a wine with plenty of oak flavor, a new 225liter/60 gallon barrel can be used for the full aging period. It depends on your taste. The delicacy of some wines can be over-shadowed by too much oak.

The catch is--full sized barrels are far more economical per gallon. A full-sized, 60 gallon American oak barrel oftentimes only costs about $60 more than the 30 gallon unit. What ever happened to your wine making buddy? Couples—do the math. A 225 liter barrel provides us with 24 cases. Assuming you are daily wine drinkers--if you are reading this you should be—you can somehow manage to deal with two cases per month. Assuming you do have friends—if you are winemakers you must have some—they should be able to help with this.

By far, the most economical option for the amateur winemaker is to use a neutral barrel gleaned from a winery, augmented with oak adjuncts (quality chips) if one seeks an oak flavor. After four years of use, wineries will often eject barrels even if they are still good for wine, because they are prioritizing floor space, and the older barrels have little oak flavor left. A neutral barrel may not give a wine much oak flavor, but since it is wooden, it will still work it's magic on the wine.

Winemakers—here's the key: Trust your nose. Insert it into the bunghole of the barrel you are considering purchasing. If a neutral barrel smells like something you would want to drink--- it's still good. If not, don't buy it. The only glitch to that paradigm is the residual odor of the sulfur wick, which you may detect. How long has it been since this barrel was wicked? If it was only two weeks prior, the sulfur will be strong. If it was four weeks ago however, the barrel should smell good—like older wine, but with a hint of sulfur tang. If it was six to eight weeks you may detect a little VA, but modest levels of VA should disappear if you treat it with soda ash.

Barrel Styles

Whether the barrel is assembled in France, the USA, or elsewhere, there are several different styles to choose from: "Transport"/"Export", "Chateau Ferré", "Chateau", and "Chateau Tradition" styles.

The Export barrel is the workhorse of the wine industry. It will usually feature six metal hoops and 27mm stave thickness. Chateau Ferré style barrels also usually have six metal hoops, but are thinner, with 22mm stave thickness, which facilitates more rapid exchange between the wine and the environment. Chateau, and Chateau Traditional style barrels stave thickness is 22mm, and typically have 6-8 metal hoops, plus 2 - 6 decorative chestnut hoops. The chestnut hoops may present a charming curb appeal in a winery, but are totally useless otherwise. Once they begin to chip off they become annoying, and mold can grow in between the wood hoop and the barrel surface. Chateau Traditional are the most expensive of the styles.

Toast levels

The toast level is oftentimes branded on the barrel head: LT (light toast), MT (medium toast) MT+ (medium plus toast), and HT (heavy toast) (see front cover). Medium toast is a common standard worldwide for many red wines, but MT+ has also become quite popular. Some cooperages also have their own proprietary trademarked toast definitions.

Barrel heads represent up to 30% of the wood-to-wine contact surface. Some opt for paying extra for toasted heads, which will impart more oak flavor. I prefer the standard untoasted heads, due to the complex interactions untoasted oak has with the phenolics in wine.

Some cooperages will assemble a single barrel for customers based on the type of wine that it will be used for. It is the artistic side of cooperage they may enjoy and revel in. Since the cooper gets feedback directly from winemakers as to what wood/forest/toast selection works well for various varieties, he is likely well qualified to select material to create a barrel for specifically Tempranillo, Pinot Noir, Merlot, or Viognier etc.

Botany in Brief

In France, some of the trees we are still using now for barrels were planted 200 years ago by Napoleon for the production of wooden ships.

French oak barrels are crafted from the two predominant, closely related Eurasian species, *Quercus petraea* (syn. *Q. sessiliflora*), and *Quercus robur* (syn. *Q. pedunculata*). These two species have an overlapping range that extends from the British Isles and Atlantic coast of Europe across to the Ural Mountains and into Asia.

I shall refer to these species using their correct botanical nomenclatures. Even though it may ruffle a few well-heeled feathers, it must be pointed out that most of the biggest, glossiest, superbly written and published wine books have presented both the species in a confusing jumble of synonyms and common names.

In terms of quality, *Quercus petraea* is our star performer. It is naturally found in upland areas over 300m (984ft) with higher rainfall and shallow, acidic, sandy soils. The trees therefore, tend to be slow growing, with fine annular growth rings. This is the species responsible for the much sought after barrels from the Tronçais, Bertranges, and Châtillon forests (amongst many others). On the other side of the English Channel, *Quercus petraea* is honored as being the national oak tree of both Wales and Cornwall. The flavor profile of this species is characterized in brief by vanilla, toffee, and sweet coffee.

Quercus robur, on the other hand, prefers deeper, richer soils at lower altitudes. In France, the faster growing trees produce medium to wide grain staves predominantly from the Limousin forest. In the British isles, *Quercus robur* is known as the English oak, that once, long ago grew in vast forests, blanketing the islands. The flavor profile of this species lies more in it's strong expression of tannins.

European (non-French) oak barrels are sold with a given nationality (Hungarian, Russian etc.), and are often crafted from the *Quercus robur* species.

Historically, the better French oak barrels were often marketed as being from a given source forest. Today, some are still marketed as forest-specific, but many French barrels are made from mixed woods that are purchased at the giant stave auction that is held every year in France.

We, as users of the barrels would like to believe that they originate from a designated forest planted with a specific species, but the foresters know better. In reality, where the two species ranges overlap, they grow in mixed forests. Since the two species are so closely related they readily cross-pollinate and fertile hybrids appear. Botanists typically refer to the crosses between *Q. robur* and *Q. petraea* as: *Quercus × rosacea*.

French Forests:

Allier
  Tronçais
  Grosbois
Nievre
  Nevers
  Bertranges
Bourgogne
  Châtillon
Vosges
  Darney
  Schirmeck
Sarthe
  Jupille
Ile de France
  Seine et Marne
  Fontainebleau
  Saint-Germain
  Compiegne

Center of France
Limousin
Mayene
  Bellêne
  Persiegne
NW France
  Blois
  Cîteaux
  Russy
  Bercé
  Gavre
  Loches
  Ecouves
  Senonches
  Chandelais
  Reno-Valdieu
  Boulogne-Chambord

American Oak--*Quercus alba*

The American White Oak forest covers most of the eastern United States and is the largest contiguous forest in the world. Staves are sourced from forests in Minnesota, Missouri, Iowa, Arkansas, Kentucky, Pennsylvania, Virginia, and Illinois. Sometimes the sources are generalized, expressed as originating in either the Ozarks or the Appalachian mountains. As with any species of tree, forests in colder northern latitudes or higher elevations produce wood with finer grain.

Tonnelerie Radoux describes the characteristics of three selections they offer:

Minnesota oak-- "a roasted nut in the nose, with a long, warm integrated finish in the palate. The oak brings the fruit forward creating a beautiful support with the wine."

Missouri oak-- "a great all-purpose barrel, for white wines the characteristics are coconut in the nose with a sweet vanilla cream in the palate. For red wines, the fruit is highlighted in the nose and a "juicy" fruit quality in the palate."

Appalachian oak-- "great spices in the nose and a lemon cream in the palate. Less sweet oak character which retains the perception of acidity. This is a terrific barrel for Zinfandel and Syrah, but also works well with Chardonnay."

Some complaints about American oak barrel manufacturing have been concerned with the fact that staves are often sawn, not split. American oak does not have to be split to remain water-tight. *Quercus alba* has an abundance of tyloses, natural structures that seal up the heartwood. With tyloses "clogging the pores", American oak resists leakage even when sawn. French oak does not seal its heartwood with tyloses. It must be split by hand to prevent leakage.

American oak cants are resawn in a specific way so that the boards (to become staves) retain a maximum percentage of vertical grain characteristics. Sawn staves may not all end up quite as "vertical" as split wood, but the difference is nominal. It is important that the vertical grain is exposed to the wine, because of the superior way that the wood will then release polyphenolic flavor compounds into the wine. That is one of the reasons why the aromas and flavors given off by an oak barrel are preferred over oak adjuncts, such as chips, cubes, or spirals, which are for those most part omnidirectional grain orientated.

Oregon Oak---*Quercus garryana*

Quercus garryana is a species with a range stretching from southern California to southwestern British Columbia. Some proponents of Oregon White Oak, swear by its similarity to French oak. And yet—it is not French oak, neither in species, nor flavor and aroma profiles. *Quercus garryana* has its own unique characteristics. Like French oak, the flavors are more subtle than its bold continental neighbor *Quercus alba*—American white oak.

Bowing to regional pride, we can understand why some Oregon winemakers like using their local Oregon oak. It will likely remain however, as a boutique oak, due to the questionable sustainability of the species. Unless there are large-scale plantings of the trees on private land—specifically for barrel production, it will continue to be a declining resource. In British Columbia, and in some counties in Washington state the species is legally protected. Parks Canada claims that *Quercus garryana* woodlands support more species of plants than any other terrestrial ecosystem in British Columbia.

Quercus garryana is a slow growing tree with fine annular growth rings and ivory-white wood. Typical of oaks, it tends to be branchy when growing in an unshaded location. Existing stands are wild, which may affect the flavor profile positively, but creates difficulties for cooperages, who struggle to find clear material free of knots and branches. Unlike eastern American oak, Oregon oak must be split, not sawn, because like French oak it does not totally seal it's heartwood with tyloses. Sawn Oregon oak barrels may leak, and it is becoming more and more difficult to find cants that will split straight enough to mill staves from.

Compounding the problem is the simple fact that even though Oregon's timber industry is huge, there exists no historically embedded wine culture powerful enough to compete with furniture and veneer manufacturers, and firewood cutters that wrestle with the cooperages for the declining resource. Higher level executives working for the Weyerhauser corporation (that owns about a third of Oregon State) may be fine wine drinkers themselves but profits from sustainable Douglas Fir plantings remain all too reliable.

Amphorae

Pottery is certainly not a new material for winemaking. In fact, barring stone, it's probably the oldest. Now winemakers want to work with it again. I am excited about it. Pottery is naturally very porous, depending on the type of clay it's made out of. Prehistoric vintners smeared beeswax on the inside of the vessel to keep the wine from seeping out. Since clay types and firing temperatures affect it's porosity, the modern potter has control over a vessel's breathing characteristics--more so than a wooden barrel.

Ideally, for red wines I want amphora designed primarily for malolactic fermentation—with a higher porosity than a wooden barrel. I want more micro-oxygenation during ML than a wooden barrel provides. New world winemakers are beginning to experiment with pottery for fermenting and aging red and white wines in vessels, many 60 gallon and larger. I would prefer smaller vessels, both for the increased wine to surface ratio, and for ease of handling.

Here is a design idea: Vertical 31 gallon capacity amphora—four of which would fit standing on a standard palette. They would rest on a special stand on the palette, which could be moved with a palette jack or fork lift. They could be strapped snuggly together with a cargo strap, with small pieces of padding stuffed in between.

I would want a domed top, with a standard bunghole. The 31 gallon capacity would allow the cellarmaster to rack 30 gallons out of it after ML, leaving one gallon of sediment. The wine from two amphora would thus rack tidily into one 60 gallon wooden barrel.

The special stand could be polyethylene, with indentations for the amphora to rest in, and holes in the bottom of each of the four indentations. Empty amphora could be cleaned by inverting by hand into the indentations and cleaned as a quad with a standard spinning barrel washer inserted through each hole in the bottom of the stand. The stand would first be placed on top of a standard metal barrel rack to raise it off the ground enough to insert the barrel washer tool in.

Barrel Maintenance

It seems there are as many ways to maintain barrels as there are winemakers.

Ideally barrels are kept in continual use, but practical realities often inhibit us from doing so. Northern hemisphere winemakers may bottle in early September and refill two months later after fermentation. That schedule is practical, but some bigger, tannic wines yearn to be held for more than seven months in the barrel. Bottling later--in the Spring requires that the barrels are dry-stored until the following Autumn.

A standard 225 liter wine barrel holds about a gallon of liquid absorbed in the wood of the barrel itself. After a used barrel is soaked and rinsed with cold water it will still smell of wine. Even after a barrel is soaked in hot water all night it will still faintly smell of wine.

Beneficial ML bacteria (and hopefully not many spoilage organisms) burrow over 6mm deep into the wood along with the wine. The microbes *encyst*, or hibernate in a wet or dry barrel as they are tucked into the pores of the wood. Due to that, the general rule of thumb is; one does not need to add ML culture to a barrel that has already been used for malolactic fermentation—the ML bacteria wake up once they are again in the presence of wine.

On that same theme, spoilage organisms may also lurk in the interior of a barrel, particularly if it has not been cared for well. *Brettanomyces* is particularly stubborn, and cannot be easily removed from a barrel or wooden press parts. Since all wine contains spoilage organisms in greater or lesser numbers, it only follows that they are in the barrels as well. The question is; how many and how nasty are they?

Generally barrels are healthy and can be reused many times—for years.

The winemaker uses the proverbial nose for gauging the health of an empty barrel. There is no other instrument. Unruly individuals may be retired to the planter barrel area, but if a barrel does not smell quite 100% it may receive a heavy duty cleaning with hot water and soda ash (or baking soda), or with ozoneated water to refresh it.

Please resist the urge to use soda ash on a newer barrel based solely on human paranoia. The alkaline soda ash strips tannins and flavor out of the wood.

Cleaning and storage requires following protocols where timing is important.

General rules of thumb for used barrel maintenance:

Hydrate barrels prior to use by filling with cold water

Never leave plain water in a barrel over 48 hours

If a barrel has had water in it and is to be used, it should be filled with wine in less than 48 hours.

Always drain water out of barrels to be stored completely. Drain for 30 minutes, then place a double paper towel wad in the bunghole and drain at least 24 more hours. There should be no pooling in the bottom after the barrel is righted. Use a flashlight.

Barrels will dry in about a week

Do not burn a sulfur wick in a wet barrel (2 seconds SO2 gas may be injected into a wet barrel)

When barrels are dry, burn ¼ sulfur wick or 10-20 grams for 10 minutes only (60 gallon).

Use a ventilated cover on the bung hole afterwards

Wick barrels outside or in a ventilated room. (It stinks!)

Sulfur wick a barrel in storage every 4-6 weeks.

Ideal relative humidity for dry storage is 70-80%

Do not put wine in a recently wicked barrel. Wait 4 weeks after wicking.

Rinsing

Winemakers working with barrels often use metal barrel racks for storage, general use, and barrel cleaning procedures. Home winemakers can fashion a sturdy all-purpose wooden rack that holds the barrel 10" or more off of the floor to enable access to the bunghole for cleaning when the barrel is in the six o'clock position.

In smaller wineries, barrels are cleaned by placing the barrels on a metal rack with the bung holes down in an outdoor rinsing area. A special omni-directional, high pressure barrel washing spray head is inserted, and hot or cold water is blasted into the barrel until the water running out is clear. Some wineries will then blast ozoneated water into the barrels to further sanitize them.

The home winemaker should use a clean garden hose that has been sanitized (inside) with iodine or SO2 solution, and a small spray nozzle. Rotate the nozzle inside the bung hole to try and blast off as much surface as possible. Allow the barrel to drain for 30 minutes. Then, if fruit flies are present, loosely wad up two paper towels and stuff them into the bung hole. The paper will become soaked with water and will need replacing once. The barrel can remain inverted.

Contrary to what some of the home winemaking sources recommend, you should not perform a soda ash treatment on a new barrel. The soda ash will strip out some of the flavor you paid well for. Professional wineries never do that. New oak is considered basically sterile. Your new barrel really only needs a cold water rinse to wash out a few of the harshest tannins, but it is wise to fill it with cold water to make sure it does not leak before you put valuable wine in it.

The wine industry, as huge as it is, ensures that few winery-sized (60 gallon and up) barrels linger in warehouses for long. Since those warehouses are operated by barrel manufacturers or distributors, it is in their best interest to ensure that the storage facilities are hermetically controlled environments, maintained a 65% - 80% relative humidity.

If one purchases a smaller than standard barrel, it is wise to buy it directly from a barrel distributor or manufacturer. Retail wine and brew making outlets purchase most of their products from only one full-line distributor in the US. As previously mentioned, that is why you may have noticed product lines are generic between various retailers. Therefore, one must wonder how long the ten gallon barrel you purchased sat in the warm retail shop, and in turn how long it was in the home wine and beer distributors warehouse prior to that. What humidity has it been stored at, and for how long? Neither business is dedicated to the storage of barrels, but rather products in general. If you don't feel like dealing with a barrel distributor, ask your favorite brew shop owner to order a barrel from a distributor specified by you.

On that note, the same paradigm is also a huge problem with retail wine sales. No matter how much care importers and distributors take to protect their inventory, once the bottles of wine are on a retail shelf, they are inevitably subjected to higher than optimal temperatures, fluorescent light, and sometimes even sunlight.

That said, make sure new barrels do not leak by filling them with water. Most new barrels will not leak. If the barrel you purchased is a dry one, water may gush out between the staves, but it will probably tighten up and seal within 24 hours. Examine the position of the metal hoops to ensure they are in their original positions. Some barrels have square nails to keep the hoops in position and some do not.

Used barrels in extended dry storage that is less than 65% relative humidity may have to be re-hydrated every several months; how often depending on the humidity.

New barrels—Preparation for immediate use.

Method A

Fill barrel with cold water for 4-48 hours. No leaks.

Empty, then invert to six o'clock, rinse once with fresh water, and drain at least one hour.

Fill with wine in less than 48 hours

Method B

Fill 60 gallon barrel with about 5 gallons/20 liters of very hot water (175F/80C)

Insert silicon bung, and roll the barrel to wet all interior surfaces.

Stand barrel on each head for 10 minutes to ensure it seals around the crozes

Lay barrel sideways and slosh the water throughout at least four rotations.

Remove the bung and drain for an hour.

Fill with wine in less than 48 hours

Storage of new barrels:
Leave barrel in plastic wrap, and protect from sunlight.
Store up off of the floor
Relative humidity should be 70-80%
Use method A when ready to use

Maintenance and storage of used wine barrels:
Rinse with either or both hot and cold water until it runs clear (5 minutes)
Invert and drain 24 hours
Allow to dry to touch from 1-5 days
Once the wood is dry, sulfur immediately
Sulfur with 10-20 grams sulfur wick for 10 minutes (60 gallon/225 liter barrel)
Store barrels with bung hole open or a screen/course cloth taped over hole

The sulfur wick burner is a medieval looking tool, like a monk's incense burner. A metal pipe with holes in it is attached to a wooden bung with heavy metal wires, and hangs inside the barrel while the stick of sulfur burns. (The metal pipe type are better than the screened type).

A modern sulfur wick comes in the form of a small stick, pieces of which are snapped off. The piece of sulfur stick is lit, dropped into the burner, which is then lowered into the bung hole and allowed to burn for ten minutes. Do not leave the burner in the barrel for longer than ten minutes—even if the wick has burnt out. It will taint the barrel with a sulfur smell that is difficult to remove.

I keep everything I need for the process in one stinky box: the burners, sulfur, gloves, chalk, cigarette lighter, masking tape, squares of nylon screen, and most important—human nature as it is—an old- fashioned kitchen timer that proclaims loudly when the ten minute period is over.

The chalk is used to record the date boldly near the bunghole. Chalk works well, and is easily rubbed off. During dry storage, the sulfur wicking process is repeated every 4-6 weeks for each barrel.

I use squares of nylon screen cut from a paint strainer bag obtained from the paint store. The screen is taped over the bung hole to keep out fruit flies, which are present almost year-round in the mild climate where I live. Some wineries store barrels in racks with the bungholes open, inverted to six o'clock in humidity-controlled rooms. One way or another, barrels should be allowed to breath during extended dry-storage. A bunged-up barrel creates a humid atmosphere that promotes microbial growth, especially at higher temperatures. Lower temperature dry-storage helps to inhibit spoilage organisms.

Old school winemakers will store 60 gallon neutral barrels filled with water and 1 full cup of Sodium metabisulfite, and 1 full cup of citric acid. Apparently barrels can be used for years if stored in this manner.

Soda Ash cleaning procedure
Rinse the barrel with the bunghole down until the water runs clear (up to 5 minutes)
Fill half way with hot water
Add soda ash dissolved in hot water
Fill completely with hot water, and insert bung
Allow to stand for 24 hours Rinse for 5 minutes with cold water

Fining

Fining is a simple technique used to clarify a wine, more popular in France than in the new world, where the practice has been supplanted in part by filtration. Fining was popular, if not standard procedure in the old days in Bordeaux, where the technique became somewhat of a refined art form. The Bordelaise often want the wine to be not just clear, but possessing a kind of crystal, brilliant clarity. Whether that level of clarity renders a wine better tasting is questionable, but anyone who has dealt with a wine that is less than clear knows that a cloudy wine will taste far better after it has been reasonably clarified. Properly executed, fining serves both to clarify, and as well as a stabilizing treatment. It carries down colloidal particles that could give rise to potential turbidity.

Here is how it works: The protein-based fining agents' particles have a positive electrical charge, while the cloudiness particles are negatively charged. The negative particles naturally cling to the positive particles and slowly fall, or precipitate to the bottom of the vessel. This is termed *flocculation.*

The beauty of the technique is that it requires no special equipment, except a chef's whisk to mix the fining agent into the wine. Products sold at home brew shops like Kieselsol, bentonite, isinglass, or gelatin are good for fining white wines, but for reds the premier fining agent is egg albumin (egg whites). Egg whites respect the delicacy of red wines. The albumen has been sold as dried powder or flakes, but it is simple to use the egg whites themselves--from fresh, quality eggs.

For best results, the practice is best done in the winter, or when the wine is colder. The egg whites are separated, lightly salted to make the globulin soluble, beaten until not quite foamy, mixed with an equal proportion of water, then immediately whisked into the wine. The wine is allowed to settle for a month, then carefully racked off of the soft sediment. 6 eggs will treat one 60 gallon barrel. One egg is too much for a 5 gallon carboy. Over-fining is not recommended, and can strip color and flavor from a wine. In fact, if a wine is already clear—do not fine it.

Filtration

Filtration has received a lot of bad press. It's true—world class red wines are not filtered. But filtered red wine is far more common than most consumers realize. It's just not advertised as such. When have you ever seen a bottle of wine that proudly states, "filtered" on the bottle? The truth is, most of the reds and all of the whites resting on the shelves under fluorescent light at Safeway or Walmart have been filtered. Today, it is standard procedure to filter white wines, but most folks are not aware that prior to WWII white wines were made in a completely different style. They required aging, oftentimes for over ten years—but they were all the better for it.

The Germans are largely responsible for pioneering filtration systems in the late 1940's, producing "Grey Riesling" and the infamous "Blue Nun". The Portuguese capitalized on the idea with their "Mateuse", and "Isabelle Rose". It was a smart marketing idea based on a new technology. With sterile filtration and SO2, low-alcohol white wines with a little residual sugar could be produced for the mass market. It worked. On a positive note, it was many Americans introduction to wines that were not fortified--a step forward in evolution shall we say. Unfortunately however, it has altered our concept of white wines.

The plate & frame filter has become a common fixture in small wineries because of both white wine production and as a form of insurance policy for reds. Most boutique wineries will filter a red only if they have to. Why? Unruly bacteria and yeasts. Remember, wine naturally contains small amounts of many microbial species. Even though our goal is to produce wines where all microbial dramas have been allowed to play out in the cellar prior to bottling, if lab results indicate that a wine has too much *Lactobacillus, Pediococous, Brettanomyaces* or other nasties, the winery is faced with the reality of either sterile filtering or opening up a valve and pouring it all down the drain. I don't know about you, but I don't like to waste wine—even table wine.

Contrary to attitudes of purists, the taste of a table wine is not altered much by careful filtration. Fine wines however, loose character. Some important larger phenolic colloidal structures will not pass through 0.45 micron (sterile) filter pads, destroying the cellaring abilities of tannic, otherwise age-worthy wines.

Home winemakers. If you have a minor problem with a wine you can run it through one of those little hobbyist plate & frame filter systems. Some of the brew shops will rent them out.

I hear they are messy, but they do work, and you can run about 20 gallons through a set of pads. Your wine will need to be clarified first, either naturally or by fining, or it will plug up the pads quickly. Run it through the filter system twice. The first pass should be through course 1 micron pads, and the final pass through the finest pads (they are only 0.50 micron, but that will suffice).

Bottles

In the wine industry, bottles come in many shapes, sizes and grades. In wineries, and even on sales web pages, wine bottles are often referred to simply as *glass*--winery glass.

It is generally customary to put the varietal type of wine in the appropriate bottle shape, but the rule is loosely followed. The Burgundy bottle is traditional in eastern France for Pinot Noir, Syrah, Gamay, the Grenache blends of the Rhone valley and Cabernet Franc in the Loire valley. The Bordeaux bottle, in its seemingly unlimited incarnations encompasses most other red varietals, and is the most popular shape in the new world. It is a good bottle for home winemakers because the shape of the bottle facilitates the capture of sediment when it is poured into a glass or a carafe.

The *punt* is the exaggerated indentation in the bottom of a quality wine bottle. A bottle without a punt is thinner, lighter weight, cheaper to produce and is synonymous with inexpensive wines.

The common industry-standard colors for winery glass in the new world are: green, antique green, dead leaf green, smoke, and flint (clear).

The 750 ml. bottle is the most common size, five of which are roughly equivalent to one US gallon. We are all familiar with the larger 1.5 liter size used for table wines. Wineries producing fine wines will oftentimes bottle some of their products in half-sized 375 ml. glass, because they are popular with sommeliers in restaurants—one little bottle fills two tidy glasses.

Home winemakers may enjoy saving quality used glass, but will find that the bottling and cellaring process is simplified by owning uniform bottles in their appropriate cardboard cartons. A wedding can provide an auspicious opportunity to acquire multiple uniform cases. Beware of Italian glass because, despite the quality, the neck size on some (not all) bottles are 2mm smaller than standard, making hand-corking difficult.

If home winemakers purchase new glass, consider buying bottles with screw caps, as it will simplify the process. Flint, or clear glass may not be traditional for red wines, but they are easier to fill and clean. The wine looks good in them, and since you should be storing the bottles in the dark in their cases you need not worry about oxidation caused by sunlight. This is assuming you will treat the bottled wine with respect and not leave a bottle half filled in the sunlight on the counter for days.

Corks

Natural corks are punched from renewable, responsibly harvested bark of the cork oak *Quercus suber* in Portugal, Spain, and North Africa. Even though the trees are not cut down in the process, there are a limited population of trees old enough for the bark to be harvested. Demand is fierce, which drives the price up on natural cork of all grades. It takes 50 years for a young cork oak to begin to produce bark suitable for corks.

The quality of oaken cork appears to be in a gradual decline. Recent genetic studies of trees that produce high and low-quality cork have not as yet been conclusive, but divulge some clues behind this decline, hinting at a possible link to climactic changes.

Poor quality cork has thin layers of bark that possess lots of lenticular channels--little air-penetrating conduits in the plant tissue. Better cork has a higher abundance of heat-shock proteins, which help other proteins form their correct shapes even under stressful conditions. Heat-shock proteins also aid cellular division, permitting the growth of thicker bark. Previous studies have found that heat-shock proteins guard cork trees from ultraviolet light, high temperatures and drought--all of which have steadily become bigger problems in Portugal over the last century.

In lower quality cork, researchers observed less gene activity for heat-shock proteins--but those trees may have an alternative defense against similar stresses. Genes that produce phenolic compounds, brownish UV-absorbing chemicals that pool in the bark's lenticular channels, are more ample in poor cork, resulting in twice the load of phenolic compounds as in good cork.

Other genes that are more active in low-quality cork also suggests a reaction to UV exposure and water shortages. Genes that temper oxidative stress and repair DNA damage were elevated in poor cork. Cell division also seemed stunted in poor cork, explaining the trees' thinner bark. Slowing growth may help the trees during harsh times--such as drought. Minimizing cell division could protect a tree's DNA from UV-triggered mutations or help conserve energy.

The well known problem with natural cork is the occasional presence of TCA, which can show up in every 40-80 corks. When a wine industry worker or a sommelier mentions that a specific bottle of wine is *corked*, they are referring to the wine having been infected with a fungus introduced by a cork that gives the wine a particular musty nose, and worse—taste.

That is the only reason why a customer will sniff a cork prior to accepting a bottle of wine in a restaurant. They are not gauging the quality of the wine, rather merely discerning if it is one of those occasional bottles with a tainted cork. As the reader can imagine, this occurs with bottles no matter how much they cost. Ouch! Cork taint used to occur more often. Today, cork producers, like Cork Supply, and M.A. Silva have gone to extremes to treat the corks in an effort to reduce the occurrence of cork taint.

Natural corks will dry out with time in the bag. Manufacturers recommend using natural corks within six months of purchase. In reality, they can be used after they have been stored longer than that, particularly if the winery is using a pneumatic corker. Bench-top and floor standing manual corkers will put older corks in as well, but a few cork particles may end up floating in the wine.

Natural corks

There are several grades of corks, the highest (costing over $1.00 each in 2014) used by wineries, and the lowest become colmated corks or are sold to the home wine making suppliers. Special sizes can be ordered, but the standard sizes are 45mm x 24mm, and 38mm x 24mm--the longer 45mm corks being used for premium wines. Wineries purchase corks from suppliers in bags of 1000.

Agglomerated corks are made of granular bits of cork that have been glued together.

Colmated corks look like natural corks, but are actually either agglomerated corks, or lower-grade natural corks that have a layer of cork dust adhered to all outside surfaces.

Technical corks are agglomerated corks that have a pure cork disc glued to each end.

Synthetic corks

We are all familiar with synthetic corks, which, over the years have become to look more like natural cork. Mostly gone are the blue, green, red, yellow and black (I liked the black) corks that boldly proclaimed their syntheticness. Alas, the colored closures failed the market test. Consumers--baby-boomers in particular seem to posses an almost religious, insecure need to be natural. I, being a boomer, must confess to prefer pulling a natural cork out of a bottle, and admit that they are certainly easier to stuff back in. However, the wine is my focus, not the closure. I can always seal an open bottle with my bar topper—even if the ornate little dragon affixed to the topper keeps a red eye glaring, threatening to scold me if I over-indulge.

Synthetic corks are not deemed for long-term aging of wines—a practice few engage in anyway. As mentioned, bottles with synthetic corks can be stored upright. Synthetic corks are harder to compress than natural corks, which makes inserting with a small, hand "winged" style corker very difficult. Home winemakers will need a single-levered floor standing corker with brass inserts to put them in easily.

Synthetic corks are slippery, and can push up out of a bottle that becomes too warm far easier than natural corks, which grip the glass better.

Wineries with pneumatic corkers: Recommended space between the bottom of either a natural cork or a synthetic cork and the top of the wine---1cm/7/16".

Home winemakers with hand corkers: Recommended space between the bottom of a synthetic cork and the top of the wine---16mm/5/8".

Recommended space between the bottom of a natural cork and the top of the wine---13mm/1/2"

Wine Storage 101

I always cringe when I see one of those open wine racks filled with good wine in someone's warm, light living room. Heat and light are damaging to bottled wine. Proximity to vibration has also been proven to be detrimental to wine (furnaces, refrigerators, washing machines and dryers). Wine should be stored in the coolest, darkest, calmest place in your house. On the floor in a bedroom closet or hall closet next to an exterior wall may suffice. Wines age slower at low temperatures. Most wines will not freeze unless the liquid temperature drops below 25F/-4C.

In a winery, the cases of bottled wine with natural corks are inverted on the palettes, and remain that way in warehouses until they are sold to retail outlets.

Traditionally, bottles with natural corks are stored on their sides to keep the corks wet. Since home made wines tend to have more sediment than commercial products, amateurs may find it more practical to use synthetic corks or screw top bottles, allowing the bottles to be stored upright in their cases. The cases can then be stacked normally, and bottles pulled out as needed. Red wines should be allowed to warm gradually up to a cool room temperature (65-68F) before serving.

Generally, young wines less than five years old will benefit by pouring the wine into a carafe before serving, as long as the color of the wine is still bright purple-red. If a wine is aged, or for any reason shows the effects of oxidation—orange to brown colors—it should be poured directly out of the bottle into the glass, and may suffer after being opened for a day.

What happens to a wine as it ages has been studied extensively, but much of the process remains phenomenal. It is wise to wait at least six months for the wine to settle in after it recovers from the bottling process before trying it. If you try a bottle every month, it will at first seem unresolved and introspective, like a young adult that hasn't yet figured out a direction to pursue in life.

One day you will pour yourself a glass and be pleasantly surprised to find that it has changed dramatically. More often than not the metamorphosis will occur quickly, but after about a year or more in the bottle. After that, who knows? You have nurtured a child, and as children do, it is now up to them to evolve and express themselves. You may now raise a glass to yourself, and the mature wine of the future.

International Wine Production Data

For those that think of wine as merely a cute little boutique market, think again. It is a huge industry. The data is impressive.

Wine plays a major role in the economies of many nations, which produce over 7 billion gallons (265 million hectoliters) of wine annually. Worldwide wine consumption is estimated to be around 6.5 billion gallons --party-planet Earth-- (no wonder the ET's are showing up).

The International Organization of Vine and Wine (OIV) announced in 2013 that global wine production was forecast to climb 8.8%, to the highest level in seven years, as grape harvests rebound in Spain, Argentina and France. Italy, France and Spain are typically neck to neck, competing to be the largest producer in the world for any given year.

World wine production by volume is expected to jump by 22.8 million hectoliters, equivalent to 3 billion bottles.

Italy's production is at about 45 million hectoliters, France at 44 million hectoliters, Spanish output may rise to 40 million hectoliters, with US volumes at about 22 million hectoliters.

Argentina's production weighs in at about 15 million hectoliters.

Among major producers, Romania is posting the biggest gain, lifting output 79 percent to 5.94 million hectoliters after a heat wave in 2012, followed by Hungary with a 44 percent jump to 2.62 million hectoliters, and New Zealand with a 28 percent increase to 2.63 million hectoliters.

Exports

Italy was the world's largest wine exporter by volume in the first half of 2013 with 20.9 million hectoliters, followed by Spain with 17.3 million hectoliters, and France with 14.9 million hectoliters. By value, France took the biggest share of exports with 7.86 billion euros ($10.8 billion), followed by Italy with 4.87 billion euros and Spain with 2.41 billion euros.

The U.S. was the biggest importer at 4.04 billion euros, followed by the U.K. at 3.86 billion euros and Germany with inbound shipments valued at 2.47 billion euros, the industry group reported.

California's 2013 harvest alone yielded over 4 million US tons of grapes

North American Provinces or States With 100-Plus Wineries

California 3,674
Washington 689
Oregon 566
New York 320
British Columbia 257
Virginia 223
Texas 208
Ontario 192
Pennsylvania 174
Ohio 144
Michigan 136
North Carolina 130
Missouri 122
Colorado 106
Illinois 100
Total U.S. Wineries 7,762

Annual case production
Number of wineries by production size
Large (>500,000 cases) 56
Medium (50,000-499,000 cases) 253
Small (5,000-49,999 cases) 1,436
Very Small (1,000-4,999 cases) 3,189
Limited Production (< 1,000 cases) 2,828

On behalf of the ascendance of the North American boutique winery, check out how many businesses there were in 2013 that produced less than 5000 cases per year—6017 wineries!

Which states drink the most wine per person?

By far the most wine is consumed in the District of Columbia, which of course is not really a state. At least our elected and appointed officials are having a good time--and the lobbyists too! New Hampshire logs in as second, followed by Vermont, Massachusetts, New Jersey, Nevada, Connecticut, and California. West Virginia comes in last place.

Resources

American Tartaric Products Inc. Windsor, CA 707-836-6840 www.americantartaric.com
Davison Winery Supply McMinnville OR 503-472-1711 www.dwinesupplies.com
G.W. Kent nn Arbor, MI 734-572 1300 www.gwkent.com
Gusmer Wine Lab Napa, CA 707-224-7903 www.gusmerwine.com
Oenofrance Santa Rosa, CA 707-484-4378 www.oenofrance.com
Pacific Coast Chemicals Berkeley CA 510-549 3535 www.pcchem.com
Presque Isle Wine Cellars North East, PA 800-488-7492 www.piwine.com
Scott Laboratories, Inc. Petaluma, CA 707-765-6666 www.scottlaboratories.com
Vinquiry Windsor, CA 707-838-6312 www.vinquiry.com
Winetech LLC Napa, CA 707-552-2080 www.winetech.us
www.wineequip.comau (Australia)
www.art-of-brewing.co.uk (UK)
www.lallemandwine.com
info@cellartek.com
www.tcw.web.com
www.wineryequipment.com
www.buchervaslin.com
www.carlsenassocites.com
www.collopack.com
www.conetech.com
www.criveller.com
www.euromachinesusa.com
www.klrmachines.com
www.coquardpresses.com
www.napafermentation.com
www.stpats.com

Corks

corksupply.com
masilva.com

Native grass seed

www.bfinativeseeds.com
www.seedsofnature.net

Education

www.wineserver.ucdavis.edu (UC Davis)
www.wineeducation.wsu.edu (WSU)
www.usc.adelaide.edu.au/assitm/winemaking (University of Adelaide)
www.nysaes.cornell.edu (Cornell)
www.univ-montp2.fr (Universitie de Montpellier)
www.u-bourgogne.fr (Universitie de Bourgogne)
www.unicatt.it/ucsc (Italy)
www.geisenheim.hs-m.de (Germany)

Barrels

A&K Cooperage Higbee, MO 660-456-7227 www.akcooperage.com
Alain Fouquet French Cooperage Napa, CA 707-265-0996 www.alainfouquet.com
Barrel Associates Napa, CA 707-257-0714 www.premierwinecask.com/barrel_associates.html
Barrel Mill, The Avon, MN 800-201-7125 www.thebarrelmill.com
Budapesti Kádár Budapest, Hungary +36 1 283-0033 www.kadarhungary.com
Canton Cooperage Windsor, CA 707-836-9742 www.cantoncooperage.com
Dargaud et Jaeglé Tonnellerie Romanèche Thorins, France 707-257-0714 www.dargaud-jaegle.com
Demptos Napa Cooperage Napa, CA 707-257-2628 www.demptos.fr
Tonnellerie François Frères Meursault, France +33 3 80 21 23 33 www.francoisfreres.com
Gamba USA Napa, CA 707-696-9005 www.bottigamba.com
Kelvin Cooperage Louisville, KY 502-366-5757 www.kelvincooperage.com
Le Grand USA Walla Walla, WA 707-738-7465 www.legrandusa.com
Mercier USA (Tonnellerie Mercier) Napa, CA 707-567-5711 www.tonnellerie-mercier.com
Mistral Barrels Sonoma, CA 707-996-5600 www.mistralbarrels.com
Nadalie USA (Tonnellerie Nadalie) Calistoga, CA 707-942-9301 www.nadalie-usa.com
Oregon Barrel Works   503 472 8883   rick@oregonbarrelworks.com
PO Box 748 ---2780 SE St. Joseph rd. McMinneville OR 97128
Seguin Moreau Napa Cooperage Napa, CA 707-252-3408 www.seguinmoreaunapa.com
Tonnellerie Allary Archiac, France 510-339-0170 www.tonnellerie-allary.com
Tonnellerie Baron Les Gonds, France 707-328-8207 www.tonnelleriebaron.com
Tonnellerie Bel Air Calistoga, CA 707-987-8905 www.tonnellerie-bel-air.fr
Tonnellerie Berthomieu St. Helena, CA 707-968-0664 www.groupecharlois.com
Tonnellerie Billion Beaune, France 707-257-3582 www.tonnellerie-billon.com
Tonnellerie Bordelaise Carmel, CA 707-225-5783 www.tonnellerie-bordelaise.com
Tonnellerie Boutes Bordeaux, France 510-799-1518 www.boutes.com
Tonnellerie Cadus Ladoix-Serrigny, France 707-257-3582 www.bouchardcooperages.com
\Tonnellerie Damy Meursault, France 707-257-3582 www.tonnellerie-damy.fr
Tonnellerie Ermitage St. Helena, CA 707-968-0664 www.groupecharlois.com
Tonnellerie Leroi Healdsburg, CA 707-508-5006 www.leroibarrels.com
Tonnellerie Marchive Barbezieux, France +33 5 4598 3334 www.tonnellerie-marchive.fr
Tonnellerie Marsannay Calistoga, CA 707-942-5037 www.nadalie-usa.com/cooperages-marsannay.asp
Tonnellerie Ô Benicia, CA 707-752-6350 www.tonnellerieo.com
Tonnellerie Quintessence Sonoma, CA 707-935-3452 www.tonnelleriequintessence.com
Tonnellerie Radoux Santa Rosa, CA 800-755-4393 www.tonnellerieradoux.com
Tonnellerie Rousseau Couchet, France 510-339-0170 www.tonnellerie-rousseau.com
Tonnellerie Saury Napa, CA 707-944-1330 www.sauryusa.com
Tonnellerie Saint Martin Buzet/Baise, France 510-339-0170 tonnelleri.st.martin.free.fr
Tonnellerie Sirugue Nuits Saint George, France 310-403-8398 www.sirugue.com

Tonnellerie Sylvain Napa, CA 707-259-5344 www.tonnellerie-sylvain.fr
Tonnellerie Vernou Cognac, France 415-474-1588 (Pickering); 800-333-4288 (GW Kent) www.tonnellerie-vernou.com GW Kent, Pickering Winery Supply
Treuil Tonnellerie de Brive Brive, France +33 5 5587 6339 www.tonnellerie.fr
Trust International West Palm Beach, FL 561-540-4043 www.barrelmakers.com
T W Boswell Napa, CA 707-255-5900 www.twboswell.com
VinOak Benicia, CA 707-746-5704 www.vinoak.com
World Cooperage Napa, CA 707-255-5900 www.worldcooperage.com

Select US barrel brokers and agents representing multiple cooperages and/or brands
Artisan Barrels Oakland, CA 510-339-0170 www.artisanbarrels.com Tonnellerie Rousseau, Saint-Martin, Allary, A&K Cooperage, Balázs Cooperage
Barrel Builders St. Helena, CA 707-942-4291 www.barrelbuilders.com Tonnellerie Marchive, EBC American Oak (AKA East Bernstadt Cooperage), Barrel Builders
The Boswell Company San Rafael, CA 415-457-3955 www.boswellcompany.com Tonnellerie Bousuet, Tonnellerie de Mercurey, Kelvin Cooperage, Tonnellerie Margo
Bouchard Cooperages Napa, CA 707-257-3582 www.bouchardcooperages.com Tonnellerie Billon, Tonellerie Cadus, Tonellerie Damy, Vicard Tonnelleries, Laglasse [alternatives & stave mill]
Cooperages 1912 Napa, CA 707-255-5900 www.cooperages1912.com Tonnellerie Quintessence, Heinrich Cooperage, T.W. Boswell, World Cooperage
Heritage Barrels Reno, NV 707-257-1374 www.heritagebarrels.com Heritage Barrels, Giraud, Tonnellerie Vallaurine
Mel Knox Barrel Broker San Francisco, CA 415-751-6306 www.knoxbarrels.com Tonnellerie François Frères, Tonnellerie Taransaud
Nadalie USA Calistoga, CA 707-942-9301 www.nadalie-usa.com Nadalie USA, Tonnellerie Nadalie, Tonnellerie Marsannay
Oak Tradition Walla Walla, WA 707-318-0002 www.oaktradition.com Tonnellerie Radoux, Tonnellerie Millet, Tonnellerie Baron
Oregon Barrel Works McMinnville, OR 503-472-8883 www.oregonbarrelworks.com François Frères, Taransaud, Tonnellerie de Ferrari, Budapesti Kádár
Pickering Winery Supply San Francisco, CA 415-474-1588 www.winerystuff.com Tonnellerie Vernou, Tonnerllerie Meyrieux Fils, Tonnellerie Doreau, Keystone Cooperage
Premier Wine Cask Napa, CA 707-257-0714 www.premierwinecask.com Barrel Associates, Dargaud & Jaeglé Tonnellerie, Marcel Cadet
Trust & Treuil Cooperages Glen Ellen, CA 707-939-9790 www.barrelmakers.com Treuil Tonnellerie de Brive, Trust International
VinOak Benicia, CA 707-746-5704 www.vinoak.com Tonelería Quercus, Barrel 21

Bibliography

Adventures on the Wine Route: A Wine Buyer's Tour of France by Kermit Lynch: Farrar, Straus and Giroux, 2013

America B. C. - Ancient Settlers in the New World, Barry Fell: Artisan Publishers 2008

Ancient Wine: The Search for the Origins of Viniculture, by Patrick E. McGovern: Princeton University Press 2007

Angels' Visits: An Inquiry into the Mystery of Zinfandel, David Darlington, Henry Holt 1991

The Art and Science of Wine, Halliday, James, : Firefly Books, 2007.

The Billionaire's Vinegar: The Mystery of the World's Most Expensive Bottle of Wine Benjamin Wallace Crown Publishers 2008

The Botanist and the Vintner: How Wine Was Saved for the World, by Christy Campbell Algonquin Books 2005

The Chemistry of Wine Flavor Waterhouse, Eberler, Oxford University Press 1998

Cooperage for Winemakers, Geoffrey Schahinger & Bruce Rankine, Ryan Publications Effects of American Oak Barrels from Various Regional Sources on the Sensory Attributes of Wines by Patricia A. Howe of UC Davis and Duane Wall of Nadalie USA

Compost Tea Making, Marc Remillard: Ascension Press 2009

Concepts in Wine Technology: Small Winery Operations, Yair Margalit, Wine Appreciation Guild 2012

To Cork or Not to Cork : tradition, romance, science, and the battle for the wine bottle George M. Taber: Scribner, 2007.

The duration effect of natural seasoning of Quercus patraea L. and Quercus robur L. on the diversity of existing fungi flora and some aspects of its ecology. Nicolas Vivas, Nathalie Saint-Cricq de Gaulejac, Bernard Doneche, and Yves Glories. 1.Tonnellerie Demptos détaché à la Faculté d'Enologie Laboratoire de Biochimie Appliquée, unité associée INRA Faculté d'Enologie

Eleanor of Aquitaine: Lord and Lady, Bonnie Wheeler, John C. Parsons: Palgrave Macmillan 2008

The Geography of Wine : how landscapes, cultures, terroir, and the weather make a good drop, Brian J. Sommers : Penguin Group, 2008.

The Global Encyclopedia of Wine Global Book Publishing 2000

The Grape Grower: A Guide to Organic Viticulture Lon Rombough, Chelsea Green 2002

The Great Domaines of Burgundy: A Guide to the Finest Wine Producers of the Cote d'Or, Remington Norman, Charles Taylor: Sterling 2010

The Heartbreak Grape: A California Winemaker's Search for the Perfect Pinot Noir: Marq De Villiers, Harpercollins 1994

History of a Grape and Its Wine, Charles L. Sullivan, University of California Press 2003

A History of wine in America-From Prohibition to Present, Thomas Pinney, University of California Press 2005

Hugh Johnson's the Story of Wine, by Hugh Johnson: MITCH 2007

Knowing and Making Wine by Alan F Spencer and Emile Peynaud: Houghton Mifflin Harcourt 1984

Monks and Wine by Desmond Seward: Crown Publishers 1979

Bibliography

The Notion of Grain in Cooperage, Nicolas Vivas, Chercheur de la Tonnellerie détaché à la Institut d'Oenologic, Université, de Bordeaux

The Oxford Companion to Wine, Jancis Robinson, Oxford University Press, 2006.

Oz Clarkes Encyclopedia of Grapes Websters International 2001

Postmodern Winemaking Clark Smith University of California Press 2013

The Romance of Wine H. Warner Allen, E.P. Dutton & Co 1932

Rhone Renaissance: The Finest Rhone and Rhone Style Wines from France and the New World, by Remington Norman, Wine Appreciation Guild 1996

Saint Julien 1984 Bernard Ginestet, Jacques LeGrande

Sotheby's Wine Encyclopedia Tom Stevenson, DK Publishing 1997

The Science of Wine : From Vine to Glass: Jamie Goode : University of California Press, 2005.

Taste Buds and Molecules: The Art and Science of Food, Wine, and Flavor, Francois Chartier, Houghton Mifflin Harcourt; 2012

Understanding Wine Technology, David Bird Wine Appreciation Guild 2011

Understanding Vineyard Soils, Robert White, Oxford University Press 2009

The Vines of San Lorenzo by Edward Steinberg, A Slow Food Editore 2006

Voodoo Vintners—Oregons Astonishing Biodynamic Winegrowers Katherine Cole, 2011 Oregon State University Press

Vintner's Apprentice : the insider's guide to the art and craft of wine making, taught by the masters, Eric Miller, Beverly, Mass. : Quarry Books, 2011.

Washington Wines and Wineries, Paul Gregutt, University of California Press Schahinger G. and Rankine, B. (2002).

The Wines of Burgundy by Clive Coates, University of California Press 2008

Wine from Sky to Earth : growing & appreciating biodynamic wine Nicolas Joly: Acres 1999.

Wine and War: The French, the Nazis, and the Battle for France's Greatest Treasure Donald Kladstrup, Petie Kladstrup: Broadway 2001`

Wine Grapes: A Complete Guide to 1,368 Vine Varieties, Jancis Robinson, Ecco 2012

Wine Faults: Causes, Effects, Cures John Huddelson Ph.D. Wine Appreciation Guild 2011

A Wine-Grower's Guide, Philip M. Wagner : The Wine Appreciation Guild, 1996.

Wine Into Words James Garber, Bacchus Press 2003

Wine Science: Principles and Applications, Ronald S. Jackson, Academic Press 1994

1421 The Year China Discovered America Gavin Menzies, Transworld Publishers 2002

The World Atlas of Wine by Hugh Johnson, Jancis Robinson: Mitchell Beazley, 2006

Zinfandel: A History of a Grape and Its Wine Charles L. Sullivan, University of California Press 2003

Conversion Table for Units

1 Gallon = 3.785 liters
1 Fluid Ounce = 29.573 milliliter
1 Quart = 16 fluid ounces = 0.946 liter
1 Milliliter = 0.0338 fluid ounce
1 Liter = 1000 milliliters = 1.0567 quarts
1 Ounce = 2.83 grams
1 Pound = 16 ounces = 0.455 kilogram
1 Pound = 455 grams
10 Milligrams = 0.000353 ounce
1 Gram = 1000 milligrams = 0.353 ounce
1 Kilogram = 1000 grams = 2.2 pounds
1 Inch = 2.54 centimeters = 25.4 millimeters
1 Foot = 30.48 centimeters = 304.8 millimeters
1 millimeter = 0.03937 inch
1 cubic centimeter = 0.06102 cubic inch
1 cubic inch = 16.387 cubic centimeters

Typical Wine Grape pH~~~TA Ratios
(General Guideline Only)

pH~~~~~~~~~TA
3.00~~~~~~~~~9.0
3.10~~~~~~~~~8.5
3.20~~~~~~~~~7.8
3.30~~~~~~~~~7.2
3.40~~~~~~~~~6.9
3.50~~~~~~~~~6.6
3.60~~~~~~~~~6.2
3.70~~~~~~~~~5.7
3.80~~~~~~~~~5.2
3.90~~~~~~~~~4.7
4.00~~~~~~~~~4.3

ACIDIC --- LESS ACIDIC

Potassium Metabisulfite

Potassium metabisulfite powder is 57.6% sulfite by weight, and is what we add to the wine.

It is loosely referred to as "SO2", and also abbreviated as PMS, PMBS, and KMBS.

Always purchase fresh PMBS every year, and store it in a sealed container in a dry, dark, cool place. PMBS will dissolve metal lids. Use plastic or glass.

Always mix it into a little hot water to ensure that it fully dissolves before adding it to the wine.

Avoid skin contact and breathing PMBS.

Sodium Metabisulfite

Sodium metabisulfite is 67.4% sulfite by weight, making it more powerful than it's cousin potassium metabisulfite.

Sodium metabisulfite is superb for sanitation purposes, but not recommended for wine additions.

In the past Campden tablets have been made out of it.

Avoid skin contact and breathing SMBS.

Winery Schedule
2027 Vintage

Year	Month	Process
2027	September	Harvest
	October	Primary Fermentation
	November	
	December	Malolactic Fermentation
		74 F./23 C.
2028	January	
	February	
	March	
	April	
	May	
	June	
	July	
	August	Barrel
	September	Cellaring
	October	59 F./15 C.
	November	
	December	
2029	January	
	February	
	March	
	April	
	May	
	June	Bottling
	July	
	August	
	September	
	October	
	November	Bottle Ageing
	December	59 F./15 C.
2030	January	
	February	
	March	
	April	
	May	2027 Vintage Release

Practical SO2

Beginning on page 67, I discussed the rather complicated topic of SO2 in wine. Since we all process information in unique ways, I recommend checking out online how other writers have tackled the subject. There are some excellent renditions on SO2 ranging from basic to advanced chemistry--whatever your cup of tea is. This is where the chemist/writers shine.

I must clue the reader in on some confusing aspects of the SO2 enigma.

First, remember that once the potassium metabisulfite powder has been addded to a wine it dissembles. Some of it is **bound** SO2, some becomes **free** SO2, and a very small amount that performs the most work is **molecular** SO2. When you are reading about SO2 make sure you are aware of which form is being discussed.

There are many factors contributing to varying levels of free, bound, and molecular SO2 in any given wine at different times. A few of the obvious factors are:

Molecular SO2 is directly pH dependant.

Free SO2 is temperature dependant. At lower temperatures a wine will have less free SO2 than the same wine at a higher temperature.

Free SO2 decreases in the presence of oxygen (like due to racking).

Free SO2 decreases with time.

Also adding some confusion is the varying opinions of different winemaking education institutions concerning recommended levels. In general, it seems that the more "chemically" oriented the institution is, the more SO2 they recommend using. In the U.S.A. the FDA allows wineries to legally add up to 350 ppm **total** SO2 to a wine. Yikes!

More reasonably, some institutions recommend maintaining 0.5 mg/L molecular SO2 in a red wine, while others weigh in at 0.6, 0.8, 0.85, and even as high as 2.0 mg/L. You can observe how their charts represent all of those different levels. I am adhering to 0.5 mg/L for reds, and 0.8 mg/L for white wines.

Also, how the experts choose to abbreviate "potassium metabisulfite" varies: Either PMS, PMBS, or for the technical--KMBS.

Some home winemaking sources advocate the use of a liquid solution of SO2. That is--powdered potassium metabisulfite mixed with water to make a solution that can be measured by volume instead of by weight. The old technique is based on the idea that the winemaker does not own a scale. Yes, in 1970 a mechanical gram scale was expensive, but today we have access to cheap, accurate digital scales. Buy a scale. I recommend a 1000 gram capacity everyday scale for the winemaker. 1 gram measurments will be accurate, but you can still weigh over two pounds on it.

---

ppm

ppm is an abbreviation for *parts per million.* ppm is equivalent to milligrams/Liter (mg/L)

Since there is 1/1000 of a gram in a milligram

And, there is 1000 grams of water in a liter

So---1000 x 1000 = 1,000,000

Unless the winemaker is one of those brave souls that is experimenting with "no sulfite" wines, PMBS/SO2 is added at least three times during the winemaking process:

1. During crush, typically 40-50 ppm SO2
2. After MLF, typically 40-60 ppm SO2
3. Before bottling, at molecular SO2 level of choice (dependant on pH)

Other additions may be introduced between step 2 and step 3, to maintain the SO2 molecular level of choice. I am recommending 0.5 molecular for red wines.

I will endeavor to simplify SO2 addition calculations by making basic recommendations:

If the grapes are in good condition use **40 ppm SO2 during crush**.
If the grapes are in poor condition or over-ripe use **50 ppm SO2 during crush.**
If the grapes are under-ripe, or below 3.20 pH use **30 ppm SO2 during crush**

For red wines I recommend shooting for 0.5 mg/L molecular level of SO2 after MLF.
That is the <u>lowest</u> amount of SO2 recommended by researchers and universities worldwide. Ideally, this will yield the best tasting (SO2 masks fruit), and the healthiest wine for the body. If using 0.5 mg/L level of SO2, please follow immaculate sanitation procedures during the winemaking process, and at bottling.

Typical Levels of SO2 During the Winemaking Process

After fermentation the wine is usually harboring only about 5 ppm free SO2. Following MLF the wine will typically have less than 5 ppm free SO2 40-60 ppm SO2 is added after MLF. After 18 months of aging in the cellar, the wine will most likely contain from 3-10 ppm free SO2--if it has not received any extra additions after the 40-60 ppm SO2 it received following MLF. During cellaring, each wine consumes free SO2 at it's own unique rate.

Formula for Acidulating Musts with Tartaric Acid

1 g/L (0.13 oz/gallon) of tartaric acid for every 0.10 unit of pH short of the ideal

---

De-Acidificaton
2.5 grams of calcium carbonate per gallon of wine will lower the TA by about 0.1%

Formulas for Potassium Metabisulfite (PMBS) Addition

1 Gallon = 3.785 liters

$$\frac{\text{Liters of wine x ppm of addition}}{576} = \text{grams of PMBS to add}$$

OR

Gallons of wine x ppm of addition x .0066 = grams of PMBS to add

Free SO2 for 0.5 Molecular SO2 Level

pH	% of Free Sulfur Molecular SO2	ppm Free SO2 For 0.5 Molecular
3.00	6.1	8
3.05	5.3	9
3.10	4.9	10
3.15	4.3	12
3.20	3.9	13
3.25	3.4	15
3.30	3.1	16
3.35	2.7	18
3.40	2.5	20
3.45	2.2	23
3.50	2.0	25
3.55	1.8	29
3.60	1.6	31
3.65	1.4	36
3.70	1.3	39
3.75	1.1	45
3.80	1.0	49
3.85	0.9	57
3.90	0.8	62
3.95	0.7	71
4.00	0.7	78

SO2 Amounts

An accepted practice in the wine industry is to target a top molecular SO2 level of 0.5 ppm for red wine. The idea is to add as little SO2 as possible while still preventing spoilage.

However, after MLF has completed most winemakers add 40-60 ppm SO2. Technically we are supposed to add twice the recommended level from the chart on the left at that time, but the amount becomes excessive above about 3.70 pH, so most winemakers will add no more than 60 ppm after MLF.

Afterwards, during cellaring and at bottling maintain the level from the column in bold on the right of the chart (Free SO2 for 0.5 molecular).

Lets say your wine is at 3.50 pH following MLF. Prior to bottling, you will need to bring the SO2 level up to 25 ppm. However, wise vintners will add 10 ppm to that number because they know that about 10 ppm free SO2 is lost during the racking (~4 ppm) and bottling (~6 ppm) process. They would thus bring the level up to target 35 ppm to bottle a 3.50 pH wine at 0.5 molecular SO2.

Potassium Metabisulfite Powder Additions
In grams

Gallons of wine x ppm of addition x .0066 = grams of PMBS to add

Gal.	Liters	~~~~~~~~~ SO₂ PPM INCREASED BY ~~~~~~~~~~~												
		5	7.5	10	12.5	15	20	25	30	35	40	45	50	55	60
5	18.9	.16	.25	.33	.41	.50	.70	.80	1.0	1.1	1.3	1.5	1.6	1.8	2.0
10	37.8	.33	.50	.66	.80	1.0	1.3	1.6	2.0	2.3	2.6	3.0	3.3	3.6	4.0
15	56.7	.50	.70	1.0	1.2	1.5	2.0	2.5	3.0	3.5	4.0	4.5	5.0	5.4	6.0
20	75.6	.70	1.0	1.3	1.6	2.0	2.6	3.3	4.0	4.6	5.3	5.9	6.6	7.3	7.9
25	94.5	.80	1.2	1.6	2.1	2.5	3.3	4.1	4.9	5.8	6.6	7.4	8.2	9.0	9.9
30	113	1.0	1.5	2.0	2.5	3.0	4.0	4.9	5.9	6.9	7.9	8.9	9.9	10.9	11.9
35	132	1.1	1.7	2.3	2.9	3.5	4.6	5.8	6.9	8.0	9.2	10.3	11.5	12.7	13.9
40	151	1.3	2.0	2.6	3.3	4.0	5.3	6.6	7.9	9.2	10.6	11.8	13.2	14.5	15.8
45	170	1.5	2.2	3.0	3.7	4.4	5.9	7.4	8.9	10.3	11.8	13.4	14.8	16.3	17.8
50	189	1.6	2.5	3.3	4.1	4.9	6.6	8.2	9.9	11.5	13.2	14.8	16.5	18.1	19.8
55	208	1.8	2.7	3.6	4.5	5.4	7.3	9.0	10.9	12.7	14.5	16.3	18.1	20	22
60	226	2.0	3.0	4.0	4.9	5.9	7.9	10	11.9	13.9	15.8	17.8	19.8	21.8	23.8
65	246	2.1	3.2	4.3	5.4	6.4	8.6	10.7	12.9	15	17.2	19.3	21.4	23.6	25.7
70	265	2.3	3.5	4.6	5.8	6.9	9.2	11.5	13.9	16.2	18.5	20.8	23.1	25.4	28
75	283	2.5	3.7	4.9	6.2	7.4	9.9	12.3	14.8	17.3	19.8	22.3	24.7	27	30
80	302	2.6	4.0	5.3	6.6	7.9	10.5	13.2	16	18.5	21	24	26	29	32
85	321	2.8	4.2	5.6	7	8.4	11.2	14	16.8	20	22	25	28	31	34
90	340	3.0	4.4	5.9	7.4	8.9	11.8	15	18	21	24	27	30	33	36
95	359	3.1	4.7	6.3	7.8	9.4	12.5	16	19	22	25	28	31	34	38
100	378	3.3	5.0	6.6	8.2	10	13	17	20	23	26	30	33	36	40
110	416	3.6	5.4	7.3	9	11	14	18	22	25	29	33	36	40	44
120	454	4.0	6.0	8	10	12	16	20	24	28	32	36	40	44	48
130	491	4.3	6.5	9	11	13	17	21	26	30	34	39	43	47	51
140	529	4.6	7	9	12	14	18	23	28	32	27	42	46	51	55
150	567	5	7.5	9.9	13	15	20	25	30	35	40	44	49	54	59
160	605	5.3	8	10.5	13.5	16	21	26	32	37	42	47	53	58	63
170	643	5.6	8.4	11.2	14	17	22	28	33	39	45	50	56	62	67
180	680	6.0	8.9	12	15	18	24	30	36	41	47	53	59	65	71
190	718	6.3	9.4	12.5	15.7	19	25	31	38	44	50	56	63	69	75
200	756	6.6	9.9	13.2	16.5	20	26	33	40	46	53	59	66	73	79
210	795	6.9	10.4	13.9	17	21	28	35	42	48	55	62	69	76	83

Temperature Conversions
Celsius~~~Fahrenheit
0 `````` 32
1 `````` 34
2 `````` 36
3 `````` 38
4 `````` 39
5 `````` 41
6 `````` 43
7 `````` 44
8 `````` 46
9 `````` 48
10 `````` 50
11 `````` 52
12 `````` 54
13 `````` 55
14 `````` 57
15 `````` 59
16 `````` 61
17 `````` 63
18 `````` 64
19 `````` 66
20 `````` 68
21 `````` 70
22 `````` 72
23 `````` 74
24 `````` 75
25 `````` 77
26 `````` 79
27 `````` 81
28 `````` 82
29 `````` 84
30 `````` 86
31 `````` 88
32 `````` 90
33 `````` 92
34 `````` 93
35 `````` 95
36 `````` 97
37 `````` 99
38 `````` 100
39 `````` 102
40 `````` 104
41 `````` 106
42 `````` 108
43 `````` 110

Raising Sugar Levels---Chaptalization

Add 1.5 ounces of cane sugar per gallon for every point of Brix short of the ideal (23 Brix).

Hydrometer Temperature correction

Modern hydrometers are usually calibrated at 20C., while the older cheap ones are usually at 60F. **You can adjust the temperature of your sample to match the hydrometer**, or add .25 degrees Brix to the reading for each 9 degrees F. if the temperature of the must is higher than the calibrated temperature; if the actual temperature is below, deduct .25 Brix from the reading for each 9 degrees F.

Typical Yeast Quantities

For musts under 25 Brix---per gallon of must:
1 gram of yeast
10 ml 102F/39C water

For musts over 25 Brix---per gallon of must:
1.2 grams of yeast
12 ml 102F/39C water

YRN-Yeast Rehydration Nutrient Quantities
(Go-Ferm)

For musts up to 25 Brix--per gallon of must:
1 gram yeast
1.25 grams YRN
25 ml 110F/43C water

For musts over 25 Brix—per gallon of must:
1.2 grams yeast
1.5 grams YRN
30 ml 110F/43C water

Potassium Metabisulfite Powder Additions
In grams

Gallons of wine x ppm of addition x .0066 = grams of PMBS to add

Gal.	Liters	5	7.5	10	12.5	15	20	25	30	35	40	45	50	55	60
						SO₂ PPM INCREASED BY									
5	18.9	.16	.25	.33	.41	.50	.70	.80	1.0	1.1	1.3	1.5	1.6	1.8	2.0
10	37.8	.33	.50	.66	.80	1.0	1.3	1.6	2.0	2.3	2.6	3.0	3.3	3.6	4.0
15	56.7	.50	.70	1.0	1.2	1.5	2.0	2.5	3.0	3.5	4.0	4.5	5.0	5.4	6.0
20	75.6	.70	1.0	1.3	1.6	2.0	2.6	3.3	4.0	4.6	5.3	5.9	6.6	7.3	7.9
25	94.5	.80	1.2	1.6	2.1	2.5	3.3	4.1	4.9	5.8	6.6	7.4	8.2	9.0	9.9
30	113	1.0	1.5	2.0	2.5	3.0	4.0	4.9	5.9	6.9	7.9	8.9	9.9	10.9	11.9
35	132	1.1	1.7	2.3	2.9	3.5	4.6	5.8	6.9	8.0	9.2	10.3	11.5	12.7	13.9
40	151	1.3	2.0	2.6	3.3	4.0	5.3	6.6	7.9	9.2	10.6	11.8	13.2	14.5	15.8
45	170	1.5	2.2	3.0	3.7	4.4	5.9	7.4	8.9	10.3	11.8	13.4	14.8	16.3	17.8
50	189	1.6	2.5	3.3	4.1	4.9	6.6	8.2	9.9	11.5	13.2	14.8	16.5	18.1	19.8
55	208	1.8	2.7	3.6	4.5	5.4	7.3	9.0	10.9	12.7	14.5	16.3	18.1	20	22
60	226	2.0	3.0	4.0	4.9	5.9	7.9	10	11.9	13.9	15.8	17.8	19.8	21.8	23.8
65	246	2.1	3.2	4.3	5.4	6.4	8.6	10.7	12.9	15	17.2	19.3	21.4	23.6	25.7
70	265	2.3	3.5	4.6	5.8	6.9	9.2	11.5	13.9	16.2	18.5	20.8	23.1	25.4	28
75	283	2.5	3.7	4.9	6.2	7.4	9.9	12.3	14.8	17.3	19.8	22.3	24.7	27	30
80	302	2.6	4.0	5.3	6.6	7.9	10.5	13.2	16	18.5	21	24	26	29	32
85	321	2.8	4.2	5.6	7	8.4	11.2	14	16.8	20	22	25	28	31	34
90	340	3.0	4.4	5.9	7.4	8.9	11.8	15	18	21	24	27	30	33	36
95	359	3.1	4.7	6.3	7.8	9.4	12.5	16	19	22	25	28	31	34	38
100	378	3.3	5.0	6.6	8.2	10	13	17	20	23	26	30	33	36	40
110	416	3.6	5.4	7.3	9	11	14	18	22	25	29	33	36	40	44
120	454	4.0	6.0	8	10	12	16	20	24	28	32	36	40	44	48
130	491	4.3	6.5	9	11	13	17	21	26	30	34	39	43	47	51
140	529	4.6	7	9	12	14	18	23	28	32	27	42	46	51	55
150	567	5	7.5	9.9	13	15	20	25	30	35	40	44	49	54	59
160	605	5.3	8	10.5	13.5	16	21	26	32	37	42	47	53	58	63
170	643	5.6	8.4	11.2	14	17	22	28	33	39	45	50	56	62	67
180	680	6.0	8.9	12	15	18	24	30	36	41	47	53	59	65	71
190	718	6.3	9.4	12.5	15.7	19	25	31	38	44	50	56	63	69	75
200	756	6.6	9.9	13.2	16.5	20	26	33	40	46	53	59	66	73	79
210	795	6.9	10.4	13.9	17	21	28	35	42	48	55	62	69	76	83

Mark Stanley

THE SACRED SPRING OF THE BLOOD ROYAL

Available on Amazon in Paperback and Kindle

During World War II, an American paratrooper on a covert mission drops into eastern France to find mystery, romance, murder, espionage and becomes involved with the Prieuré de Sion, an ancient secret order that has been quietly influencing western society for centuries.

And that is only the beginning.

For over a thousand years, members of the Prieuré de Sion have been the targets of assassinations. Why? The tale weaves a thread that begins in the alpine meadows of the Jura mountains, and moves into mystical journeys of self-realization in the labyrinth and secret underground temple complex near Rennes le Chateau in southwestern France.

Mystical, Magical, Esoteric Entertainment--Edward J. Barton-VineVoice

This was one of those books I couldn't put down. It seemed to have a little bit of everything. A thriller, a love story, a spiritual quest, a fantasy, a history primer, and a travelog all rolled up into one grand adventure. Charles

Well Done--Riveting--Inspector 12

Stanley has woven a mystic tale with a historic background and mysterious throughout. This is a story of love and intrigue but it seems with a underlying content of the spiritual development of the soul. Roger

All elements were there for an entertaining and enjoyable book. I found it a plus that the writing style took me into the environment in a refreshing way. I would enjoy further efforts by this author VanDeMark

Made in the USA
San Bernardino, CA
23 February 2016